Contents

Acknowledgements	5
Foreword	7
Introduction	11
Why Carnegie Hall?	15
The Build-up to the Concert	21
Plans for a Concert	25
Hot Music in a Cold Town	31
Guests	35
Rehearsals	41
Leaving the Madhattan Room	47
The Concert Program	51
Tickets	71
"How Long Does Mr Toscanini take?"	75
A Cold Evening to Queue	77
The Concert	81
The Music	85
Don't Be That Way	85
Sometimes I'm Happy	86
One O'Clock Jump	88
Twenty Years of Jazz – Sensation Rag	90
I'm Coming Virginia	91
When My Baby Smiles at Me	93
Shine	93
Blue Reverie	94
Life Goes To A Party	95
Honeysuckle Rose	97
The Trio - Body and Soul	101
Avalon	103
The Man I Love	104
I Got Rhythm	104
Intermission	104

The Music *continued*

    The second set: Blue Skies 107
    Loch Lomond 108
    Blue Room 110
    Swingtime In The Rockies 112
    Bei Mir Bist Du Shoen 113
    China Boy 114
    Stompin' At The Savoy 114
    Dizzy Spells 115
    Sing, Sing, Sing 119
    The Encores 121

Battle of the Bands 125
Mozart 129
The Photographs 133
Newsreel Film 137
Carnegie Hall Museum and Archives 141
The Recording 145
How was it recorded? 149
The Acetates are Re-discovered 157
The Records 161
The Album Design 165
The Record is Released 169
The Complete Concert for the First Time 173
What Next? 177
The Anniversaries 181
Bibliography 185
Appendix 1:
    Irving Kolodin's Original 1938 Program Notes 193
Appendix 2:
    Benny Goodman's Carnegie Hall Appearances 207
Index 213
Photograph Credits 218

BENNY GOODMAN

The Famous 1938 Carnegie Hall Jazz Concert

CELEBRATING BENNY GOODMAN'S CENTENARY!

To Tony

*Keep Swingin'!
Jon Hancock*

Copyright © 2008 Jon Hancock

The Gables • Ruyton XI Towns • Shrewsbury • Shropshire • SY4 1HU • UK

+44 (0)1939 260308

jon@bg1938.com

DEDICATION

For my brother Vincent

Text copyright © 2008 Jon Hancock.
Illustrations copyrighted as marked

First published in the UK in 2009
by Prancing Fish Publishing

British Library Cataloguing-in-Publication Data
A catalogue record for this book is available from the British Library

ISBN 978-0-9562404-0-8

The right of Jon Hancock to be identified as author of this work
has been asserted in accordance with the Copyright, Design and Patent Act 1988.

The information in this book is true and complete to the best of
our knowledge. All recommendations are made without any
guarantee on the part of the Publisher, who also disclaims any
liability incurred in connection with the use of this data
or specific details.

All rights reserved. No part of this book may be reproduced or
transmitted in any form or by any means, electronic or mechanical
including photocopying, recording or by any information storage and retrieval system,
without permission from the Publisher in writing.

Designed and Printed in the UK by
Creative Digital Printing Limited, Shrewsbury, Shropshire
01743 263030

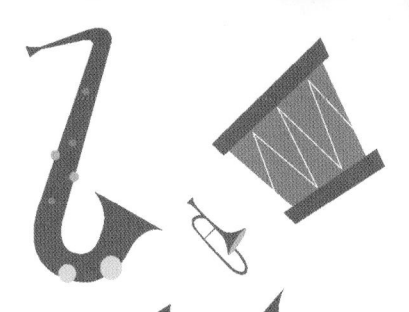

Acknowledgements

By its very nature, a project like this would not work without the input and cooperation of many different people and organisations. Without exception, everybody that I have asked for help and information has been very forthcoming and generous with their precious time. I am particularly grateful to Gino Francesconi and his staff at the Carnegie Hall Archives. Over a four year period, I bombarded Gino with emails asking silly questions about Goodman's performances in Carnegie Hall, his answers always came back very quickly, in great detail and good humour.

I would also like to thank the Benny Goodman Estate for their enthusiasm for this book and for allowing me to reproduce documents that have never been published before.

The Benny Goodman authority, David Jessop has been very generous and patient with me; David has given me enormous help and encouragement. I would recommend that you search out his forthcoming book on Benny Goodman.

Many other people have helped me, and they all deserve a huge round of applause! In alphabetical order they are:

Frank Alkyer
    at *Down Beat Magazine*
Alan Bunting
Dr Joan Bronte-Stewart
Naomi Edelson
Rachel Edelson
Mike Gray
Carmelina Hancock
Bob Hancock
John Hornsby
Anna Holcombe
    at Sony BMG Music Entertainment
Sjef Hoefsmit
    - *Duke Ellington Music Society*
Phoebe Jacobs
Andrew Johnston

Suzanne Lovejoy
    at *Yale University Music Library*
Jim Lowe
    at the *Manchester Jazz Society*
Mike Meddings
Sonny McGown
Bill McQuaide
    - *Audio Engineering Society*
Richard Morrison
Susan Satz - The Estate of Benny Goodman
Steven Smith
    - *Kenton Kronicles*
Lewis Wyman
    at the *Library of Congress*
The staff at New York Public Library

The life of anybody who has an interest in Benny Goodman would be greatly enhanced by reading Russ Connor's lovely books.

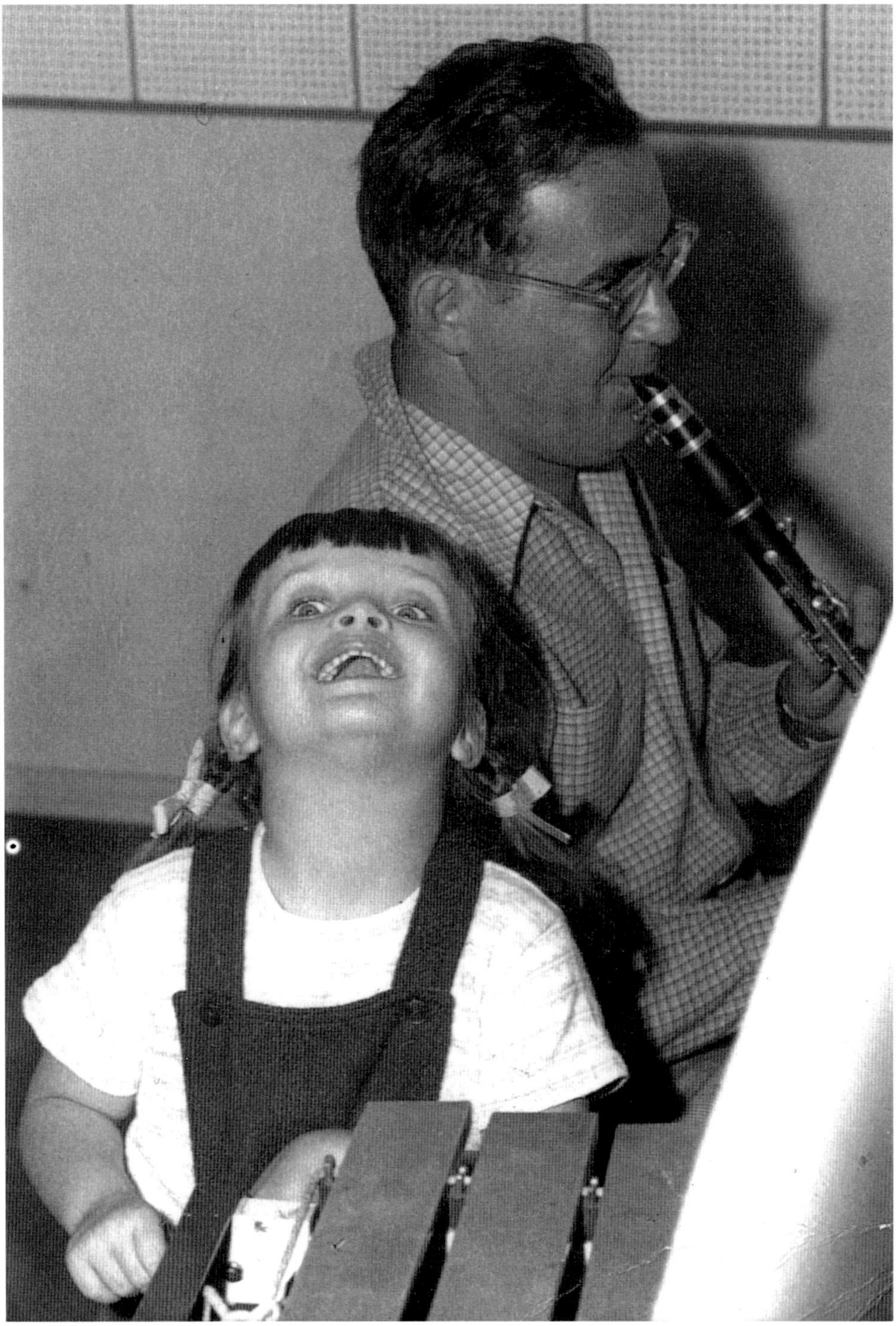

• FOREWORD •

The Quest for the Perfect Reed

Rachel Edelson

I wonder when my father's Quest for the Perfect Reed began — when, at age ten, he was first loaned a clarinet at the Kehalah Jacob Synagogue? When he began practicing so assiduously, during the after school times that his friends were playing marbles in the streets? When he was given his first gig at age twelve, making five dollars? When he was studying clarinet technique for those two years with the demanding and white-haired Hans Shoepp? But it couldn't have been any of those times, because reeds cost money.

Maybe that reed obsession came over him slowly, as his fame grew — trapping him within the costly bargain made between the world's adulation and the artist's self expectations. I'd never considered the trade-off between these two, until considering what a burden it must have been for him to have achieved the fame he achieved at Carnegie Hall, age twenty-eight: how and how long could he maintain that mastery and the public favor that accompanied it? I think now of all the rock stars, Kurt Cobain among them, who couldn't manage the intensity of that glory. He, at least, died before having to ponder whether to adapt his musical style, whereas my father had to live with being able and willing to play only swing. I remember a goofy photo of him with a Gillespie-style beret as he took unwilling steps into Bebop, steps he reversed very quickly. Those rhythms and harmonies were not who he was; he lived forever in the kingdom of swing. Nor, of course, was he an Ellington, whose style did evolve over the decades, along with his compositions. No, my father's music was the classical pieces of the twenties and thirties, most of the arrangements done by Fletcher Henderson.

As most fans of his know, he did evolve into the world of classical music, still playing in a way that made fellow clarinettists marvel, "How does he *do* that?" Although I never dared encroach on the improvisational world he had mastered (just as well: I am convinced he would have been highly territorial), he and I did often play classical music for clarinet and piano: the Brahms F minor clarinet sonata and the trio for clarinet, cello and piano; as well as music by Debussy, Mozart and von Weber. I played some concerts with him and practiced solo music with him as my "coach." But he was completely ungifted as a teacher: whereas he had in his ear a clear sound of how the phrase or piece was supposed to go, he was unable to articulate this sound to anyone else. I now know that the members of his orchestra endured the same misery I did: an unspoken but fierce "Well, just play it till you get it right. I don't care how many times you have to do this — play it till it sounds OK." The spoken version with me went, "Hmm, *pretty* good." Or he'd whistle what he wanted, the notes unrecognizable. Or he'd try the melody on the piano, fingers clunking. Then another "Hmm," at a different

Rachel, age 3, with her Dad.

pitch than the first one. Etc. etc, as I kept trying to please him. Until he'd say, "OK, now you've got it." But the reason why the new sound was better always remained a mystery to me; I wanted the reasons for what his musical intuition supplied, and he didn't have those. And sometimes he would apply his own mastery of the clarinet to my lack thereof at the piano, such as when I was twelve and struggling with an early Beethoven piano sonata, trying to get the subtle rhythmic integration of three versus two notes per beat, known as "three against two." We both sat on the bench, he at my left. Endlessly, under the rain of his impatience, I played separately the left hand triplets and then the right hand quarter notes, then trying to merge the two rhythms smoothly, like eggs and oil in mayonnaise. But the rhythm always curdled unsteadily. I whimpered. He responded, "C'mon, Rache – this is easy."

My father dedicated around four hours a day to his music, practicing as he searched for his reeds – acts integral to each other. My mother, whose passion besides gardening was architectural drawing, designed plans for a new garage at our Stamford, CT house, a kidney-shaped pool where he swam for his bad back and a conversion of the old garage into a studio / recording room / pool house. The studio contained the Steinway grand piano, an antique high-backed chair on which my father sat as he practiced, his antique music stand, and a table at his right. The A-frame ceiling had a darkly multi-colored Moroccan glass lamp suspended from it; opposite the piano was a curved coral tuile sofa seating six. In the middle of the wall in back of the piano hung a formal portrait painted in England of my elegant mother in her thirties, wearing a mink wrap and a spray of orchids. To her right was a glass-fronted corner cabinet. In the recording room at the back he kept all his Grundig equipment, at that time reel to reel, all behind locked doors.

My father had a collection of approximately two thousand reeds: I speak with certainty because after he died, my sister Benjie and his secretary Muriel Zuckerman and I went through the Stamford house and his penthouse apartment at 200 East 66th St in New York: reeds, used and unused, split or perfect, both in and out of the French periwinkle blue and gold cases, were scattered everywhere in drawers and clarinet cases. A recollection: one day, I came out to the studio to talk to him where he was seated in front of the plain wooden chest that held his turntable and a lot of LPs. Two different recordings of "Rigoletto" lay askew on the floor. He was trying out a reed, in a ritual that went like this: holding the clarinet, its mouthpiece slightly above eye level and a bit to the left, he squinted as he put on a new reed, turning the little screws. Then he ran through his reed test, an unpredictable mishmash which varied according to whatever classical pieces he was practicing at the time - Bartok, Nielsen, Mozart, Brahms, Weber - the standards – plus whatever jazz phrases were flowing through his brain and fingers – Sweet Georgia Brown, Avalon, Body and Soul, the blues – plus scales that may or may not have been in the key of any of those pieces: a "BrahmsGershwinScales Medley." The scales always began in the high register, and ended there; it was that register in which a reed, for my father at least, proved its merit. I often wondered if he even heard that test to which he subjected each reed; sometimes it appeared a more obsessive and mindless ritual than a practical way to test reeds. My evidence here is that having tried them out, he'd always toss them on the table, but not throw them away – in irrational recycler. Someone walked into the studio that day and, noticing the tiny heap on the table, asked, "Are those reeds ones that you're throwing out, Benny?" Distracted from his Quest, my father glanced in the direction of the reeds, then answered. "No. You might just say they're temporarily out of favor."

He was a man of moods, treating not only his reeds, but others with unpredictability.

Everyone who knew him felt what it was like to be out of favor in his eyes; but no one felt that disfavor as fully as he did with himself. In one of his self-hating states, he uncharacteristically confided in me "This one's the Big Dipper." He always pushed himself, always fearful of losing the ability, reputation and money that he'd gained. In 1959, after a not so successful engagement at the Waldorf Astoria, Phoebe Jacobs, his publicity agent then and now, wanted him to play at Basin Street East, owned by her cousin Frank Watkins. She and Watkins were convinced that this more intimate setting would bring in larger and more responsive crowds. My father balked: "No, I'll be a flop, I know it. I don't want to do this to Frank. He's got a business to keep going, and a family to feed, just like I do. "But after much cajoling from them, he assented. Opening night, he sat in his dressing room, trying out one reed after another. Phoebe came in, to announce that it was five minutes before show time. Through his preoccupation, he asked, "Is there anyone at all in the audience?"

That was the negative; but it was balanced out, who knows how much of the time, with his elation at playing the right gig with the right reed. He once confessed to me, sitting comfortably in his black leather chair in New York, a temporary universe away from self-doubt about his musicianship: "I can't believe I get paid to do this."

Rachel Edelson – April 2009

After the memorial party for BG given by Rachel Edelson, her family, Muriel Zuckerman and Phoebe Jacobs at New York City's Century club, Ms. Edelson had booklets made to send to the guests. Each booklet contains a transcription of funny anecdotes about her father that the six guest speakers, all close friends of him, gave. As well, each contains a bookmark made from one of those two thousand reeds that BG left behind. Ms Edelson has set up a foundation through which proceeds from the booklet, selling at $25.00 apiece, go to a scholarship for music students at the University of California at Davis.

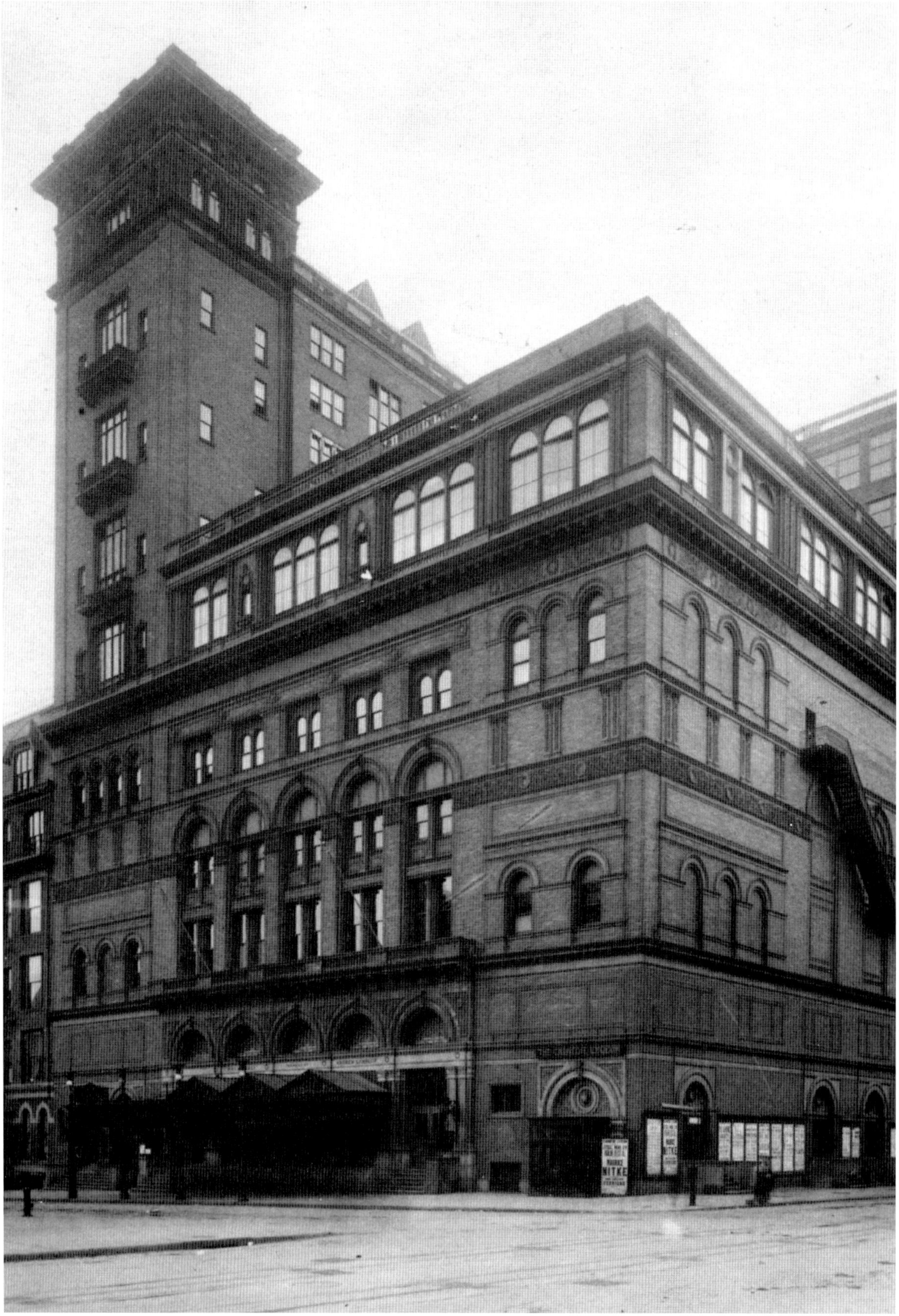

Introduction

Through his own upbeat and swinging style of music in the middle and late 1930s, Benny Goodman had earned the title of the 'King of Swing'. He was a virtuoso on the clarinet and indeed, many believe him to be the greatest clarinettist ever. For as long as swing music was in vogue, Benny Goodman was its foremost practitioner. He belonged to the nobility of Jazz along with other jazz greats like Count Basie and Duke Ellington. Nowadays, it is not unusual to find a musician who straddles the classical and jazz worlds but in the 1930s, there was a strict divide between the two musical camps. In addition, at a time when colour distinction was a normal part of American society, Benny Goodman was unusual in that he did not seem to see the colour of a musician's skin, he judged them by their musical abilities. Goodman was equally at home as a classical soloist as he was as a swing band leader and his great facility with the clarinet became his trademark, instantly recognised by audiences and fans around the world.

Benny Goodman's 1938 Carnegie Hall concert is the stuff of legend and is probably the most widely talked about event in the history of Carnegie Hall. Immortalised for us all to enjoy on a set of scratchy acetate discs which turned up 12 years after the concert, jazz fans everywhere have a special affection for this concert which has come to define a special era of Big Band and Swing music. Those remote recordings which were made on the evening of 16th January 1938 have become the best selling live jazz record ever and have been retained in the current catalogue since their release in 1950. Columbia's original blue record album, with its classic 1950s styling and boasting a stellar assembly of jazz giants, is still prized amongst jazz fans and collectors today.

The concert itself was a landmark in American music but eyebrows were raised across Manhattan society when it was announced that the prestigious Carnegie Hall, the home of the nation's classical music, was to be used for a concert given by a swing orchestra with black and white musicians playing together! There was clearly some consternation that popular jazz music was presuming to become acceptable to the Establishment.

In addition to the members of his own swing orchestra, Goodman assembled some of the best jazz musicians of the day for his Carnegie Hall appearance. These included Buck Clayton, Count Basie, Johnny Hodges and Lester Young to name just a few. They were all to become giants of jazz in their own right.

This concert was a true one-off event, never to be successfully repeated, never bettered. Although the concert is often 'recreated', the passion, virtuosity and most of all, conviction with which these young musicians played is something that cannot be matched. A listener to the Carnegie Hall recordings today will still experience the thrill of Benny's fabulous orchestra at their very peak.

Carnegie Hall at the junction of W 57th Street and 7th Avenue as it stood in 1909.

Goodman's concert there was eagerly awaited by his fans. Tickets sold out in days and seats were crammed onto the stage to cope with the overwhelming demand. Archive photographs and film of the concert show the lucky members of the audience sitting alongside the orchestra. But the music played that evening by those skilled young musicians was quite extraordinary. The end of the Depression of the early Thirties, the sudden explosion in popularity of jazz and the thrill of playing Carnegie Hall all came together by some strange alchemy to produce these enduring recordings. Along with the wonderful music there is the folk-lore that goes with it. Speculation has thrived amongst fans over the years about the single overhead microphone, the supposed discovery of the acetates in Benny's closet and the long-lost missing tunes and truncated choruses! The high points of the concert are many. Who can forget Ziggy Elman's devastating attack in 'Swingtime In The Rockies' let alone Lester Young at his creative best in 'Honeysuckle Rose' and Jess Stacy's beautiful diversion in 'Sing, Sing, Sing'?

As for the maestro himself, Benny had made his mark as 'the kid in short pants who played hot clarinet', and then graduated through the ranks of popular music and jazz. For Benny to have established his own style of swing music across America and to have led his own swing orchestra onto the stage of Carnegie Hall, all before his 30th birthday, was a colossal achievement. Few, if any, achieved such legendary status so early in their careers.

There is already a huge body of material written about Benny Goodman, 'King of Swing', covering in great detail his early career as a freelance session musician in the late 1920s and early 1930s right through to, and beyond his death in 1986. This extensive library includes two fascinating biographies written by Ross Firestone and James Lincoln Collier. In 1939, Goodman published an early autobiography which was written with the help of music critic, Irving Kolodin. Russell Connor has written a handful of exquisitely detailed and witty Bio-Discographies about his friend and hero without which, accurate research into Benny Goodman's life and music would be impossible. Russ's books are an absolute must for any BG fan. There have been more articles and stories in the Press about Goodman than are possible to count. Benny was the subject of intense public interest for more than fifty years, so why write more?

A casual riffle through the Benny Goodman section at any music shop will almost always find one item: 'The Famous 1938 Benny Goodman Carnegie Hall Jazz Concert'. It is one of the biggest selling jazz records ever. As of today, either on LP or CD, these recordings have been continuously available for 58 years! Constantly reissued and repackaged, worldwide the total sales of this album are impossible to calculate but it will run into several millions.

By 1950, the Swing era had long since passed, the Bee-Bop movement had been and gone too. Benny had disbanded and played only occasional small group appearances in parallel with his career as a classical soloist. He was also doing weekly radio work on WNEW, the New York radio station that had always been very supportive of Benny. He was a classical disc jockey and reviewer and a very good one at that, but he was still passionate about his music and concerned about his reputation. On the re-discovery of the Carnegie Hall recordings and with the enthusiastic help of Martin Block of WNEW, Swing music began to make something of a revival. Block had decided to revive his Sunday swing sessions, 'Make Believe Ballroom' and these sessions were not just playing records, he would invite musicians to come into the studio and play live. The first of these sessions in April 1951 featured the Benny Goodman trio in a session that was released later on record, as a benefit for the great

– Introduction –

arranger, Fletcher Henderson, who had recently suffered a stroke. Block got in contact with disc jockeys up and down the country and urged them to start their own swing programs and it really caught on.[1] Speaking in 1953, two years after the release of the concert recordings, Benny made this revealing comment about swing music: "You know, the records they made of that Carnegie Hall Concert, I had to be an egomaniac about that. I had to see that swing wasn't just a fad. I told myself, if it doesn't sell then my whole life's work is worth nothing"[2]. The impact of this one album on the music scene in the 1950s was phenomenal, sales of the record soared. (Sales of record players took off too, for the long playing Microgroove record was a new format then.) In the first two and a half years the album sold over 220,000 copies. Big Bands began to re-form and later, interest in Benny Goodman became sufficient for him to become the subject of a Hollywood movie along the lines of the 'Glen Miller Story'. 'The Benny Goodman Story' is a sugar-coated version of Benny's life up to the Carnegie concert which bears little resemblance to real life events.

It is over 70 years since that cold and spectacular night in January 1938 when the Benny Goodman Orchestra nervously walked out onto the Carnegie Hall stage and played a set that has gone down in history as one of the greatest concerts ever. The success of the record album in its various forms and the longevity of the music must surely mean that the occasion deserves a book all to itself.

Gathered together in this book are as many of the first hand reports and reminiscences of the concert that many years of research could uncover. The long time editor of Down Beat magazine, John McDonough, once described this concert as 'The most widely watched and written about event of the decade'.[3] This might well have been so, but tracking down all of this writing has been quite an undertaking. Although much of the material included here has been published before in a range of journals, it has never been brought together to form a comprehensive and rigorous study of the concert. Some of the publications are long since gone and forgotten, and many of them are very difficult to find. In an effort to avoid the 'Chinese Whispers' phenomenon where a story is repeated over and over until it becomes far removed from the original facts, I have, wherever possible, traced the legends surrounding this concert back to the earliest source available. Of course, believing everything that you read in the Press can be a dangerous occupation, and there are bound to be inaccuracies and contradictions when comparing long-held memories with reports written in the news media at the time. Regrettably, none of the musicians survive today so all we have is a catalogue of documentary evidence, and archive material.

In these pages, we can take the time to explore in great detail why a swing concert at that venue was so important, how the musicians felt about appearing there and how the concert came to be recorded. Along the way we can look at newly-discovered photographs, delve into the newspapers that reported the events of that night and find out more about the plans and preparations that went into making it such a monumental event. This then, is the story of a legendary concert, the story of a group of musicians who rarely, if ever sounded better, the story of a true landmark in American musical history: Benny Goodman's 'Famous 1938 Carnegie Hall Jazz Concert'.

1 Metronome Magazine – July 1951
2 Melody Maker – May 2 1953
3 Down Beat – 60 Years of Jazz. P. 20. Hal Leonard.

Music News from Coast to Coast

Down Beat

BALLROOM · CAFE · RADIO · STUDIO · SYMPHONY · THEATRE

B. G. INVADES SANCTUM OF LONG-HAIRS

See Story On Page Two

Above is a candid shot of Benny Goodman's famous Quartet, which with Benny Goodman's orchestra and several guest stars play a concert in New York's famous home of the Symphonic Long-Hairs, staid Carnegie Hall, Jan. 16. Left to right are Teddy Wilson, piano; Lionel Hampton, vibraphone; Gene Krupa, drums; Benny Goodman, clarinet.

VOL. 5, No. 1   (Foreign 25 Cents)   CHICAGO, JANUARY, 1938   U. S. and Canada 15 Cents Per Copy

• CHAPTER 1 •

Why Carnegie Hall?

To gain a better understanding of what it meant to play at Carnegie, it is worth having a look at the hall itself. Conceived by Leopold Damrosch and financed by the steel magnate and philanthropist Andrew Carnegie, Carnegie Hall is not just a simple concert hall. In the Carnegie Hall complex there are three halls: The Main Hall which seats 2800, the Recital Hall which is located below the Main Hall with seats for 1200 and the Chamber Music Hall which seats 250. Above the halls there were 170 studios, 30 offices and apartments and 9 shops. Carnegie Hall was and is a true community arts centre. It was designed to be the best facility of its kind. Petr Ilich Tchaikovsky and Leopold's son Walter Damrosch conducted the Symphony Society Orchestra on the opening night of May 5th 1891 and a host of other celebrated classical giants like Rachmaninoff, Vladimir Horowitz, Gustav Mahler, Richard Strauss and Thomas Beecham also played there in the early days. At the time of BG's famous concert in 1938, newspaper headlines urged us to believe that Carnegie Hall was a sacred place only to be graced by classical virtuosi and elite composers. 'BG Invades Sanctum of Long-hairs!'[4] was the banner headline in Down Beat Magazine announcing Benny's planned concert. "Andrew Carnegie's polite plaster shrine"[5] was how Time Magazine described the venue. Carnegie Hall, however, has always been open and eager to attract a wide variety of musicians and performers, not just the classical elite. At Carnegie Hall, the people of New York have always been keen to revel in the art, science, politics, philosophy and religion that were routinely on display alongside the feast of top quality music and dance. It was the regular 'serious' musicians playing at Carnegie Hall who were the most vociferous against Goodman's concert. They objected to the hall being used for such irreverent music.[6] Even seventy years after his Carnegie debut, Benny Goodman is still today the most celebrated of all clarinettists and contrary to the impression given in some parts of the Press at the time, he richly deserved the opportunity to perform there.

The warren of apartments and offices above the Carnegie Hall was home to artists, musicians and poets of all descriptions. There you could find recording facilities, photographic studios and rehearsal rooms. These studios and apartments have been referred to as 'upper bohemia' because of the eclectic mix of tenants and visitors. Having a large number of people coming and going at all hours often presented problems for

4 Down Beat Magazine – January 1938
5 Time Magazine – January 24 1938
6 Melody Maker – February 5 1938

The cover of Down Beat Magazine for January 1938 announcing BG's forthcoming 'invasion'.

the Carnegie Hall management. In order to prevent the tenants wandering in as they pleased when there was a performance in the hall, staff had to be strategically positioned in the maze of doors and corridors that led directly to the auditorium and backstage areas. On the other hand, it was very convenient for the many artists who lived there at one time or another, like the conductor Leonard Bernstein.

If you had lived in New York during the first 30 or so years of the twentieth century, you would have had a chance to go to Carnegie Hall to hear lectures by Roald Amundsen and later Ernest Shackleton on the subject of their expeditions to the South Pole. Arthur Conan Doyle gave lectures there and Winston Churchill gave an illustrated talk in 1901 entitled "The War As I Saw It" (The Boer War). Theodore Roosevelt lectured there many times, there were meetings organised by the Suffrage movement and various religious groups gathered there too. The world-famous impresario Sol Hurok had almost made Carnegie Hall his home and had presented many of the greatest dance artists and musicians from around the globe on the Carnegie stage. The day after he had showcased Benny, Sol Horuk presented the Hindu ballet company led by Uday Shan-Kar who was making his final visit to New York before the first of his retirements from dancing!

As far as music goes, audiences at Carnegie Hall saw an equally varied mix of performers and genres. The first Jazz heard at Carnegie was probably on May 2 1912. On that occasion, the Clef Club Orchestra which featured 120 black musicians, under the leadership of James Reese Europe rented the Hall for the first of many concerts they held there. Paul Whiteman had appeared there several times in the 1920s to present a program of concerts called 'Experiments in Modern Music'. Vincent Lopez and Zev Confrey ('Kitten on the Keys') had played Carnegie Hall. George Gershwin was commissioned to write a piece for the Philharmonic Orchestra and gave the first performance of his piano concerto there in 1925[7]. One of the pioneers of jazz, W C Handy played Carnegie in 1928, in a long and wide ranging concert of Spirituals, Blues and Jazz which featured Fats Waller at the piano and organ. (This was one of Fats' big early successes.)[8] In fact, Benny Goodman's music had been presented in Carnegie Hall on January 19 1937, almost exactly one year before the 'famous' concert, in a program of 'all types of Jazz from the classic to the hot idiom'. This was under the leadership of pianist and arranger Ferde Grofé, 'The Jazz Maestro', with an orchestra of forty-five musicians. Various pieces were performed that night including 'Mardi Gras' from Grofe's 'Mississippi Suite', and part of Gershwin's 'Cuban Overture'. Mr Grofe's 'Symphony of Steel' included a compressed air pneumatic drill along with a siren used on the overhead cranes that inspired the composition. The 'hot' section of the evening saw a performance of Bennie Godman's [sic][9] 'Stompin' at the Savoy' along with 'The Man I Love', 'Lisa', 'I Got Rhythm' and many other popular tunes, albeit in a rather

---

7 Portrait of Carnegie Hall – Theodore Cron & Burt Goldblatt
8 New York Times – April 28 1928
9 New York Times – January 20 1937

pompous form. There was also a performance of 'Cheek to Cheek' played by a string quartet and 'Top Hat' played on an electric piano.[10] Between 1912 and 1938, there had been something like 24 Jazz shows at Carnegie Hall.[11]

Benny Goodman and his orchestra's performance in 1938 was certainly not the first time Jazz was heard in Carnegie Hall but it was a momentous event, eagerly awaited by Goodman's young fans and massively oversubscribed. The speed at which the tickets sold for BG's concert prompted the Carnegie Hall management to announce, even before the concert had taken place, that they would be featuring more pop concerts, probably a series of Sunday night concerts featuring Berigan, Dorsey, Ellington and others.[12] For Benny, the success of the evening was not measured in financial terms, for even though he was to get a guaranteed sum and a percentage of the box office, the heavy costs of bringing in guest musicians and hiring Carnegie Hall and the stage hands for rehearsals, meant that Benny lost money that night. The true value to Benny came from the publicity and public esteem and that was incalculable. Even before the record sales were factored in, it was worth it, just for the 'fun of doing it'.[13] Throughout his long career, Benny performed at Carnegie Hall at least another twenty-five times, playing both classical and jazz concerts, and they were always sell-out shows.

More important to us now is the fact that Benny Goodman's 1938 concert featured, for the first time, a racially mixed group of musicians on the Carnegie Hall stage. Few of the newspapers remarked on this at the time except the 'black newspaper', the 'New York Amsterdam News' which understandably focused on the black musicians and arrangers who were on show that night; 10 of the 26 star musicians were black.

It is interesting to note that Carnegie Hall was often referred to in reverential terms as an ancient and hallowed hall. 'Swing It! And Even In A Temple of Music' was the headline in the New York Times magazine on the day of Benny's landmark concert there. The building is a very grand edifice, with richly ornamented columns and cornices, candelabras and cherubs, and gold leaf detailing. The stage is ornate and cavernous, the proscenium arch is imposing. A visitor to Carnegie Hall would be struck with awe before hearing a single note of music. Although it can accommodate nearly 3000 people, Carnegie Hall is surprisingly intimate. The building was designed by a team headed by William Burnet Tuthill and completed in 1891 using a mixture of ornate architectural styles. A small army of sculptors, moulders and artisans were used in the finishing of the interior, but underneath that styling there lies an extremely modern state-of-the-art structure. Its load-bearing walls are four and a half feet thick (1.5m), perhaps this mass could account for the wonderful quality of the hall's acoustics. It was one of New York's first all-fireproof buildings. It boasted its own steam powered electrical generation system and has never had a power cut. Deep in the basement there was a gigantic bunker which was filled with ice to provide cool air that was ducted, completely silently, around the building within the walls, under the stage and up through the auditorium. On a hot night, as much as 30 tons of ice per hour was consumed. Plans

10 Metronome Magazine – February 1937
11 Gino Francesconi – Archivist, Carnegie Hall
12 Tempo Magazine – February 1938. The Billboard Magazine – 22 January 1938
13 Variety Magazine January – January 19 1938

were being considered in 1938 to equip the hall with air-conditioning so that more use could be made of the hall during the summer months. It is a fantastic piece of architectural engineering which included every possible modern innovation of the time.

Let us not forget though, that at the time of Benny's concert in 1938, the Carnegie complex was only 47 years old. In that short time, it had become *the* greatest centre for musical progress in the land and not, as implied in the popular music Press at that time, a stuffy, backward-looking institution inhabited by sleeping, baggy-eyed 'pseudo-sophisticates' who sneered at great modern music![14] A Benny Goodman swing concert at Carnegie was not quite as incongruous as folklore would have us believe.

Benny was a backstreet kid from the Chicago slums and would have been acutely aware of the significance of playing at Carnegie Hall. His musicians too had a deep respect for the venue and were all very nervous at the thought of performing there, "Are you out of your mind, what the hell would we do there?"[15] was Benny's response when an astute publicity man floated the idea of a Carnegie concert late in 1937. A week before the concert, Benny's guitar player Allan Reuss looked forward with excitement to his appearance, "I am thrilled right now just thinking about the whole idea, I certainly never in my life expected to be playing a Carnegie Hall concert."[16] Gene Krupa, Benny's extraordinary drummer, used to pen a regular column in Metronome Magazine. Writing the day after the concert he explained "I never expected to get into Carnegie Hall – honest I didn't, I never even expected to get into the front door, let alone come through the back door the way all the really great artists have."[17] Whilst getting ready to go on stage that night, Benny's young and gifted trumpeter, Harry James came up with the much-quoted, immortal line "I feel like a whore in church."[18] Trumpeter Chris Griffin was a little more down to earth, "Just another gig" was his recollection of the evening![19] Standing in Carnegie Hall a few days before the concert for rehearsals, Benny grinned and joked with a reporter "You didn't think this was a League of Nations conference did you?"[20]

Benny Goodman's band was primarily a dance band. In those days, there were comparatively few 'sit down' jazz concerts but the idea was catching on fast on both sides of the Atlantic. On 12 December 1937, Down Beat Magazine presented a swing concert at the Congress Casino in Chicago which featured Jimmy Dorsey and Roy Eldridge. The enthusiastic crowd of 800 made it a howling success.[21] At about the same time as the tickets for Goodman's Carnegie concert went on sale in New York, the hot ticket in London was for a concert by Django Rheinhardt and Stephan Grappelli, the 'Hot Club of France'. That too sold out very quickly. Goodman's band had played concerts before, probably the most notable was at the Congress Hotel in Chicago on December 8 1935 which was promoted by the local 'Rhythm Club' run by Helen Oakley. That concert was a huge success.[22] It seems strange to us now but even with a few 'concerts' in the bag, Goodman

[14] Down Beat Magazine – February 1938
[15] The New Yorker – December 26 1977
[16] Down Beat Magazine – January 1938
[17] Metronome Magazine – February 1938 also quoted himself in Metronome, March 1956
[18] A slightly moderated 'I feel like waitress on a date with a college boy' is the earliest reference to this quote (Colliers Magazine January 1956)
[19] American History Magazine – April 2001
[20] New York World Telegram – 11 January 1938
[21] Down Beat Magazine – January 1938
[22] The Kingdom of Swing – Benny Goodman & Irving Kolodin

and his agents doubted whether they could hold the attention of an audience for the duration of a full-blown, two-hour concert at the country's most prestigious venue. Up until then, they had performed mainly at dances, cinemas (sandwiched between films) and on radio broadcasts. Here, audiences were always 'warmed up' ready for the band. Goodman's sponsored radio shows were peppered with jokes, tobacco advertising and comic actors doing their routines. This was pretty much standard fare at that time, there could be no chance of awkward silences or lack of pace on a radio show. A concert hall appearance would have to be varied and interesting to keep the audience's attention.

Benny was a rough diamond in those days, he wasn't trying to gain respectability for his music, he was just doing what he loved, "After all, this is just dance music. What's the use of trying to make something fancy and formal out of it?"[23] It was the serious Press that promoted the idea that Benny was somehow gate crashing Carnegie Hall. Jazz was frowned upon by many people and was supposed to be the cause of all sorts of degenerate behaviour. But there was a move by some musicians and their publicists to try and shift this image and give Jazz, or Swing music some kind of legitimacy. Parts of the Music Press were talking about jazz in a pseudo-highbrow manner using all sorts of 'fancy' language. A week before BG's Carnegie concert, Tommy Dorsey and his orchestra broadcast a 'masterly and scholarly treatise', entitled 'The Evolution of Swing', which depicted the development of swing, tracing its origins and following its sweep across the nation.[24] There seemed to be something of an inferiority complex amongst the jazz musicians and writers, there was a definite move to try to gain some respect for the music and make it appear more dignified.

The story of Benny's early career, his work with musicians such as Ben Pollack and Bix Biederbecke, and the formation of the trio and quartet with Teddy Wilson, Gene Krupa and Lionel Hampton, has been told often and there is no need to go over it again here.[25] We can pick up the story in 1937 when the Benny Goodman orchestra had become hugely successful and was, without question, the most sought after band in the country. By March 1937, the band was working round the clock six days a week. They were playing five or six shows *a day* at the Paramount Theatre in Times Square between matinee film shows, then in the evenings the band moved to the Pennsylvania Hotel where they would play six evenings a week. On Tuesdays, they would broadcast the Camel Caravan radio show direct from the hotel, there were other broadcasts during the week too. On top of that, after playing all evening for the dancers at the Pennsylvania, on Thursdays they would rehearse for the following Tuesday's Caravan radio show until four in the morning![26] There would also be occasional benefits and shows on Sundays too, one of which would get Benny into a spot of bother on the night of our concert the following January. Such was the life of a jazz musician in the most popular band in the country but this, of course, is the reason why the Goodman band was such a tight cohesive unit: Each section of the band thinking and breathing together, anticipating each other's thoughts, playing each other's parts, a band completely relaxed and in total command of the music.

---

23 The Kingdom of Swing – Benny Goodman & Irving Kolodin P.208
24 Radio Guide – January 15 1938
25 Ross Firestone's Biography covers Benny's career in great detail. See Bibliography.
26 Trumpet Blues – Peter Levinson P.43

To Savoy
What is better than
a sincere friend!
With appreciation

• CHAPTER 2 •

The Build-up to the Concert

The key events that set Benny on the path to the stage at Carnegie Hall started to unfold in the summer of 1937. After nearly a year in and around the New York area, where they had played to wildly enthusiastic fans at the Paramount theatre and the Hotel Pennsylvania and of course the increasingly popular broadcasts of the Camel Caravan radio program, the band took the train over to the west coast to start work on their second Hollywood movie 'Hollywood Hotel'. This would be their third summer in California. The previous year they had been in Tinsel-Town filming 'The Big Broadcast of 1937'. As the name implies, the Camel Caravan was broadcast from wherever the band were playing, so the show carried on with the Tuesday night shows when they got to the west coast.

The band was filming during July and August and the movie would be released to the public on January 12 1938, just four days before the Carnegie concert. The appalling racial tensions in the American South caused the film censors in Memphis to edit out scenes of the film which featured the mixed race Benny Goodman quartet playing 'I've Got A Heartful of Music'! There were only a few examples of mixed race bands around at that time but mostly as recording outfits not often as live bands. For a mixed band to appear on screen was a real taboo in some sections of American society. Tempo Music Magazine offered its congratulations to Warner Brothers, who made the film, and Benny for forcing the issue.[27]

Benny had been a regular guest on the incredibly popular WABC-Columbia Network 'Camel Caravan' radio show. In its early days, it had a Country and Western theme and was called 'Jack Oakie's College of Musical Knowledge' with music in the main by George Stoll's orchestra. The show also featured a spot for amateur college ensembles and soloists. Benny had first joined the Camel Caravan on June 30 1936 where he took over from the Casa Loma Orchestra who had been on the show for the previous three years. As this was his third sponsored radio show, he was already well known to radio audiences. The other two being NBC's 'Let's Dance' from December '34 to May '35 and the Elgin Watch Company's 'Elgin Review' early in 1936.[28]

The Camel Caravan show was sponsored by R J Reynolds, the makers of Camel Cigarettes and Prince Albert pipe tobacco. Many of those early commercial radio shows were sponsored by cigarette companies, perhaps they felt that the young listening audience of the pop music shows was an ideal place to promote their

Savington Crampton (right) producer of Benny Goodman's 1938 Carnegie Hall concert with Don McNeil, presenter of the long running radio show "The Breakfast Club". Crampton devised the format of BG's 'Swing School' whilst working for the William Esty Agency. Esty also sponsored the Carnegie Hall concert.

27 Tempo Magazine – March 1938
28 Listen To His Legacy – D. Russell Conner – P.45 and P.57. Also Kingdom of Swing – Benny Goodman & Irving Kolodin P.272

cigarettes. The broadcasts all had their star orchestra endorsements too. Tommy Dorsey was with Raleigh & Kool Cigarettes, Artie Shaw with Old Gold and Glen Miller and Paul Whiteman promoted Chesterfield. Then, as now, competition between radio shows for audience share was fierce and the Jack Oakie Show played opposite NBC's musical variety program 'Mardi Gras' which had featured big stars like Fred Astaire with music by the Raymond Paige Orchestra.[29] The Goodman band's contributions to the Camel Caravan show were becoming more and more popular and although the show was an hour long, Benny's performances were limited to short sections where the band would only play one or two numbers. Despite some big name stars on the Jack Oakie show like Eddie Cantor, Alice Faye and Judy Garland it was felt that since it had been running for nearly a year, the format of the show was a bit tired and needed a re-vamp[30].

The William Esty advertising agency had held the Camel Cigarettes account since the very early 30's and were asked to salvage the situation. William Esty hired radio director Savington Crampton,[31] a former Paris correspondent for the Associated Press to shake things up a bit.[32] Savington had gained his experience in radio working for J Walter Thompson on the 'Lux Radio Theatre', a long running radio program which was launched in 1934 and specialised in staging radio adaptations of plays and later on, movies. John Hammond, Benny's soon to be brother-in-law, was also hired as a writer and consultant for the Camel Caravan shows. John Hammond was a well-to-do music enthusiast and amateur musician who had a driving passion for jazz and an uncanny knack of finding and promoting new talent. Over the years he had a hot and cold relationship with Goodman, but in the thirties it was definitely hot! Hammond took on the job of talent-scout too, something at which he excelled, touring the college campuses looking for promising young performers to feature on the Camel Caravan show. "I accepted the job because it would help assure Benny a better show" John modestly recalled in his biography[33]. Such was the popularity of the Benny Goodman orchestra, Savington decided to change the format of the show to feature Benny for a full half an hour. The program was re-branded the 'The Benny Goodman Swing School' and was built around a collegiate format: everybody was addressed as 'Professor' or 'Doctor' with Professor Benny Goodman 'teaching' the audience or 'student body' about this new musical phenomenon. There were still gags and skits with ham actors playing the roles of truck drivers and test engineers whose nerves had been soothed by smoking Camel Cigarettes but there was also much, much more of BG and his fabulous orchestra.

Radio listeners coast to coast could tune-in to the Camel Caravan shows on Tuesday evenings and avid jazz fans in Europe could listen on Wednesday evenings to an 'Electrical Transcription' (a recording) of the shows re-broadcast by CBS's short-wave partner, radio station W2XE out of Wayne N.J.

The first of Crampton's new half hour shows was aired on the evening of the 29 June 1937, the same day that Benny started his third short residence at the Palomar

29 The Radio Guide 1937
30 Sarasota Herald Tribune – June 24 1986
31 New York Times – December 20 1939
32 Saratoga Herald Tribune – June 24 1986
33 On the Record – John Hammond

– The Build-up to the Concert –

Ballroom in Los Angeles. The show's host, Bill Goodwin announced that Oakie College would be closed for the summer and the format of the show remained the same until Jack Oakie returned in October to take the first half of a one hour show. It was almost as if there was a strategic plan put in place in June 1937, which would elevate Benny from doing short, scripted three minute slots on a late night radio show to the high point of his career, a concert at New York's Carnegie Hall.

That first show featured guest Rufe Davis a country singer and farmyard animal impressionist who had appeared in the film 'Mountain Music'. (They weren't quite confident enough to exclude Country music from Benny's first new format show!) Benny had just won the Metronome award for best Swing Band of the year and was presented with the award on air during this show. He modestly announced that it was the boys in the band that made it swing and dedicated the next tune, the trio playing 'Sweet Leilani', to them. Benny went on to make 182 shows for Camel Cigarettes spanning three and a half years. His last show was broadcast on 30 December 1939.[34] The Camel Caravan radio show carried on without BG into the 1950s. Speaking about the Camel Shows in 1956 Benny remarked "Our friends said that it was that radio show that made us into an institution. Wherever we went from then on we played to enormous crowds."[35]

On August 1 1937, the band played 'a concert' for 3500 people at the Palomar in Los Angeles. This was a fairly unusual event, unusual in that most gigs on the tour circuit were dance dates. This was more like a jazz festival, with Louis Prima, Ben Pollack, Hal Kemp, Stuff Smith and various others. It was around this time that Benny's long search for a singer to take the place of Helen Ward, who left the band to get married the previous December, finally paid off. Helen was a very popular singer and an accomplished pianist. She left the band to marry Albert Marx who went on to play a very important part in the Carnegie Hall story, more of which later. For eight months from December 1936, Benny had tried several singers with varying degrees of success, Margaret McCrae, Frances Hunt, Peg LaCentra, Marion Newman and Betty Van all came and went. It was not until August 1937 that Benny found what he was looking for.

Local singer Martha Tilton was determined to sing with the Benny Goodman orchestra, she had confided in her sister a year before that this was her ultimate dream. Martha was a relatively unknown singer with the Alexander Mayer Chorus, a twelve piece vocal group working on the Camel Caravan show from studios in California. Not completely unknown, she had appeared in the Cary Grant Film 'Topper' as an unnamed member of her vocal group 'Three Hits and a Miss'. Even though she had worked on the same show as Benny, she had never met him because his part was piped in from New York. Martha had become friends with the radio announcer, Bill Goodwin and it was he who suggested that Martha should audition for Benny whilst he was over in California filming 'Hollywood Hotel'. To her amazement, she was offered the job, signed a three year contract and started singing with the band almost immediately.[36]

---

34 "Summary of Company Sponsored Radio and TV Shows 1930-1960 (300000-600000)" 1960.
Bates: 505481526-505481528. http://tobaccodocuments.org/rjr/505481526-1528.html
35 Collier's Magazine – January 20 1956
36 Dream World – Love and Romance Magazine 'The Girl in Benny Goodman's Band'. August 1938

S. HUROK
presents

BENNY GOODMAN
and his
Swing Orchestra

in the first swing concert in the history of Carnegie Hall on

**SUNDAY EVENING
JANUARY 16th
CARNEGIE HALL**

TICKETS NOW AT BOX OFFICE
85c, $1.10, $1.65, $2.20, $2.75

• CHAPTER 3 •

Plans for a Concert

Solomon Hurok was from Eastern Europe. He had paid a black-market emigration operator to smuggle him out of Russia into Germany from where he sailed for New York, arriving in 1906 at the age of eighteen to find fame and make his fortune. On the first line of his autobiography he describes himself as a 'hero-worshiper', and he loved to rub shoulders with famous artists and performers. For nearly seventy years he was a driving force in New York performing arts. It was he who, almost single-handedly, brought ballet to the wide attention of the American public. Sol was not exclusively involved with ballet. He promoted acts from all branches of show business and he became known as one of the world's great impresarios. At one time or another he had presented to the American public the avant-garde dancer, Isadora Duncan, the ballerina Anna Pavlova, singer, Marion Anderson and the pianist Arthur Rubinstein to name just a few. Sol had spent the summer of 1937 in Europe, presenting the Ballet Russe in London and visiting the USSR. In October, he brought the Ballet Russe over to New York for a very successful ten day stay at the Metropolitan Opera House. In that same month, Sol had initiated a series of concerts at Carnegie Hall under his slogan, 'S Hurok Presents…', Benny Goodman's appearance there would be the third concert in the series. Sol had in effect made Carnegie Hall his home base. The management there would have welcomed his initiative as they had been without a regular subscription series for the previous ten years.[37]

The band left California early in September and worked its way back East playing concerts in Texas, Kansas, Ohio, Pennsylvania, Maryland and on October 11, Benny and the band moved back into the biggest hotel in the world in 1937, the Hotel Pennsylvania in New York City. The Big Bands in the Thirties were always in a state of flux and Benny's was no different. Trombone player Murray MacEachern had left the band around this time and moved over to Glen Gray's Casa Loma Orchestra at the Hotel New Yorker. There was talk in the Music Press that Goodman's trumpeter Ziggy Elman was thinking of going over to Glen Gray's band too but Ziggy stayed put.[38] After several auditions, the brilliant young trombone virtuoso Vernon Brown took over as first trombone. According to Metronome, Brown was the talk of the New York trombone world![39]

'Life Magazine', the most popular magazine in the country at the time, was planning a photo feature on the Goodman phenomenon for its regular excursion, 'Life Goes To A Party'. On October 16th, shortly after the band took up their three month stay, 'Life'

Sol Hurok's promotional handbill on display at the Rose Museum in Carnegie Hall.

37 'The Last Impresario' – Harlow Robinson
38 Metronome Magazine – October 1937 P.16
39 Metronome Magazine – January 1938 P.33

*The 1937 band:
Back row –
Harry Goodman,
Ziggy Elman,
Gordon Griffin,
Harry James,
Benny Goodman,
Gene Krupa,
Allan Reuss,
Jess Stacy.
Front row –
Vido Musso,
Hymie Schertzer,
Murray McEachern,
Art Rollini,
Red Ballard,
George Koenig.*

sent their photographer Rex Hardy down to the Madhattan Room at the Pennsylvania, and successfully captured in photographs the atmosphere of a Saturday evening dining and dancing.[40] 'Life' ran the Goodman story on November 1 1937. The following week, they published a story about Sol Hurok's sensational Ballet Russe! We can sense here that the Press agents of Sol and Benny were converging on each other. The Life journalist respectfully described the band's performance that night like this:

'No players to the gallery, the Goodman band neither sings, dances, recites or clowns. Earnest musicians, they improvise, extemporise, and beat the living daylights out of tunes like 'House Hop', 'Walk, Jenny, Walk' and 'Down South Camp Meetin'' with a minimum of horse play and a maximum of bland dignity'.

Bland dignity? Fortunately, we can judge for ourselves, a recording was made of the radio broadcast that evening and released on bootleg LP in the 1950s, it is now available on CD.[41]

---

40 No date for the visit is given in the article but the story in Life mentions that some of the audience had been at the Columbia-Pennsylvania football match at Columbia's Baker Field in New York that same afternoon. See: New York Times – October 16 1937
41 Viper's Nest VN-171

– Plans for a Concert –

By now, the sponsors of the Camel Caravan radio shows, R J Reynolds, were being besieged by sack loads of fan mail asking for information about Benny's band and swing music. Reynolds responded by producing a little booklet entitled 'This Thing Called Swing'. The booklet has an introduction by BG and contains a glossary of 'Swing Talk', along with a nice picture of Goodman's 'Madhattan band'. In order to stem the tide of fan mail and gain a little more publicity, Reynolds sent out a letter to their salesmen requesting that they distribute the booklet free to beauty shops, schools, colleges, universities and music stores as, a valuable good-will builder.

When Goodman's publicity man Wynn Nathanson had the idea of a concert in Carnegie Hall, it was only natural that he should speak to Sol Hurok's office. Wynn Nathanson worked for the Tom Fizdale Agency, who specialised in publicity for artists and agencies, they were advising Benny Goodman at that time along with his long-time friend Willard Alexander from MCA.[42] Photographs taken of the Goodman band at the rehearsals in Carnegie Hall and published in Metronome Magazine are credited to Tom Fizdale Inc.

One afternoon in early December 1937, so the story goes, the New York Sun music critic, Irving Kolodin, was visiting Gerald Goode who was the Press chief for Sol Hurok.

Harry James takes a solo in the Madhattan Room at the Hotel Pennsylvania. The other two thirds of the 'Biting Brass', Ziggy Elman and Gordon Griffin are sitting alongside.

42 'That Old Gang of Mine' – Collier's Magazine – January 20 1956

Whilst in conversation with Goode the telephone rang and it was Wynn Nathanson on the line suggesting that BG play a concert at Carnegie Hall.

Goode asked Kolodin "What would you think of a concert by Benny Goodman's band at Carnegie?"

"A terrific idea" was Kolodin's response, "Why?"

"It's somebody from Goodman's radio show, he wants Hurok to run it."[43]

We can add a little here to Kolodin's account of that meeting which first appeared on the original liner notes, The Billboard Magazine noted that:

Jerry Goode was heard to ask "Who is this Benny Goodman?"[44]

According to Benny Goodman, "Wynn had to do some talking to get me to agree.

"We'll die there, I kept saying."

"You'll be great" Wynn said, and Willard Alexander agreed."[45]

Sol was keen to develop his burgeoning 'S Hurok Presents' series at Carnegie Hall, so to satisfy his curiosity and maybe to allay his misgivings, he marched down to the Madhattan Room of the Hotel Pennsylvania to see and hear the Benny Goodman band for himself, perhaps he had already seen the pictures in 'Life Magazine'. Benny and the band were part way through a fifteen week residency at the famous hotel, where they would entertain in the region of 375 dancing couples on a Saturday night. The Madhattan Room was the favourite haunt of college students whose exuberant dancing was 'as good as a floor-show'.[46]

Fortunately for us, we can see in that issue of Life Magazine, just about what Sol Hurok would have seen on his venture into the Kingdom of Swing. Sol was quite taken aback by the uproar of the band and the artistry of the Goodman quartet.[47] The young fans, many of whom we can see crowded around the stage in those 'Life' pictures, just watching and listening would have helped persuade Sol that he could profit by bringing the BG orchestra into Carnegie Hall. Even in Benny's early days in 1935 and 1936, fans would gather around the stage just to take in the music. Metronome told of a crowd thirty-deep around the bandstand at a dance in Sunnybrook Pa. in October 1937, just before they moved into the Pennsylvania Hotel.[48]

Once Wynn Nathanson's suggestion for a concert at Carnegie Hall was agreed by all involved, the job of producing the concert was given to none other than the William Esty Agency, who were doing such a good job in writing the scripts and promoting the Camel Caravan shows.[49] (Variety Magazine claimed that the William Esty Agency should be credited with proposing the idea for the concert.[50] It was said in Billboard Magazine when the plans for the concert were announced, that the whole idea for the concert was 'the brainstorm of John Hammond', the renowned jazz authority and freelance talent scout. But in John's autobiography, published in 1977, he says that he

---

43 Liner notes SL-160
44 The Billboard Magazine – January 1 1938
45 'The Old Gang of Mine' – Collier's Magazine – January 20 1956
46 Stage Magazine – January 1938. P.28
47 Columbia Records SL-160 – Liner notes
48 Metronome – November 1937. P.16
49 The Billboard Magazine – January 1 1938 P.46
50 Variety Magazine – January 19 1938. P.51

had little to do with the concert other than suggesting that Benny invite members of the Count Basie and Duke Ellington orchestras to participate). The William Esty Agency felt that the added prestige of presenting a Benny Goodman swing concert at Carnegie Hall, would boost sales for their client's Camel cigarettes. The intention was to keep Benny's brand of swing on a higher plain compared to the multitude of other swing bands playing the dance halls at the time. This would be achieved by following the Carnegie Hall concert with a tour of the country's elegant concert halls, rather than the endless stream of movie theatres and ballrooms. The management of this tour was to be put into the capable hands of Sol Hurok. Speaking to Whitney Balliett nearly forty years after the concert, Benny was rather ambivalent about Sol's contribution to the evening. "Sol Hurok's name was on the evening, but he had nothing to do with it outside of sending me a wire reminding me to tell the musicians that they would be playing in Carnegie Hall and to be on their best behaviour".[51]

This was not the last time that Sol Hurok would be associated with BG. In 1962, it was Hurok who suggested that the Benny Goodman Orchestra be chosen to represent the USA on a State Department goodwill tour of the Soviet Union.

---

51 The New Yorker Magazine – December 26 1977

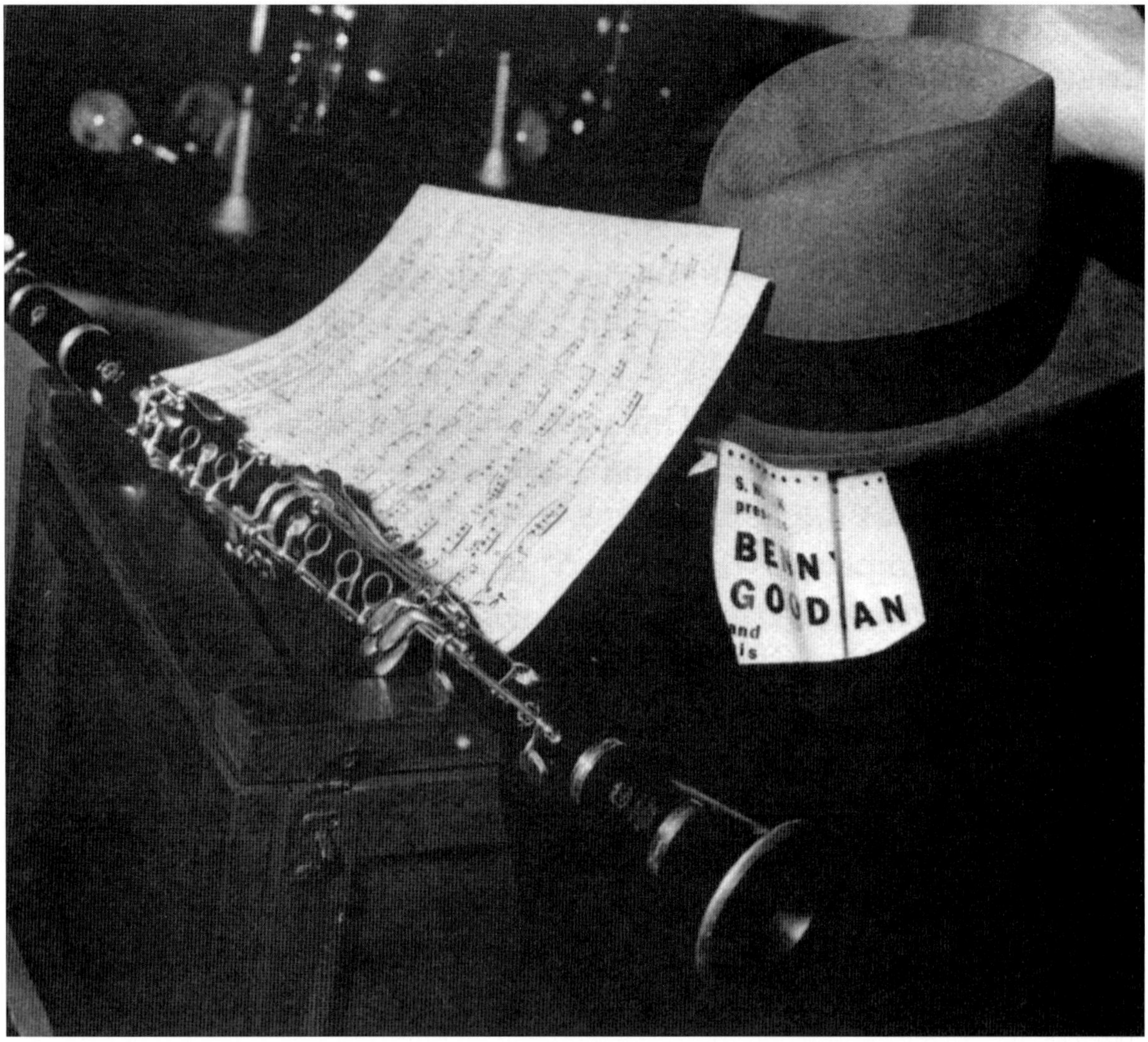

• CHAPTER 4 •

Hot Music in a Cold Town

The post-Depression American music industry was booming in 1937, Variety Magazine reported that there were 400,000 working musicians in the U.S and 18,000 of those in touring bands. Musical instrument manufacturers and music publishers were enjoying a bumper year too. Through the winter of 1937-38, New York was at the epicentre of the swing music movement. Over 25 of the big-name bands were in town over those few short months including: Cab Calloway at the Cotton Club, Louis Prima at the Famous Door, the Count Basie Band had made its debut on Broadway, Bob Crosby moved into the Madhattan Room after the Goodman Band moved on to the Paramount Theatre, Red Norvo replaced Tommy Dorsey at the Commodore Hotel, Duke Ellington was in town too, and over that Winter many more of the great names of Jazz visited, like Charlie Barnet, Les Brown, Chick Webb, Art Tatum and Fats Waller.

Papers were signed committing Benny to the concert sometime during the week of 4th December 1937[52] and Associated Press released the news of Benny's intention to perform at Carnegie Hall on the 11 December 1937. One of the first newspapers to pick it up was the Palladium Times in Oswago NY. They published the news on December 11 1937 although the format of the evening was far from settled at that time. A short article in the NY Times on the 12th December announced:

'Carnegie Hall, no stranger to jazz, is taking the next step and admitting Benny Goodman and his swing band for a concert'.[53] Note the use of the word 'admitting'. This tells us much about how the establishment felt about his appearance there. He was not 'invited' or 'welcomed' he was admitted. We can imagine Benny and the band outside of Carnegie Hall angrily beating on the stage doors... "Let us in, let us in!" Well, in a sense perhaps that is just what they were doing.

It is also worth noting that the very first announcement of the concert in the New York Times also states that Carnegie Hall is no stranger to jazz. Subsequent stories, even today, proclaim that this was to be the very first jazz concert in the hall, probably as a result of Sol Hurok's original handbill. Pre-publicity for the concert was relatively sparse. There were some handbills printed which announced 'Sol Hurok Presents Benny Goodman and his Swing Orchestra in the first swing concert in the history of Carnegie Hall', but there were no big ads in the Music Press promoting the concert. Ticket sales

Benny's clarinet and overcoat arranged for this 'still life' shot taken at rehearsals. (Notice Hurok's handbill in Benny's top pocket.)

---

52 Jack Sher – Screen & Radio Weekly – Rochester NY Democrat Chronicle
53 New York Times – December 12 1937

"What's going on at Carnegie Hall this weekend?" With a bit of stretching and enlarging of this contemporary photograph, we can have a look.

were driven by editorial in the Press, backed up by some carefully scripted mentions on the Camel Caravan radio shows.

Reports in the Press suggested that along with the Goodman band we might see Joe Turner, the blues singer and pianist that Benny had 'discovered' in Kansas.[54] W C Handy, who had played Carnegie Hall ten years before might also make a return appearance. It was said that Mary Lou Williams, one of Benny's arrangers would be writing a Jazz concerto for the concert with the possibility that she may play it as well. (Mary Lou was responsible for one of Benny's greatest successes, 'Roll'Em'). Lionel Hampton too, was reportedly composing a Swing Symphony for the occasion.[55] Tempo Magazine said that Benny would be playing variations on W C Handy's 'St Louis Blues' in various styles with Babe Russin taking the major portion of the tenor work.[56] Melody Maker magazine suggested that the news of Benny breaking the colour bar at Carnegie Hall, would in some way make up for the disappointment of the last minute failure of

54 The Billboard Magazine – January 1 193 P.46
55 Melody Maker – January 1 1938
56 Tempo magazine – January 1938

John Hammond's ambitious plan to bring Benny Goodman and Benny Carter to Europe a few years earlier![57] (Some of Goodman's earliest hits were recorded for distribution in Europe on the English Columbia label.) Pandering to the young swing fans and perhaps referring to the riotous opening at the Paramount Theatre the previous March, Metronome's editor announced the forthcoming engagement at Carnegie, under the headline 'Benny Goodman Crashes Sedate Carnegie Hall'. He went on: 'Held under the auspices of famed artists' manager Sol Hurok, the Goodman swing concert will be the first ever to infest the atrabilious atmosphere of the staid, old hall. Special arrangements are now being made to re-enforce seats, chandeliers, walls, the roof, and even the ushers in a frantic attempt to keep everything within the domain of the building. Of course, if the building, itself, should wake up and jump across to the other side of Fifty-Seventh Street – well, Carnegie Hall attachés just hope for the best!'[58] On a light-hearted note, Down Beat Magazine quipped, 'There's no truth in the rumour that Carnegie Hall directors are booking Stokowski for a week at the Apollo Theatre in Harlem, as revenge against Goodman's invasion of the symphonic sanctity of their classical auditorium!!!'.[59]

The music for the concert was carefully chosen, the band had to keep the audience entertained for nearly two hours. Benny commissioned some new arrangements and included some old flag-wavers too. The trio and quartet would have a good workout and they contributed a brand new number which they had collectively composed only a few days before. There would also be a couple of pop songs to help make the evening varied and interesting: the program was a well-balanced mixture of small group improvisations and big band orchestrations. There are four tunes in the printed program that were not played at the concert, 'I'm a Ding Dong Daddy', 'Tiger Rag', 'Who' and 'Dinah', all small group numbers. It was the respected music critic, Irving Kolodin, who proposed the idea of an historical interlude 'Twenty Years of Jazz'[60] as part of the concert. John Hammond, Benny's friend and advisor, suggested that he include star soloists from the Basie and Ellington bands for the historical section and the jam session. John also had a hand in the detailed program notes which accompanied the concert program.[61] (See Appendix 1)

---

[57] Melody Maker – December 25 1937
[58] Metronome – January 1938
[59] Down Beat Magazine – January 1938 P.5
[60] Columbia Records SL-160 – Liner notes
[61] The program notes acknowledged the help that John had given. See Appendix 1.

TELEPHONE: CIRCLE 7-8300

Cable Address
"HURAT"

HUROK ATTRACTIONS, INC.
S. HUROK, President
30 ROCKEFELLER PLAZA

NEW YORK

January 10th, 1938

S. HUROK
presents
for 1938-39
First American Season
THE NEW
AND GREATER
BALLET RUSSE
Direct from Monte Carlo
LEONIDE MASSINE
Artistic Director

DISTINGUISHED ATTRACTIONS
Presented by
S. HUROK

ANNA PAVLOWA
and her Ballet Russe
FEODOR CHALIAPIN
ALEXANDER GLAZOUNOW
RICHARD STRAUSS
EUGENE YSAYE
ERNESTINE SCHUMANN-HEINK
ISADORA DUNCAN
ALMA GLUCK
EFREM ZIMBALIST
TITTA RUFFO
LUISA TETRAZZINI
MISCHA ELMAN
RUSSIAN GRAND OPERA CO.
GERMAN GRAND OPERA CO.
ISADORA DUNCAN DANCERS
HABIMA PLAYERS
ISA KREMER
LOIE FULLER
MOSCOW ART PLAYERS
THE BLUE BIRD
MARY WIGMAN
VICENTE ESCUDERO
NIKITA BALIEFF
BRONISLAW HUBERMAN
DANA SINGING ENSEMBLE
MOSCOW CATHEDRAL CHOIR
TEATRO DE PICCOLI

PRESENTING FOR SEASONS
1937-1938-1939

MARIAN ANDERSON
CONTINENTAL ENSEMBLE
KOLISCH QUARTET
ARTUR RUBINSTEIN
JOSEPH SCHMIDT
TRUDI SCHOOP
and her Comic Ballet
UDAY SHAN-KAR
and his Hindu Ballet
VIENNA CHOIR BOYS
SAXOPHONE QUARTET
ARGENTINITA
COMEDIAN HARMONISTS
JENNIE TOUREL

SEASON 1938-39
SALZBURG
OPERA GUILD
New Repertoire
Company of 75
Orchestra : Ballet

Mr. Willard Alexander
Music Corporation of America
745 Fifth Avenue
New York City

Dear Mr. Alexander:

Before leaving for Hollywood this afternoon, I wish to go on record as disapproving of some of the preparations which are being made for Mr. Goodman's Carnegie Hall concert.

I do not think that the idea of Miss Beatrice Lillie acting as commentator is a very good one and believe that it will bring about a certain amount of ridicule from the music critics - who are the very ones you should be seeking to impress.

Also, I am told, you are planning to have Mr. Goodman play against a background of black curtains, with special lighting effects, and with the musicians clad in theatrical costumes. This is contrary to musical tradition and will only serve to neutralize the very dignity which you were seeking to obtain by having Mr. Goodman play at Carnegie Hall.

Since the arrangements with Miss Lillie have already been made, there is no use carping about that point, but I wish to object (since the concert is under my auspices) to the employment of theatrical atmosphere - when the point of this entire event is that it is a concert we are offering, subject to the tradition and decorum of such an event.

Very truly yours,

S. HUROK

copy to: Mr. Benny Goodman

• CHAPTER 5 •

Guests

The Count Basie orchestra was relatively unknown amongst white audiences at that time and like Goodman, Basie was being promoted by the booking agents Music Corporation of America, by far the largest agent for bands in the country. John Hammond was heavily promoting Basie too, he had brought The 'Count' to New York from Kansas a year before and was almost evangelical about Basie and his soloists. Whenever possible, John used to attend the band's recording sessions and ballroom appearances. To get Basie and four of his musicians on the bill with Goodman at Carnegie Hall was quite a coup. Hammond was always searching out new talent and played a big part in bringing many 'undiscovered' performers to the public eye. (His long list of talent went on to include Aretha Franklin, Bob Dylan and Bruce Springstein in later years). Touring bands had punishing schedules to cope with. Count Basie's band were playing in Scranton, Pennsylvania on the 15 January, then a select few of the band joined Benny at Carnegie Hall on the 16th. Later that same evening, Basie's band was duelling in a 'Battle of the Bands' with Chick Webb at the Savoy Ballroom in Harlem. Yet, next day on the 17th, Basie and his men were off to the Ritz in Pottsville Pennsylvania.[62]

Duke Ellington's band (Benny's favourite then) was in New York recording with Consolidated Radio Artists at that time. Three key members of Ellington's band were also invited to join with Goodman for his debut at Carnegie Hall. Benny's other choice of guest was Bobby Hackett who had just opened at Nick's Tavern in Greenwich Village playing Dixieland jazz. Bobby was becoming a very popular musician, having made several visits to the recording studios over the previous few months.

Another attraction for the evening was to be Beatrice Lillie, the comic that Noel Coward had called the funniest woman in the world. Beatrice had been a guest on Benny's Camel Caravan show a couple of weeks before the concert and he was a big fan of hers. He went to see her after he had accepted the Carnegie assignment to ask if she would do a skit, "I thought it would relieve the monotony and anyway, the stage shows we played in theatres always included comics. She was smart enough to decline".[63] Curiously, Benny's version is slightly at odds with reports printed in the Press at the time. The New York Times ran a story on consecutive days, on the 13 January it said that Bea Lillie would be acting as commentator and singing at the concert, but on the 14th they added a sentence to their regular 'Music Notes' column saying that she

---

62 Count Basie Discography. – Chris Sheridan P.1091
63 New Yorker Magazine - December 26 1977

Sol Hurok's letter to Willard Alexander of the MCA agency.

Beatrice Lillie who so very nearly appeared at Carnegie Hall with Benny.

had been called to Hollywood. Francis Perkins also noted in the New York Herald Tribune, 'Bea Lillie had also been announced for some verbal annotating, but her cinema activities recalled her to Hollywood a few days before',[64] it would seem that Bea had at first accepted Benny's invitation and notice of her participation had been released to the Press. The reason why she withdrew from the concert can be found in a letter first published in Benny's pictorial autobiography published in 1979[65]. The letter is from Sol Hurok, the promoter of the concert, to Willard Alexander of MCA Benny's booking agents and was dated 10th January. Sol wrote this: "I do not think that the idea of having Miss Beatrice Lillie as commentator is a very good one and I believe that it will bring a certain amount of ridicule from the music critics – who are the very ones you should be seeking to impress" Sol went on: "Also, I am told, you are planning to have Mr Goodman play against a background of black curtains, with special lighting effects, and with the musicians clad in theatrical costumes. This is contrary to musical tradition and will only serve to neutralise the very dignity which you were seeking to obtain by having Mr Goodman play at Carnegie Hall." Whatever the reason for Beatrice Lillie's non-appearance at the concert that night, she was back in New York and on Benny's regular Camel Caravan radio show three weeks later, where she sang with Benny and his regular singer Martha Tilton.[66] Benny and his publicity team seemed under-confident about performing at Carnegie and were hoping to present more of a traditional Vaudeville type performance rather than a straightforward concert. Willard Alexander obviously took Sol's intervention seriously as we can see from the photographs taken that night. One wonders what these theatrical costumes and lighting effects might have looked like!

The January 1938 issue of Down Beat Magazine contained the results of their annual poll, the Benny Goodman band featured highly in the results. A year before, Harry James was relatively unknown, playing with the Ben Pollack Orchestra and had not featured at all in the results. This year, having played in the glorious Goodman trumpet section since January 1937, he had won the 'Best Trumpet Player' category, Teddy Wilson carried off the top piano player award, Gene Krupa took the best drummer spot and of course Benny retained his top clarinet player position. The band also got the award for the best arrangement of the year with 'Sing, Sing, Sing'.[67] Martin Block's Make-Believe Ballroom on the New York radio station WNEW held an annual 'listeners' poll' and they also published the results in January. The Goodman outfit had come out on top of that too, beating the increasingly popular Tommy Dorsey Orchestra into second place, but not by very much....

The New Year started as the Old Year had finished, the band was very busy. On New Year's Day they were broadcasting again from the Madhattan Room and on the

64 New York Herald Tribune - January 17 1938
65 Benny, A Pictorial Biography. Stanley Baron
66 Listen to His Legacy - D. Russell Connor. P.82
67 Down Beat Magazine - January 1938

4th January, Benny did a little comedy routine with Tom Howard and George Shelton on his Tuesday Camel show. The routine finished with a plug for the concert, then less than two weeks away:

Howard: "Glad to know you Benny. Oh yeah. You're the fella that's going highbrow, playing at Carnegie Hall where they listen to the classical artists."

Benny: "No, not highbrow. Simply playing the same kind of music we are playing tonight. It seems that the people who really know and love music think we belong in Carnegie Hall."[68]

Benny and the orchestra were on the air again from the Madhattan Room on the 5th January. On the 6th, both Teddy Wilson and Harry James were recording with their own bands, including Harry's interpretation of 'One O'Clock Jump'.

Things were hotting up in Carnegie Hall on the 8th January, for a different reason, there was a serious fire in the building late that evening! It started in a dress shop on the ground floor and caused the evacuation of parts of the building. The fire spread to the second floor damaging shops and offices there, traffic was halted in the area while the fire services dealt with the incident. Luckily, they managed to get the situation under control before too much damage was done.[69]

There was a story in gossip columns that Gene Krupa was planning to leave the Goodman band during April after their theatre commitments and front his own band.[70] Contrary to popular belief, Billboard Magazine, which went to Press on the 10th January, suggested that Goodman himself would be sponsoring the new Krupa band. Melody Maker also said that Goodman would be sponsoring the enterprise. In an effort to squash these rumours, Benny renewed Gene's contract with the band.[71] The commonly accepted story is that Krupa left Goodman's band as a result of a very public row on stage at the Earl Theatre in Philadelphia on the 3rd March 1938 and that Gene's departure was a surprise to Goodman. It is now clear that Benny would have been well aware of Krupa's intention to leave the band and start up on his own, even at the time of the Carnegie Hall concert.

Teddy Wilson was back in the recording studios again on the 10th with Mildred Bailey. The New York World-Telegram published a story on the 11th January under the headline 'Goodman, Standing Where Toscanini Stands, Tells About Swing'. Their reporter Douglas Gilbert writes that Benny and the band were at Carnegie Hall, we assume on the 10th, for rehearsals. A photograph published alongside that article shows Benny with his hands cupped over his ears as the band straighten out the new arrangement of 'Blue Room'.

During the Camel Caravan radio show on the 11th January from the Madhattan Room, the band played four tunes that they would be performing at Carnegie Hall. These included the first live on-air run through of the new Edgar Sampson arrangement of 'Don't Be That Way', they also played 'Blue Room', 'Body and Soul' and 'Dizzy

---

68 Camel Caravan. William Esty. "Columbia Broadcasting System. Benny Goodman's Swing School - Program No. 13 - 2.." Jan 4 1938. Bates: 514563877-514563887. http://tobaccodocuments.org/rjr/514563877-3887.html
69 New York Times - January 9 1938
70 Billboard Magazine – January 15 1938 P.15 Melody Maker - January 29 1938
71 Radio Mirror – February 1938 P.63

Spells'. At the time of writing this, the airchecks of that Camel broadcast have not been published but the radio scripts are available and there we find a revealing exchange between Benny Goodman and the program's compere, Dan Seymour, which gives us some insight into the creation of the new quartet number, 'Dizzy Spells':

Seymour: "This week's meeting of the board of trustees brings a tune that is probably the newest number ever heard on any program. The Professor, Dr Krupa, Dr. Wilson and Dr. Hampton wrote it this afternoon during rehearsal. We've titled it "Dizzy Spell" [sic] which is a fine example of understatement."[72] (It's not clear whether they are talking about rehearsal for the radio show or rehearsal for the Carnegie concert.)

Dan Seymour also makes a little announcement about the upcoming concert for the radio listeners:

Seymour: "Professor, before the next number, I'd like to offer my congratulations on your Carnegie Hall concert next Sunday."

Benny: "Thank you, Doctor. We're very proud of it."

Seymour: "Naturally, as some of you students know, Carnegie Hall is the goal of most of the classical stars of the music world. Benny Goodman has brought Swing to the point where the musical authorities of New York feel that it should take its place among the immortal music of the world. So next Sunday night the Professor with the faculty, Martha, the trio and quartet will play the first Swing Concert ever presented in the hallowed confines of Carnegie Hall. Again, Professor, congratulations.

Goodman: Thanks, Doctor. We wish the whole Swing School could be there."[73]

On the 12th January 1938, Benny 'put in a mean rehearsal' with the Coolidge String quartet whom he had invited to join him on his Camel Caravan Show two days after his appearance at Carnegie Hall, to play some Mozart.[74] Teddy Wilson was recording at the Columbia Studio with a small group made up from members of the Basie Band and Billie Holiday. Benny and the band made their regular broadcast from the Madhattan Room that evening, having another go at 'Don't Be That Way' and also 'Swingtime in the Rockies'.

Also on the 12th January, Warner Brothers released the new Busby Berkeley movie 'Hollywood Hotel' based on the long running radio show with the same name and starring Dick Powell, Rosemary and Lola Lane and the Benny Goodman Orchestra. Ronald Reagan makes a brief appearance too. Dick Powell was the first master of ceremonies in the original Hollywood Hotel radio show and played saxophonist Ronnie Bowers in the film. The Strand Theatre in Times Square was packed with young Goodman fans for the premier, who almost drowned out the movie. The New York Times felt it proper to issue an advance warning to the management at Carnegie Hall to: 'take whatever cover is available'! Benny and the band featured heavily in the movie, causing the audience to erupt 'whenever his clarinet is poked into camera range'. Benny took on an acting role too. Melody Maker magazine revealed to its

---

72 Camel Caravan William Esty. "Columbia Broadcasting System. Benny Goodman's Swing School - Program No. 16" Tuesday, January 11, 1938. Bates: 514563888-514563894. http://tobaccodocuments.org/rjr/514563888-3894.html
73 Camel Caravan William Esty. "Columbia Broadcasting System. Benny Goodman's Swing School - Program No. 16." Tuesday, January 11, 1938. Bates: 514563888-514563894. http://tobaccodocuments.org/rjr/514563888-3894.html
74 The Billboard magazine - January 22 1938

English readers that 'he speaks lines and looks agreeably modest, although there is just a trace of camera consciousness about his work'[75]. The opening sequence has some close-ups of band members performing 'Hooray For Hollywood' all standing in the backs of open-top cars arriving at 'St Louis Airport'. They obviously could not work out a way of getting a piano on the back of a car and into the opening parade. Poor Jess Stacy is forced to march about holding a clarinet![76] The film, which was shot in the summer of 1937, contains some nice scenes of the orchestra playing a somewhat truncated version of 'Sing Sing Sing'. Benny was insistent that they were to play their music 'live' during filming of the movie and not mime to a pre-recorded soundtrack, so the performances we see on screen are the real thing shot from several angles simultaneously. Performing in front of the Hollywood cameras could not have been easy, but the Goodman quartet play marvellously for their portion of the movie, a supposed rehearsal session in which Goodman finishes up by delivering the immortal line "Alright boys, that's all. Don't forget to be on time tomorrow!"

After a very shaky start in 1934 and four hard years on the road, 'Benny Goodman and His Swing Orchestra' were now at the very pinnacle of their careers. They had become movie stars, they had their own radio show, they had been voted the top band in the music Press and they were about to play a concert at the most prestigious venue in the country.

75 Melody Maker - January 29 1938
76 Warner Brothers DVD - Hollywood Hotel

Benny Goodman

Ziggie Elman

Chriss Staley

Lionel Hampton

Herman Shertzer

Red Ballard

Jordon Griffin

Vernon Brown

Harry Goodman

Arti Rollini

Babe Rusin

Leonard Vannerson

1/16/38

CHAPTER 6
Rehearsals

How do you get to Carnegie Hall? Practice! Goodman was certainly a keen advocate of that old adage. Although the orchestra was well rehearsed, razor sharp and at the peak of its abilities, Benny brought his band and the guest musicians from the Duke Ellington and Count Basie bands along with Bobby Hackett to Carnegie Hall a few days before the concert for rehearsals. They all needed to get a feel for how the hall would respond to the 'devil's music'! The musicians needed to hear the hall. Precisely when they went into Carnegie Hall to rehearse is difficult to tell. The Carnegie Hall archives have no records of the rehearsal sessions booked by the huge number of artists that performed there during the winter months of 1937-38. There were something like fifteen performances in the hall that week alone and all of those artists would have wanted stage time for rehearsals too. We have to rely on Press reports for our information. Several publications mention that Benny had more than one rehearsal for the concert. The evidence from photographs, like the fact that Benny was wearing a different neck-tie in some of them, and Press reports, suggests that there were two, possibly even three sessions at Carnegie Hall prior to the concert. Perhaps something like this: one for the 'History of Jazz', one for the 'Jam Session' and one for the band numbers. However, three rehearsal slots is just about unheard of in the history of Carnegie Hall. In later years, Benny recalled, "We were not nervous at the unprecedented Jazz performance, we were a pretty cocky bunch and besides, we had a couple of rehearsal days there."[77]

Carnegie Hall does have one item in its museum which suggests a rehearsal, a page from a book of autographs collected by the stage manager at the time, John Totten. The signatures of most of the band members plus the road manager and band boy are there. The page is dated 1/6/38, although this of course could just be a mistake which should have read 1/16/38. This list of signatures is incomplete, the missing band members are Teddy Wilson, Harry James, Gene Krupa, and Allan Reuss. We can check up on those missing names and see what they were doing on the 6th. Teddy Wilson was recording with Billie Holiday, Harry James was recording his own band, Gene Krupa was sick and had missed the broadcast from the Madhattan the night before. That leaves Allan Reuss, Russ Connor writes in his last book 'Wrappin' It Up', that on one occasion Allan Reuss was unable to get to a rehearsal in time and had made frantic telephone calls to guitarist Allan Hanlon (who was about to join Red Norvo's band at the Commodore Hotel) to ask him to sit in his place[78]. Hanlon had subbed for Allan Reuss

John Totten's autograph book. John was the stage manager at Carnegie Hall in 1938 and collected the autographs of most of the band as well as Benny's staff at rehearsals on the 6th January 1938.

77 Palladium Times –February 9 1976
78 Benny Goodman Wrappin' It Up - D Russell Connor - P.15

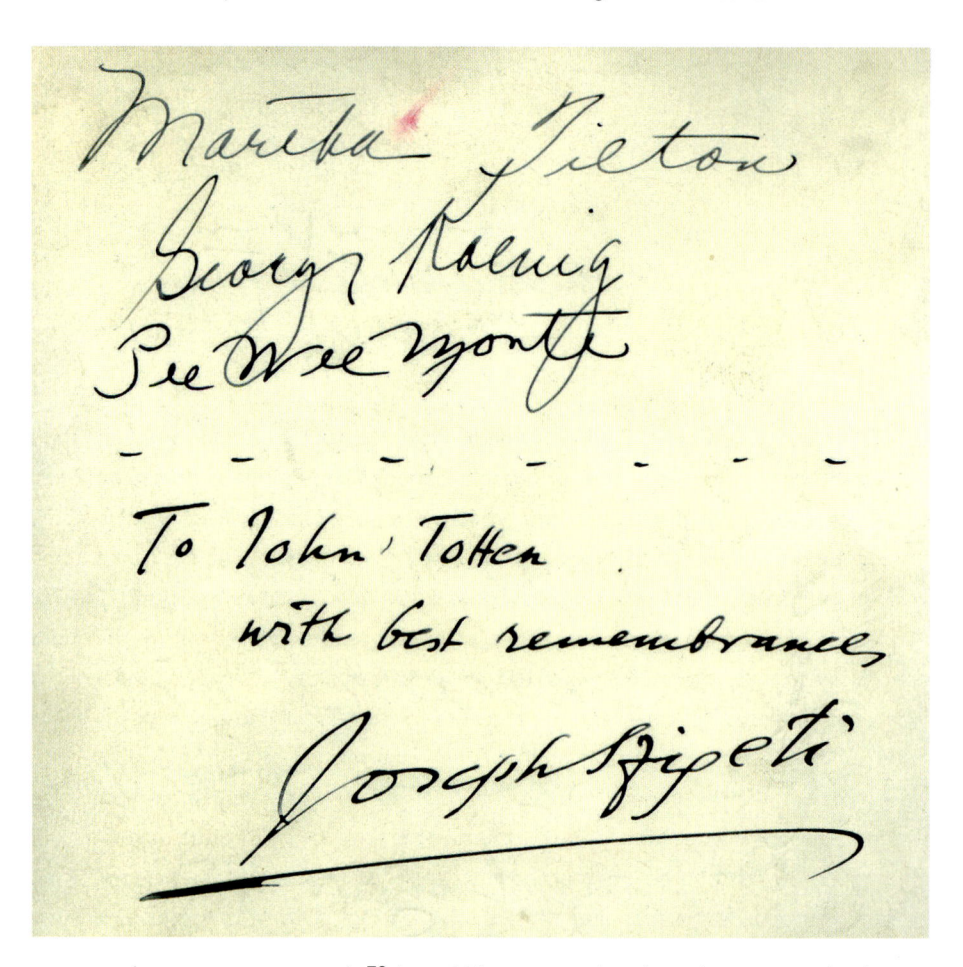

on several occasions previously.[79] Lionel Hampton is listed on the autographed page and his presence could be to replace Krupa which he had done the night before at the Madhattan.[80] Without Teddy Wilson and Gene Krupa there would be little point in rehearsing the quartet. One difficulty with this theory is that Vernon Brown and Jess Stacy were also at Harry James' recording session. We could speculate that James needed to stay on in the studio to review the play backs and choose the master, but there is no evidence for that. We do know that there was only one concert in the Hall on the 6th, an evening concert by the Boston Symphony, they probably would have warmed up in the afternoon but that would have left the morning free.

A little more concrete, is a report by Douglas Gilbert in the New York World-Telegram which confidently places Benny and the orchestra in Carnegie Hall rehearsing sometime around the 10th January, almost a week before the concert. Establishing the date for Benny's other rehearsal is a little more difficult. There was another concert in the hall at 3pm on the same afternoon as Benny's, given by the New York Philharmonic Orchestra. Benny's concert was due to start at 8.45pm. The afternoon concert was a quite lengthy program that contained some unfamiliar work and was broadcast live, at least in part, by CBS. It included a Concerto by Saint Saens conducted by Mishel Piastro with Georges Enesco as the violin soloist. Enesco then took

[79] Metronome Magazine - May 1938. P.44
[80] Swing Era Scrap Book - Ken Vail. P.308

over the baton for the 'Haffner' symphony by Mozart followed by the first two movements of the 'Rustic Suite' by Sabin Dragoi, and Beethoven's fourth symphony. This was the first time that the Dragoi piece had been performed in America[81]. For that reason, the Philharmonic probably would have rehearsed the Dragoi piece in the morning. Perhaps Benny could have squeezed in a rehearsal after the George Enesco concert but that would not have allowed much time for clearing the stage of the Philharmonic equipment and setting it up for the BG concert. The band were in the habit of rehearsing after their show in the Madhattan Room on a Thursday night/ Friday morning, so it is quite likely that they did at least one rehearsal there. Speaking at the International Association of Jazz Record Collectors (IAJRC) Conference in 1987, Jess Stacy remembered rehearsals like this: "Well, we went over to Carnegie Hall to set up, play one tune and get out. We just wanted to see it." There is a nice photo from Metronome published in 1951 which captures Benny, Jess Stacy, Vernon Brown, Cootie Williams and Johnny Hodges (sporting a snazzy hat and playing a straight Soprano.) Presumably they were going through Blue Reverie.

Jess Stacy, Benny, Vernon Brown, Cootie Williams and Johnny Hodges at rehearsals.

We do have a story about Milt Gabler which gives us some insight into a possible rehearsal date of Friday 14 January. Milt was a jazz fan and the proprietor of the legendary Commodore Radio Store opposite the Commodore Hotel in New York. His store became a gathering place for hot music enthusiasts, where they used to meet, play records and discuss solos and discographies. In 1935, John Hammond, Marshall Stearns (who later went on to found the Institute of Jazz Studies), George Frazier, Helen Oakley, Milt and a few others thought it would be worthwhile forming some Rhythm Clubs, an idea that was flourishing in Europe and it was not long before they had clubs in many of the big cities. The mandate for these clubs 'founded on a desire to facilitate the universal progress of swing music backed by the conviction that it is a worthy cultural object of study' already shows signs of an effort to legitimise jazz music which had something of a sleazy reputation. Milt started to re-release classic jazz recordings under licence on his own label: United Hot Clubs of America or 'UHCA'. Of course, having a network of Rhythm Clubs at his disposal made the records easier to sell. The 'UHCA' also had its own official monthly journal, 'Tempo – The Modern Musical Newsmagazine' which of course listed amongst its contributors John Hammond, Marshall Stearns (and his pseudonym 'Guy Sykes'). This would help sell records too. The unique thing that Milt was doing with his record releases was to name the musicians who played on the recordings and list them on the labels. This was, and is, of great interest to jazz

81 Radio Guide - Week ending January 22 1938

The full band at rehearsals.

enthusiasts. Prior to this innovation, jazz musicians other than the leader were mostly anonymous. It was not long before Milt wanted to start making some commercial recordings of his own for a new label; 'Commodore' and set about trying to fix up a date that was agreeable to the recording studio and all of the musicians involved. This proved to be very difficult but after several abortive attempts, 17th January 1938 was chosen as the date that was acceptable to all and the Brunswick Studios were booked. The musicians that were engaged to play on that date were: Jess Stacy, Bobby Hackett, Bud Freeman, Eddie Condon, George Brunis, Pee Wee Russell, George Wettling and Art Shapiro. There's a little nugget of information, important for our story here: 'On the Friday, three days before the planned session and two before Goodman's concert, the blow fell. "Eddie [Condon] walked into the store and said 'Jess can't make it on Monday he's recording with Benny before they leave town"'. That was the last straw for Milt and he marched over to Carnegie Hall where the band was rehearsing and confronted the clarinettist during a break. (Milt had been invited to attend some Goodman recording sessions in the early thirties as a reward for selling so many records, so he and Benny knew each other and Benny was aware, too, of the contribution the Rhythm Clubs had made to his popularity.) We don't know what was said between them but we do know that Benny agreed to postpone his visit to the recording studios and allow Jess to take part in Milt's inaugural session on Monday.[82] (To mark the occasion, two of the tunes that Milt recorded on January 17 were titled 'Carnegie Jump' and 'Carnegie Drag'.) Benny could not find the time to get into the studio again until February 16.

John Hammond's review of the concert jam session 'Honeysuckle Rose' included this comment: 'It would be pleasant to report that the jam session was the success that

---

82 The Lost Chords.- Richard M Sudhalter. Oxford University Press 1999. P.281
Also: -'We call it Music' by Eddie Condon and Collected works of Whitney Balliett

– Rehearsals –

Rehearsal for the jam session. Freddie Green, Benny, Lester Young, Gene Krupa and Harry James.

it should have been and actually was when the boys first got together a few days before'. Of course we cannot be sure, but Hammond's comment, along with the Milt Gabler story, would seem to put the band in Carnegie Hall on Friday 14th, the fly in the ointment is that there were two concerts in the hall on that day. At 2.30pm the New York Philharmonic played and at 8.30pm the Golden Hill Chorus were on stage, which does mean the hall was free for at least some of that morning.

On Saturday 15th there were three concerts in the hall so it's unlikely that they could have got in then. It would seem that the most probable times for another rehearsal were either on Friday morning or Sunday afternoon, after the Philharmonic concert. Photographs show the band at rehearsals in the main hall and Lester Young and Freddie Green from Basie's band are in some of those shots that appeared in Metronome, but Basie was due on stage in Scranton on Saturday night which would be at least a couple of hours' drive away. So it seems unlikely, but not impossible, that they would have found a slot to rehearse on that Saturday. It is really very unusual for a band to have more than one rehearsal in Carnegie Hall, this is an extremely busy concert hall and finding slots for everyone would have been a logistical nightmare.

Benny was always striving to get the best from his band. At the rehearsal, Benny went down into the hall to listen to the band from the audience's perspective. They were playing Honeysuckle Rose, the tune chosen for the Jam Session. (Is it cheating to rehearse a Jam Session?) In his autobiography, Benny described the session like this: "I went down in the hall to get an idea of how it sounded, but before they had done more than five or six choruses on 'Honeysuckle Rose', the thing was jumping so much that I had to rush up and get in on it. We probably would have kept on playing all night if there hadn't been jobs waiting for us."[83] Maybe John Hammond was right when he said that they had played better at the rehearsal than they did a few days later on the night of the concert.[84] Today, many people would agree that the Jam Session is the high point of the concert.

83 The Kingdom of Swing - Benny Goodman & Irving Kolodin
84 Tempo Magazine - February 1938

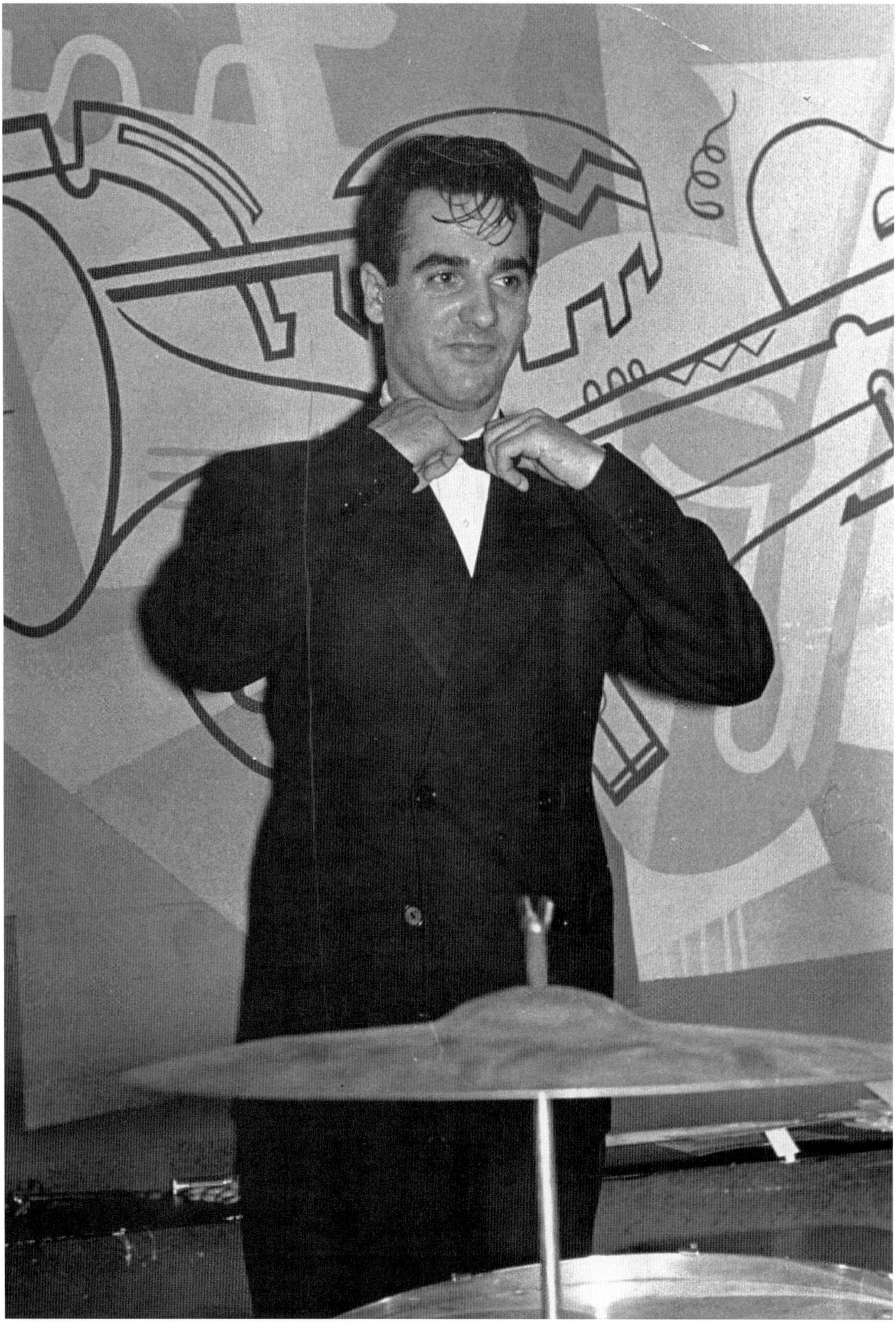

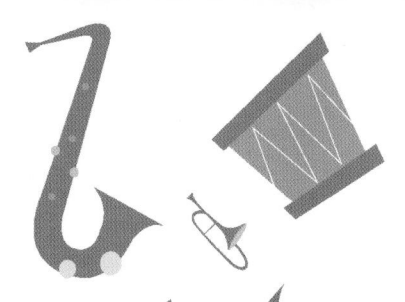

• CHAPTER 7 •

Leaving the Madhattan Room

Benny was broadcasting again from the Madhattan Room on the evening of the 13 January, where they played 'Blue Skies', 'Loch Lomond', 'Dizzy Spells' and 'Big John Special' amongst others. Then on Saturday evening, the 15 January, Benny's band ended a triumphant fifteen week stay at the Madhattan Room in the Hotel Pennsylvania, the audience on the final night was throbbing with well known music people. Gene Krupa was celebrating his 29th birthday and the band played Happy Birthday for him.[85] They also ran through an instrumental version of 'Bei Mir Bist Du Schoen', on the card for the following day's concert. George Simon wrote of the band's tenure that 'Goodman remained a warm, level-headed, gracious host. The Goodman gang should consider its triumph a personal as well as musical one'.[86] Bob Crosby's band moved into the Madhattan Room after Benny's long tenancy and stayed there for six weeks until the Goodman band returned on 4 March – without Gene Krupa.

The general popularity of Swing music and the adulation heaped onto the Goodman orchestra was starting to become tiresome for Benny and his musicians. Every night they were playing to packed houses of cavorting, screaming, jitterbug dancers and the band were finding it difficult to make themselves heard over the noise. They spent endless hours rehearsing clever passages only to find them drowned out by the fans applauding everything and anything. 'We learned to play against hell and high water. We played loud when we should have played soft and we played louder where we normally would have played loud. To make ourselves heard we rocked the rafters off with the brasses, blew our brains out with the trumpets and raised the roof with the granddad horns. Krupa banged the hide out of his drums, got arms like the village blacksmith from the exercise. Harry James' lips got like leather.'[87]

They were having problems with the fans taking souvenirs from the stand too. Goodman explained to Ted Shane of Collier's Magazine that it got so bad that they had to nail everything down, they were losing music stands when nobody was looking, any reeds that were left unattended would be stolen and any corner of an instrument case that could be pried off was attacked by souvenir-hunters. Benny had to dismantle his clarinet and slip it into his jacket whenever he left the stand and Gene could do nothing to stop his drum sticks disappearing. The relentless pressure of performance

"Another fine mess you've got me into!" Gene Krupa adjusts his tie ready for another session at the Madhattan Room.

85 Swing Era Scrap Book. Ken Vail. P.313
86 Metronome Magazine - February, 1938
87 Collier's Magazine - February 1939

'The Babe' stands for a solo.

was starting to show itself in another way. On 19 November 1937, Benny sacked his entire brass section![88] What they did to deserve expulsion we shall probably never know, but their exile was short lived and they were back onboard the following day and in good form for the Camel Caravan show on November 22.

An evening's concert at Carnegie Hall would have given them some respite from these distractions and there was the added benefit of the acclaimed concert hall's acoustics. This would have been a real treat for the musicians. Carnegie Hall was very different acoustically from the Madhattan Room. The concert hall has a superb sound. Benny's long time tenor sax player, Art Rollini wrote in his autobiography that the Carnegie acoustics were the best he had ever encountered. "You could hear yourself and each individual in the band with ease."[89] Jess Stacy put it this way: "The acoustics were perfect, only one overhead mike hanging down from the ceiling picked up the whole thing."[90] "I can play softer there than anywhere else" was how concert pianist Dame Myra Hess described the experience of a recital there.[91] By comparison, the sound in the Madhattan room, packed with dancers and diners, was stuffy, dead and dense.

Benny's band, or to use the delightful quote from the New York Herald Tribune, the day after the concert, 'Mr Goodman's group of uncommonly skilled executants', had been on the road now for four years and with almost the same personnel for the last year. Sterling 'Red' Ballard, Hymie Schertzer and Benny's brother Harry were the only

---

[88] Down Beat Magazine - December 1937 P.20
[89] Thirty Years with the Big Bands - Art Rollini P.63
[90] IAJRC 1987 Conference audience recording
[91] Portrait of Carnegie Hall. – Theodore Cron & Burt Goldblatt

members of the band to have stayed with Benny for the previous four years. Tenor sax player, Irving 'Babe' Russin was the last to join the band a month before the concert, he had replaced the colourful Vido Musso. Benny had succeeded where many band leaders had failed in luring Russin away from a stable job in the CBS Studio band, where he played the very popular radio show 'Saturday Night Swing Session' under Leith Stevens. Russin had played with Benny and Gene Krupa some eight years before in the Red Nichols band. Benny's guitarist in later years, Turk Van Lake, who was an excited 19-year-old member of the audience at Carnegie Hall noted, that 'The Babe' was still unsure of the music at the Carnegie concert and had to stoop slightly to read the music when the reed section stood for their solos.[92]

92 Liner notes Sony CD C2K 65143

CARNEGIE HALL

Copyright, 1929, by ALFRED SCOTT, *Publisher*, 156 Fifth Avenue, N. Y.

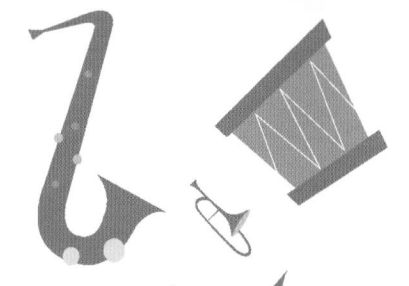

CHAPTER 8

The Concert Program

The high number of concerts at Carnegie Hall, sometimes three a day, meant that the printed programs had to follow a standard form. The Carnegie Hall programs from that period all looked the same. The cover is from a 1929 drawing of the hall by William McNaughty. The content did not vary much from one performance to another. Advertising space was sold to music stores and local restaurants and there were specific boxes allocated for the concert in question and forthcoming events. The Benny Goodman program looks more or less the same as the program the following week for the concert by the Philadelphia Orchestra, the same advertisements and the same cover. One of the forthcoming events scheduled in Benny's program was the New York debut, on January 23 at the Town Hall, of the blind Welsh pianist Alec Templeton. All Goodman fans will recognise Alec as the composer of one of Benny's more popular pieces 'Bach goes to Town' and the lesser-known 'Mozart Matriculates'. Having almost complete control over the dance band industry, to the point where some people were crying 'monopoly', the Music Corporation of America, Benny's booking agent, was planning to move into the world of the concert stage and classical music. This recital with Alec Templeton was the first experiment in its planned expansion. It was no secret at the time that MCA also had designs on movie production too.

The unnamed reporter for Down Beat wrote of how he amused himself during the dull portions of BG's concert by counting the number of tiers in the hall and calculating the distance a paper aeroplane would travel if launched from the gallery. He also suggested that the most attractive advertisement in the program was on page eleven and the dullest was on page twelve.[93] (The complete program is reproduced here, check for yourself!)

The publicity men do not always get their own way: Benny's Camel Caravan radio shows were sponsored by RJ Reynolds, the makers of Camel cigarettes; the William Esty agency were sponsoring the Carnegie concert and they were working for Reynolds. On this occasion however, the back page of the program carried a full page advertisement for Chesterfield cigarettes – the opposition!

[93] Down Beat Magazine - February 1938

There were two concerts at Carnegie Hall on the 16 January 1938, this is the complete program for BG's evening concert.

Forever Yours...
Lotte Lehmann · Lauritz Melchior
on Victor Records

Great performances become truly deathless when you own them on Victor Records.... Yours is then the power to command the great to sing and play.... All the encores you want are yours.... The time of year or day make no difference. Like all the world's greatest artists, Lotte Lehmann and Lauritz Melchior have made many fine Victor Recordings of their best-loved performances. Following are some representative selections.

DIE WALKURE, ACT 1. Sung by Lotte Lehmann, Lauritz Melchior and Emanuel List with the Vienna Philharmonic Orchestra. Victor Album M-298, $16.00

Victor Records by Lotte Lehmann
ROSENKAVALIER   Album M-196 $26.00
SONG RECITAL   Album M-292   7.50
    Includes Songs of Mozart, Schubert, Schumann, Brahms, Hugo Wolf.

Victor Records by Lauritz Melchior
GOTTERDAMMERUNG—In Leid zu Dem Wipfeln (In Grief to the Branches) (Wagner) with Helgers
     No. 7659 $2.00

MEISTERSINGER—Abendlich gluhend in himmlischer Gluth (Evening's Heavenly Light) (Wagner) with Schorr
     No. 7681 $2.00

MEISTERSINGER—Quintet—Selig, wie die Sonne Meines Gluckes lacht (Wagner) with Schumann—Schorr—Parr—Williams
     No. 7682 $2.00

SIEGFRIED (Act 3) (Wagner)   Album M-167 $8.00

TRISTAN UND ISOLDE—Isolde! Tristan! Geliebter! (Isolde! Tristan! Beloved!) (Wagner) with Lieder
     No. 7273 $2.00

TRISTAN UND ISOLDE—O sink' hernieder, Nach der Liebe (O Sink Upon Us, Night of Love) (Wagner) with Lieder
     No. 7274 $2.00

• RCA Victor Electrola R-99... Music that is vital... fresh... brilliantly natural! Hear it when you play Victor Records on this great RCA Victor Higher Fidelity instrument, the finest phonograph ever to bear this name! Has improved dynamic amplifier, 12-inch speaker, feather weight pick-up that saves your records.

Listen to: The NBC Symphony Orchestra conducted by Arturo Toscanini, every Saturday night at 10:00 E.S.T. over the NBC Blue and Red Networks.... The Metropolitan Opera broadcasts every Saturday afternoon at 2:00 E.S.T., over the NBC Blue Network.... The "Magic Key of RCA" every Sunday afternoon at 2:00 E.S.T. over the NBC Blue Network.

RCA VICTOR RECORDS
A SERVICE OF THE RADIO CORPORATION OF AMERICA

CARNEGIE HALL PROGRAM

"FOR A GREAT 1938 EIGHT"
"BETTER BUY BUICK"
FOR NEAREST BUICK DEALER, SEE YOUR TELEPHONE DIRECTORY

Carnegie Hall Announcements
JANUARY

Sunday Eve.	Jan. 16	Benny Goodman *and His Swing Orchestra*
Monday Eve.	Jan. 17	Uday Shan-Kar *and His Hindu Ballet*
Tuesday Eve.	Jan. 18	New York Women's Symphony Orchestra
Thursday Eve.	Jan. 20	Philharmonic-Symphony Society
Friday Aft.	Jan. 21	Philharmonic-Symphony Society
Friday Eve.	Jan. 21	Lambros Demetrios Callimahos *Flute Recital*
Saturday Aft.	Jan. 22	Mischa Elman, *Violinist*
Saturday Eve.	Jan. 22	Moriz Rosenthal, *Pianist*
Sunday Aft.	Jan. 23	Philharmonic-Symphony Society
Monday Eve.	Jan. 24	National Orchestral Association
Tuesday Eve.	Jan. 25	Philadelphia Orchestra
Wed. Morn.	Jan. 26	Hunter College Commencement Exercises
Wed. Eve.	Jan. 26	Artur Schnabel, *Pianist*
Thursday Eve.	Jan. 27	Philharmonic-Symphony Society
Friday Aft.	Jan. 28	Philharmonic-Symphony Society
Friday Eve.	Jan. 28	Vitya Vronsky *and* Victor Babin *Duo-Pianists*
Saturday Morn.	Jan. 29	Philharmonic Concert for Young People

M. Murray Weisman, *President of Carnegie Hall*

SINCE 1842 OUR HAND HAS NEVER LOST ITS SKILL
Schaefer — BEER AT ITS BEST
THE F. & M. SCHAEFER BREWING COMPANY, BROOKLYN, N. Y.

Meeting Place
before or after a
CARNEGIE CONCERT

Dinner from a delectable, reasonably priced menu—or for an after-concert-snack or liqueur, join music lovers at the

OMAR RESTAURANT OF ESSEX HOUSE
One block from Carnegie Hall

If you prefer to dance before or after the Concert the **CASINO-ON-THE-PARK** blends superb food with Richard Himber's delightful dance music.

155 WEST 58TH STREET
160 CENTRAL PARK SOUTH

CARNEGIE HALL

HOFMANN

by public demand
repeating his April 9th, 1938
Carnegie Program on

APRIL 10th, SUN. EVE.
at 8.30

Hofmann April 9th recital
sold out Dec. 11th, 1937

Tickets for **APRIL 10th** now on sale
at Carnegie Hall Box Office

Management **Richard Copley**

Steinway Piano Used

A Piano Recital in Your Home
MORIZ ROSENTHAL
VICTOR RECORDS
Nocturnes in D flat major, E flat major—Waltzes in A flat major, C sharp minor—Mazurkas in A flat major, B minor—Preludes Nos. 3, 6 and 7.

VESEY MUSIC SHOP
57 VESEY ST. — CO.7-5781
Records Shipped Anywhere
DOWNTOWN NEW YORK'S LARGEST RECORD SHOP

THIS PIANO, favorite of Wagner and Liszt, is the chosen instrument of Hofmann... Horowitz... Paderewski... Rachmaninoff... of virtually every great artist of our day.

It is, as well, the piano used most frequently by the great broadcasting stations... and the preferred instrument of leading schools and conservatories, here and abroad.

And it is pre-eminently the piano for the home. There are sizes for the drawing-room, and for the room of modest proportions — and for the most modest income.... The new Steinway Grand is only $885. Generous purchase terms can be easily arranged.

STEINWAY & SONS
STEINWAY HALL
109 W. 57th Street, New York City
(between Sixth and Seventh Avenues)

STEINWAY
THE INSTRUMENT OF THE IMMORTALS

TOWN HALL
Wed. Aft., January 19, at 3
All-Bach Recital

ALBERT-LÉVÊQUE
PIANIST

RENÉ LE ROY
FLUTIST

Sonata, No. 5
  René Le Roy and Albert-Lévêque
Well Tempered Clavichord (1st Book):
  *Prelude and Fugue in C minor
  Prelude and Fugue in C sharp major
  **Choral "Werde munter, mein Gemüt"
    (Cantata 147)
  Gigue in B flat major
  Overture of the 28th Cantata
    Albert-Lévêque
Sonata
  René Le Roy
Well Tempered Clavichord (1st Book):
  Prelude and Fugue in D major
  Prelude and Fugue in B flat major
  **Aria "Schafe können, sicher weiden"
    (Cantata 208)
  Choir of the 30th Cantata
    Albert-Lévêque
Sonata, No. 6
  René Le Roy and Albert-Lévêque

*Gramophone Records K7502
**Albert-Lévêque's Transcriptions:
  Fortin Edition, Schirmer
Steinway Piano

Scale of Prices (including tax):
Box Seats $2.75. Parquet $2.20, 1.65, 1.10.
  Balcony 40c. Special Student Rates.

Management, **Annie Friedberg**

TOWN HALL
Sunday Aft., January 23, at 3

ELISABETH SCHUMANN
SONG RECITAL
PROGRAM

I.
Schneegloeckchen .... Schumann
Mondnacht .... Schumann
Staendchen .... Schumann
Loreley .... Schumann
Auftraege .... Schumann

II.
Geheimnis .... Brahms
Gang zum Liebchen .... Brahms
Nachtigall .... Brahms
Vergebliches Staendchen .... Brahms

III.
Komm wir wandeln .... Cornelius
Wiegenlied .... Wagner
O quand je dors .... Liszt
Wieder moecht ich Dir begegnen .. Liszt

IV.
Heimkehr .... Richard Strauss
All mein Gedanken .... Richard Strauss
Morgen .... Richard Strauss
Muttertaendelei .... Richard Strauss

Coenraad V. Bos
at the Steinway Piano

•
Management
Annie Friedberg
250 West 57th St.

MUSICAL—DRAMATIC
NOVELTY of the YEAR!

WENDELL PHILLIPS DODGE
presents

London Intimate Opera Co.

FREDERICK   WINIFRED   GEOFFREY
WOODHOUSE · RADFORD · DUNN

in a Repertory of Early English, Mozart and other One-Act Operas, Humorous Dialogues and Mirth-Provoking Songs ... Comedy at its Best!

WEEK OF JANUARY 11th
"LOVE IN A COFFEE CUP"..... (J. S. Bach)
"COLIN AND HIS WIFE"... (Henry Purcell)
"THE GRENADIER"........ (Charles Dibdin)
"EVERY MAID HER OWN MISTRESS"...
  (G. B. Pergolesi)

Evenings Except Monday at 8:30
Matinees Wednesday and Saturday at 2:30
Sunday Nights at 9 o'clock
Change of Bill Weekly

LITTLE THEATRE
44th St. West of B'way   Tel. LAc 4-9791
PRICES: Orch. $3.30
Balc. $2.75, $2.20, $1.65, $1.10

CARNEGIE HALL PROGRAM

ON THIS WEEK'S PROGRAMS
Superb COLUMBIA Recordings are available of
Beethoven: Symphony No. 2 in D major. 4-12" discs in an album.
Berlioz: Overture. "The Roman Carnival." One 12" disc.
Both played by the London Philharmonic Orchestra conducted by Sir Thomas Beecham.

"The World's Best Recorded Music"

The Gramophone Shop, Inc. 18 East 48th St., New York
WIckersham 2-1876

NEWEST SWEDISH RESTAURANT
CASTLEHOLM
featuring
FAMOUS SMÖRGÅSBORD
Luncheon - Dinner
Cocktail Lounge
SUPPER DANCING 9 p.m. to 1 a.m.
344 WEST 57th ST. - PARC VENDOME
CIrcle 7-0873

CARNEGIE HALL PROGRAM
SEASON 1937-1938

FIRE NOTICE—Look around *now* and choose the nearest exit to your seat. In case of fire walk (not run) to *that* Exit. Do not try to beat your neighbor to the street.

JOHN J. McELLIGOTT, *Fire Commissioner*

CARNEGIE HALL
Sunday Evening, January 16th, at 8:30

S. HUROK
presents
(by arrangement with Music Corporation of America)

BENNY GOODMAN
and his
SWING ORCHESTRA

I.

"Don't Be That Way" .... *Edgar Sampson*
"Sometimes I'm Happy" (from "Hit the Deck") .... *Irving Caesar & Vincent Youmans*
"One O'clock Jump" .... *William (Count) Basie*

II.

TWENTY YEARS OF JAZZ
"Sensation Rag" (as played c. 1917 by the Dixieland Jazz Band)
E. B. Edwards

PROGRAM CONTINUED ON SECOND PAGE FOLLOWING

Recapture Your Musical Experience of This Concert

If your favorite is recorded, you can get it at Schirmer's where you will find not only a complete stock of the better type of records (domestic and imported) but radios and phonographs—instruments and accessories, books, a recording studio for personal recordings—and a wide stock of piano, vocal, instrumental, and choral music of all publishers.

Mail and Telephone Orders Promptly Filled

G. SCHIRMER, INC.
America's Music Headquarters

RCA VICTOR RECORDS
ALBUM M-301 (SET OF 5 RECORDS)
SYMPHONY No. 1, in C MINOR
(BRAHMS)
STOKOWSKI-PHILADELPHIA ORCH.
LIBERTY MUSIC SHOPS
450 Madison Ave. at 50th St. • 795 Madison Ave. at 67th St.
10 East 59th St. (Savoy-Plaza)

BALDWIN—TODAY'S GREAT PIANO
Used exclusively by such famous artists as

BACHAUS • BAUER • BORI • BOGUSLAWSKI • ECHANIZ • ERICOURT
GIESEKING • GOOSSENS • ITURBI • KELBERINE • JOHNSON
LHEVINNE • MASON • PONS • ROSENTHAL • SCHMITZ
SLENCZYNSKI • SZIGETI • P. WITTGENSTEIN • WHITHORNE

Choose Your Piano as the Artists Do

BALDWIN PIANOS • 20 EAST 54th STREET
BALDWIN • HAMILTON • HOWARD PIANOS

Come in and let us answer your questions about the HAMMOND ORGAN

Why do musicians call this remarkable instrument "the greatest musical development of the last 100 years?" Is it really so fascinating—and so *easy*—to play? How can an organ that fits in a four-foot square create such exquisite tones—tones of flutes, violins, woodwinds and countless other instruments?

To anyone who cares for music, it's an intensely interesting experience to see and *hear* the Hammond Organ. Why not give yourself this pleasure . . . soon? Drop in and let us *show* you why the Hammond Organ is bringing such tremendous enjoyment to thousands of families here and abroad!

$1275
and up, f.o.b. New York.
Slightly higher for large installations.

The **HAMMOND ORGAN** *Studios*
Drop in any time, 50 W. 57th St.
Phone CIrcle 6-2290

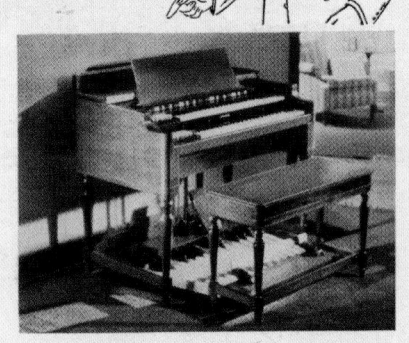

In other cities see classified directory under "Organs" or "Organs, Electric"

WED. EVE. JAN. 26th
5th Event
Hurok Carnegie Hall Series

SCHNABEL

BACH, WEBER and
BEETHOVEN'S
"33 VARIATIONS"
(53 minutes without a stop)
CARNEGIE HALL BOX OFFICE
1.25 to 2.75   (Steinway Piano)

Management RICHARD COPLEY announces

BARBIZON-PLAZA CONCERT HALL
Friday Eve., JANUARY 21, at 8:30

NATHALIE
PAUL
VLADIMIR
DROZDOFF
PIANISTS
Steinway Pianos

•

TOWN HALL
Friday Eve., JANUARY 21, at 8:30

MAURICE
AMES
MEZZO-SOPRANO
(Steinway)

•

TOWN HALL
Tuesday Eve., JANUARY 25, at 8:30

JOSEF
RAIEFF
PIANIST
(Steinway)

CARNEGIE HALL
Tuesday Eve., JANUARY 18, at 8:45

New York Women's Symphony Orchestra

ANTONIA BRICO, Conductor

Assisting Artists
JOYCE BARTHELSON
ANTONIA BRICO
LEE PATTISON
LUISA MORALES STOJOWSKI
Harpsichordists

PROGRAM
Symphony in D major................Haydn
(The Clock Symphony)
Concerto in A minor, for Four Harpsichords....................Bach
Intermission
"Versang" (Spring Song)............Sibelius
Two Pieces for Orchestra............Delius
1. On Hearing the First Cuckoo in Spring
2. Summer Night on the River
Capriccio Espagnol........*Rimsky-Korsakow*

Harpsichords by courtesy of
Steinway & Sons

TICKETS: Box Seats $3.00, $2.00;
Orchestra $2.50, $2.00; Dress Circle $1.50;
Balcony $1.00, 75c.

The Steinway is the official piano of the New York Women's Symphony Orchestra

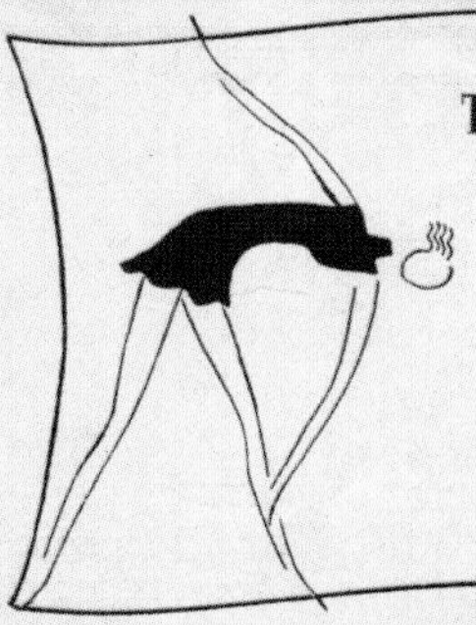

CARNEGIE HALL PROGRAM

THE *Exercise Way* TO BEAUTY

An attractive figure... quickness of motion... and a spontaneous vitality are priceless possessions. Join a class of Rhythmic Exercises in the Gymnasium Moderne of the Elizabeth Arden Salon and follow the exercise way to health and loveliness.

COURSE OF 12 LESSONS ... $15.00—*Each course includes diet supervision, individual instruction, and a carefully recorded progress chart.*

New classes forming immediately.. Telephone PL 3-5846—Ext. 21

Elizabeth Arden
691 FIFTH AVENUE • NEW YORK

PROGRAM CONTINUED

"I'm Comin Virginia" (as played c. 1926 by "Bix" Beiderbecke) .... Cooke-Heywood
"When My Baby Smiles at Me" (as played c. 1927 by Ted Lewis) .... Munro-Sterling-Lewis
"Shine" (as played c. 1929 by Louis Armstrong) Mack-Brown-Dabney
"Blue Reverie" .... Duke Ellington
"Life Goes to a Party" .... Harry James-Benny Goodman

III.
JAM SESSION
Collective improvision by a group of soloists to be announced. The length of the session is indeterminate, and may include one or more tunes.

IV.
"Tiger Rag" .... Nick La Rocca
"Body and Soul" .... John Green

The Goodman Trio
Teddy Wilson, *Piano*
Gene Krupa, *Drums*
Benny Goodman, *Clarinet*

PROGRAM CONTINUED ON SECOND PAGE FOLLOWING

RCA VICTOR RECORDS
ALBUM M-301 (SET OF 5 RECORDS)
SYMPHONY No. 1, in C MINOR
(BRAHMS)
STOKOWSKI-PHILADELPHIA ORCH.
LIBERTY MUSIC SHOPS
450 Madison Ave. at 50th St. • 795 Madison Ave. at 67th St.
10 East 59th St. (Savoy-Plaza)

RUSSIAN TEA ROOM RESTAURANT
150 W. 57 ST. (CARNEGIE HALL BLDG.)
New Exclusive "BOYAR ROOM"
LUNCHEON AFTERNOON TEA DINNER AFTER THEATRE
OUR BAR For Quality Variety RUSSIAN DRINKS
SOUND ABSORBING SYSTEM • AIR CONDITIONED

BENNY GOODMAN
Plays the Swing Classic
"Sing, Sing, Sing" on
VICTOR RECORDS
Available separately at $1.25 or in Complete Swing Album of four-12" records, $5.50

MABSONS RECORD SHOP
DIAGONALLY OPPOSITE CARNEGIE HALL
100 WEST 56th ST., NEW YORK
Phone and Mail Orders Filled • Circle 7-0070

A NEW HIGH IN
CONTINENTAL ENTERTAINMENT
Enchanting music • delicious food exciting atmosphere
Dinner and Supper Dancing Nightly
Delightful Entertainment
RESTAURANT de la PAIX
and Around the World Bar
at the ST. MORITZ On-the-Park
50 Central Park So., New York
Personal Direction: S. Gregory Taylor

CHANGE OF ADDRESS
EMIL HERRMANN
RARE VIOLINS, Inc.

Moved to

130 WEST 57 STREET

You are cordially invited to visit our attractive new studio

BRUNSWICK RECORDS PRESENT
America's Great Swing Pianist and Trumpeter

TEDDY WILSON and his Orchestra
- 7859 I MUST HAVE THAT MAN / WHY WAS I BORN
- 8015 NICE WORK IF YOU CAN GET IT / THINGS ARE LOOKING UP
- 7943 THE HOUR OF PARTING / COQUETTE

TEDDY WILSON Piano Solos
- 8025 BETWEEN THE DEVIL AND THE DEEP BLUE SEA / DON'T BLAME ME
- 7563 LIZA / ROSETTA

HARRY JAMES and his Orchestra
- 8038 JUBILEE / I CAN DREAM, CAN'T I?
- 8035 LIFE GOES TO A PARTY / WHEN WE'RE ALONE (Penthouse Serenade)

TEDDY WILSON'S QUARTET
Teddy Wilson, Piano Red Norvo, Xylophone
Harry James, Trumpet John Simmons, Bass
- 7973 JUST A MOOD Part I / JUST A MOOD Part II
- 7964 HONEYSUCKLE ROSE / AIN'T MISBEHAVIN'

BENNY GOODMAN'S ORCHESTRA
- 7645 BASIN STREET BLUES / BEALE STREET BLUES
- 7644 BUGLE CALL RAG / DIXIELAND BAND

Coming Attractions on Release of January 22nd, 1938

TEDDY WILSON and his Orchestra
- 8053 MY FIRST IMPRESSION OF YOU / IF DREAMS COME TRUE

HARRY JAMES and his Orchestra
- 8055 ONE O'CLOCK JUMP / IT'S THE DREAMER IN ME

THE GRAMOPHONE SHOP, Inc.
18 East 48th Street, New York WIckersham 2-1876

★ NBC ARTISTS SERVICE ★
announces

TOWN HALL
Tuesday Afternoon, January 18, at 3
RUTH LUTY
PIANIST
Steinway Piano

TOWN HALL
Tuesday Eve., January 18th, at 8:30
Raya GARBOUSOVA
'CELLIST
Ralph Berkowitz at the Steinway Piano

TOWN HALL
Saturday Eve., January 22, at 8:30 o'clock
Second in the
BEETHOVEN SONATA SERIES
BUSCH + SERKIN
VIOLINIST   PIANIST
Steinway Piano

Only N. Y. Appearance This Season
MILSTEIN
VIOLINIST
CARNEGIE HALL
Saturday Afternoon, January 29th, at 2:30
Leopold Mittmann at the Steinway Piano

Only New York Recital This Season
CARNEGIE HALL
Monday Eve., January 31st, at 8:30
RUDOLF SERKIN
PIANIST
Steinway Piano

CARNEGIE HALL PROGRAM

IF YOU THIRST FOR EXTRA THRILLS—MEASURE THE PLEASURE IN

Dubonnet

WINE—ALCOHOL 18% BY VOLUME

THE FRENCH WAY — Straight, well chilled. No fuss, no bother, very smart!

THE AMERICAN WAY — The Dubonnet Cocktail... half gin, half Dubonnet.

Copyright 1937, Schenley Import Corp., New York

V.

"Avalon" .... Al Jolson-Vincent Rose
"The Man I Love" (from "Strike Up the Band")
　　　　　　　　　　　　　　　George and Ira Gershwin
"I Got Rhythm" (from "Girl Crazy") ...... George and Ira Gershwin
　　　　The Goodman Quartet
　Wilson, Krupa, Goodman and Lionel Hampton, *Vibraphone*

—— Intermission ——

VI.

"Blue Skies" .... Irving Berlin
"Loch Lomond" .... Traditional Scotch

VII.

"Blue Room" (from "The Girl Friend") .... Richard Rodgers
　　　　　　　　　　　　　　　　　　　and Lorenz Hart
"Swingtime in the Rockies" .... James Mundy
"Bei Mir Bist du Schoen" .... Jacobs-Secunda-Cahn-Chaplin

VIII.

"Who" (from "Sunny") .... Jerome Kern-Otto Harbach
"Dinah" .... Harry Akst
"Stompin' at the Savoy" .... Edgar Sampson
"I'm a Ding Dong Daddy" .... Phil Baxter
　　　　Goodman Trio and Quartet

PROGRAM CONTINUED ON PAGE 12

CONVENIENT TO CARNEGIE!

It's just down the block to food at its finest, cocktails and sodas at their best. Before a concert—after a concert, make a habit of stopping at Schrafft's!

SCHRAFFT'S

220 W. 57TH ST.　　222 W. 57TH ST.

After the Concert attend the

BATTLE OF SWING

between

CHICK WEBB
and his Orchestra

with

Ella Fitzgerald

and

COUNT BASIE
and his Orchestra

with

Billie Holliday

TONIGHT

SAVOY BALLROOM
Lenox Ave. & 140th St.
N. Y. C.

Chesterfield Cigarettes
On sale in Buffet and Ladies' Rooms off of Parquet and First Tier Boxes.

RCA VICTOR RECORDS
ALBUM M-272
SYMPHONY No. 2, in D MAJOR
(SIBELIUS)
KOUSSEVITZKY-BOSTON SYMPHONY ORCH.
LIBERTY MUSIC SHOPS
450 Madison Ave. at 50th St. · 795 Madison Ave. at 67th St.
10 East 59th St. (Savoy-Plaza)

Distinctive Eye Glasses & Spectacles

Gall & Lembke, Inc

OPTICIANS
7 EAST 48th STREET, N. Y.
(Just East of Fifth Ave.)

Opera Glasses, Oxfords
Lorgnettes, Binoculars,
Field Glasses, Thermometers,
Kodaks, Projectors
and Supplies
Established 1842
94 years of dependable service

COLUMBIA CONCERTS CORPORATION of COLUMBIA BROADCASTING SYSTEM
announces

TOWN HALL
Monday Evening, January 17th, at 8:30

ISIDOR ACHRON

PIANIST

•

Steinway Piano

Division:
Concert Management Arthur Judson, Inc.

CARNEGIE HALL
Friday Evening, January 21st, at 8:30

Lambros Demetrios
CALLIMAHOS
GREEK-AMERICAN FLUTIST

Paul Ulanowsky *at the Steinway Piano*

•

Division:
Metropolitan Musical Bureau, Inc.

TOWN HALL
Saturday Aft., January 22, at 3

Last N. Y. Recital Prior to Extensive European Tour

RAY LEV
PIANIST

•

Tickets 83c to $2.20   *Steinway Piano*

Division:
Concert Management Arthur Judson, Inc.

CARNEGIE HALL
Saturday Afternoon, January 22, at 3

Mischa
ELMAN

VIOLINIST

Vladimir Padwa at the Steinway Piano

Tickets: $2.20, $1.65, $1.10. Boxes: $22.00 and $17.60
On sale at Box Office

Division: **Haensel & Jones**

CARNEGIE HALL
Friday Evening, JANUARY 28, at 8:30

Only New York Recital This Season

THE RENOWNED DUO-PIANISTS

Vronsky & Babin

Tickets $1.10, 1.65, 2.20 Now at Box Office

Steinway Pianos

Division: **Metropolitan Musical Bureau, Inc.**

TOWN HALL
Sunday Afternoon, January 30, at 3

Only New York Recital This Season

SIGRID
ONEGIN
WORLD-FAMOUS CONTRALTO

Division: **Metropolitan Musical Bureau, Inc.**

CARNEGIE HALL PROGRAM

FRANCOIS TOURTE
PARIS 1747-1835

The world's finest collection of his unsurpassable Violin and 'Cello bows, as well as Violins by Stradivari, Guarneri, Guadagnini and other 17th and 18th Century makers, very reasonably priced, are on display at

WURLITZER

120 WEST 42nd STREET   NEW YORK CITY

THE PHILHARMONIC-SYMPHONY SOCIETY OF NEW YORK
CARNEGIE HALL

Under the Direction of

GEORGES ENESCO
Guest Conductor

Thursday Evening, January 20, at 8:45
Friday Afternoon, January 21, at 2:30

BEETHOVEN	Overture, "The Dedication of the House"
SCHUBERT	Symphony in B-flat major, No. 5
PISTON	Suite for Orchestra
ROGALSKI	"Burial at the Cemetery of the Poor"
ANDRICO	Dance in C major
ENESCO	Roumanian Rhapsody No. 1, in A major

Sunday Afternoon, January 23, at 3:00

MacDOWELL	Symphonic Poem, "Lancelot and Elaine"
ENESCO	Suite for Orchestra, No. 1, Op. 9
BERLIOZ	Fantastic Symphony

ARTHUR JUDSON, *Manager*
BRUNO ZIRATO, *Assistant Manager*
The Steinway is the Official Piano of
The Philharmonic-Symphony Society
Victor Records

For space in CARNEGIE *and* TOWN HALL *Programs*
Call
ALFRED SCOTT
CHelsea 3-0334
156 FIFTH AVENUE, NEW YORK

NAEGELÉ

Town Hall
Sunday Eve.
January 16
8:30 p.m.

Tickets
83c
to
$2.75
Boxes $19.80

Baldwin Piano

Exclusive Management
WILLMORE AND POWERS

FRITZ KREISLER
Transcriptions in stock at all times at
J. F. HILL & CO., Inc.
151 WEST 57th STREET
(Just across the street)
Open 9-6   Deliveries   CI 7-4798

"There is a Maiden Form for Every Type of Figure!"

"Allo" and "Intimo" are only two of the wide selection of Maiden Form brassieres, for different figure types. Maiden Form Brassiere Co., Inc., New York

Maiden Form
LOOK FOR THIS TRADE-MARK ON
BRASSIERES · GIRDLES · ONCE-OVERS

"INTIMO"   *"ALLO"*
**Reg. App. for
*Reg. U.S. Pat. Off.

CARNEGIE HALL PROGRAM

The Auxiliary Board of
THE PHILHARMONIC-SYMPHONY SOCIETY OF NEW YORK

GOVERNING BOARD

Chairman, Mrs. Vincent Astor
Vice-Chairmen: Mrs. Charles S. Guggenheimer, *First*
Countess Mercati, *Second* Mrs. Christian R. Holmes, *Third*
Mrs. J. West Roosevelt, *Fourth*
Recording Secretary, Mrs. Henry Martyn Alexander
Corresponding Secretary, Mrs. Frederick T. Steinway
Treasurer, Mrs. Elbridge Gerry Chadwick
Mrs. Charles E. Mitchell........*Chairman, Educational Comm.*
Mrs. Harris R. Childs....*Vice-Chairman, Educational Committee and Chairman, Ensemble Musical Training and Scholarships*
Mrs. Charles S. Guggenheimer......*Vice-Chairman, Educational Committee and Chairman, Popular Concerts (Students')*
Mrs. Melvin E. Sawin, *Chairman, Young People's Concerts Comm.*
Mrs. Bartlett Arkell...*Vice-Chairman, Educational Committee; Chairman, Contacts for Music Interest in Colleges and Public Schools*
Mrs. Henry Martyn Alexander, *Chairman, Pension Fund Comm.*
Mrs. Elbridge Gerry Chadwick......*Chairman, Committee on Subscription Activities*
Mrs. Walter Maynard............*Chairman, Junior Committee*

Mrs. Barrett Andrews   Mrs. Morris Loeb
Mrs. William C. Breed   Mrs. Charles E. F. McCann
Mrs. Melbert B. Cary, Jr.   Mrs. Julian W. Robbins
Mrs. George L. Cheney   Mrs. Moritz Rosenthal
Mrs. William B. Dinsmore   Mrs. Alva Benjamin See
Mrs. Henry Evans   Mrs. Hokan B. Steffanson
Mrs. Felix Fuld   Mrs. von Jeszenszky
Miss Annie Burr Jennings   Mrs. Richard Whitney

MEMBERS

Mrs. Winthrop Aldrich   Mrs. James Lees Laidlaw
Mrs. Robert Bacon   Mrs. Joseph B. Long
Mrs. Robert Low Bacon   Mrs. Edward Loomis
Mrs. Zlatko Balokovic   Mrs. Clarence H. Mackay
Mrs. Harry R. Baltz   Mrs. John Phillips Marquand
Mrs. Courtlandt D. Barnes   Mrs. Charles H. Marshall
Mrs. Frederick W. Beckman   Mrs. Conrad H. Matthiessen
Mrs. Robert Woods Bliss   Mrs. Thomas H. McInnerney
Mrs. Willis H. Booth   Mrs. George Mesta
Mrs. George T. Bowdoin   Mrs. Gilbert H. Montague
Mrs. E. Cochran Bowen   Mrs. Henry Morgenthau
Mrs. Calvin Bullock   Mrs. Frederick A. Muschenheim
Mrs. William D. Carmichael, Jr. Mrs. Kenneth O'Brien
Mrs. Ward Cheney   Mrs. Donald M. Oenslager
Mrs. Walter P. Chrysler   Mrs. A. Perry Osborn
Mrs. Winthrop Murray Crane Mrs. William S. Paley
Mrs. Drexel Dahlgren   Mrs. Rembrandt Peale, Jr.
Mrs. Marius de Brabant   Mrs. H. Hobart Porter
Mrs. Reginald de Koven   Mrs. George B. Post
Mrs. Charles H. Ditson   Mrs. Harold I. Pratt
Mrs. James P. Donohue   Mrs. John T. Pratt
Mrs. Frank Doubleday   Mrs. Robert C. Ream
Mrs. David Dows   Mrs. John King Reckford
Mrs. Charles Dana Draper   Mrs. Johnston L. Redmond
Mrs. William P. Draper   Mrs. Dudley Roberts
Mrs. C. B. Dresselhuys   Mrs. James Roosevelt
Lady Duveen   Mrs. Ernst Rosenfeld
Mrs. Marshall Field   Miss Marie L. Russell
Mrs. Oliver Filley   Countess Sala
Mrs. Reginald Fincke   Mrs. Morton L. Schwartz
Mrs. Harry Harkness Flagler Mrs. Edward B. Sexton
Mrs. Julius Forstmann   Mrs. George Shaw
Mrs. George Barton French   Mrs. John S. Sheppard
Mrs. Otto Frohnknecht   Mrs. Alexis W. Stein
Mrs. Henry J. Fuller   Mrs. John Stilwell
Mrs. Richard Gambrill   Mrs. J. Frederic Tams
Mrs. Busch Greenough   Mrs. Bryce W. Turner
Mrs. George F. Handel   Mrs. Robert Watts
Mrs. Edward S. Harkness   Mrs. George K. Weeks
Mrs. Clarence L. Hay   Mrs. Henry White
Mrs. Walter B. James   Mrs. Sheldon Whitehouse
Mrs. Edouard L. Jonas   Mrs. Caspar Whitney
Mrs. Otto H. Kahn   Mrs. Arnold Whitridge
Mrs. Cornelius F. Kelley   Miss Mary Hoyt Wiborg
Mrs. Fiorello H. LaGuardia

JUNIOR COMMITTEE

Mrs. John B. Aspegren   Mrs. Herman Harjes
Mrs. John Jacob Astor   Miss Alice Hunt
Mrs. Hugh Bullock   Mrs. John Parkinson
Mrs. Daniel Catlin   Miss Alice Polk
Miss Mary deMumm   Mrs. George A. Rentschler
Mrs. Spencer Eddy, Jr.   Mrs. Carleton Sprague Smith
Mrs. Ogden Goelet   Miss Virginia Thaw
Mrs. Randolph Guggenheimer Miss Lucy Truesdale

DONORS

Mrs. Charles C. Auchincloss Mrs. William Chapman Potter
Mrs. Andrew Carnegie   Mrs. Herbert L. Satterlee
Mrs. Stephen C. Clark   Mrs. Eugene C. Savidge
Miss Rose Frankenheimer   Mrs. Woodford T. Stewart
Mrs. John Henry Hammond   Miss Charlotte R. Stillman
Mrs. Charles Neave   Mr. James A. Stillman
Mrs. William Church Osborn Mrs. Carll Tucker
Mrs. Lionello Perera   Mrs. George Whitney

IX.

"Sing, Sing, Sing" .... Louis Prima

X.

Reprise

•

Baldwin Piano Used

The Program is Subject to Slight Alteration

Members of the Orchestra

Benny Goodman, *Clarinet*

Reeds: Babe Rusin, George Koenig, Herman Shertzer and Arthur Rollini

Trumpets: Harry James, Ziggy Elman and Gordon Griffin

Trombones: Red Ballard and Vernon Brown

Harry Goodman, *Bass;* Allan Reuss, *Guitar;* Jess Stacy, *Piano;* Gene Krupa, *Drums;* Martha Tilton, *Vocalist*

Cornet soloist in "I'm Comin' Virginia": Bobby Hackett

Soloists in "Blue Reverie": Johnny Hodges, *Soprano Saxophone;* "Cootie" Williams, *Trumpet;* and Harry Carney, *Baritone Saxophone*

•

Guest soloists in the Jam Session:

Count Basie, *Piano*

Lester Young, *Tenor Saxophone*

"Buck" Clayton, *Trumpet*

Freddie Green, *Guitar*

Walter Page, *Bass*

Johnny Hodges, *Alto Saxophone*

Harry Carney, *Baritone Saxophone*

and

Members of the Goodman Orchestra

•

This performance by courtesy of the Hotel Pennsylvania

Concert Management: HUROK ATTRACTIONS, Inc.
30 Rockefeller Plaza, N. Y. C.

CARNEGIE HALL PROGRAM

TOWN HALL
Sunday Eve., January 23

New York Debut of the Distinguished English Pianist

Alec Templeton

Mr. Templeton will devote part of his program to the delightful improvisations which have brought him International acclaim.

Tickets: $1.10, $1.65, $2.20, $2.75
Boxes: $19.80
at Town Hall Box Office
Tel. BR. 9-9447

•

Management
Music Corporation of America

(Steinway Piano)

MARTIN BECK THEATRE
45th Street West of 8th Ave.

BURTON HOLMES TRAVELOGUES

NEW SCREEN TRAVEL ADVENTURES — ALL IN COLOR AND MOTION PICTURES

THREE COURSES EXACTLY ALIKE

5 Thursday Matinees at 2:45
JANUARY 13-20-27 — FEBRUARY 3-10
5 Sunday Matinees at 2:45
JANUARY 16-23-30 — FEBRUARY 6-13
5 Sunday Evenings at 8:30
JANUARY 16-23-30 — FEBRUARY 6-13

A 1937 Motor Tour in BRIGHTEST SOUTH AFRICA, ITALY and the New ROMAN EMPIRE, The World Wide BRITISH EMPIRE, Picturesque GERMANY, Down to RIO through MEXICO and Over the ANDES.

Tickets on sale at the Box Office

Course Tickets
Thursday Matinees: $4.40, 3.30, 2.20
Sunday Matinees: $5.50, 4.40, 3.30, 2.20
Sunday Evenings: $6.60, 5.50, 4.40, 3.30, 2.20
Single Tickets
Thursday Matinees: $1.10, 85c, 55c
Sunday Matinees: $1.65, 1.10, 85c, 55c
Sunday Evenings: $2.20, 1.65, 1.10, 85c, 55c

MAKE RESERVATIONS EARLY

THE TOWN HALL
ENDOWMENT SERIES

8th Season - 7th Event

Presents

ENESCO

in a Violin Recital

at

TOWN HALL
Wed. Eve., March 9, at 8:30

•

Limited number of tickets available now at Box Office, 113 W. 43rd St.
BRyant 9-9447

Steinway Piano

NEW SCHOOL FOR SOCIAL RESEARCH

The Complete Pianoforte Sonatas of SCHUBERT

WEBSTER
AITKEN

4 Tuesday Evenings
at 8:30

January 25th   February 1st
February 8th   February 15th

Subscriptions for the Series
$10 - $5 - $2

Address: **The New School**
66 West 12th Street, N. Y.

Oratorio Society of New York

SPECIAL ANNOUNCEMENT
BACH
MASS IN B MINOR
(Unabridged)

CARNEGIE HALL
Tuesday Eve., March 1st
7:30 o'clock

ETHYL HAYDEN, Soprano
PAULINE PIERCE, Mezzo-Soprano
*GEORGE RASELY, Tenor
*JOHN GURNEY, Bass
*Metropolitan Opera Association

ALBERT STOESSEL, Conductor
HUGH PORTER at the Organ
THE CHORUS OF THE ORATORIO SOCIETY
AN ORCHESTRA OF SIXTY

(Steinway Piano)

Tickets at Carnegie Hall Box Office and Office of Society, 113 West 57th Street

Prospectus sent on request

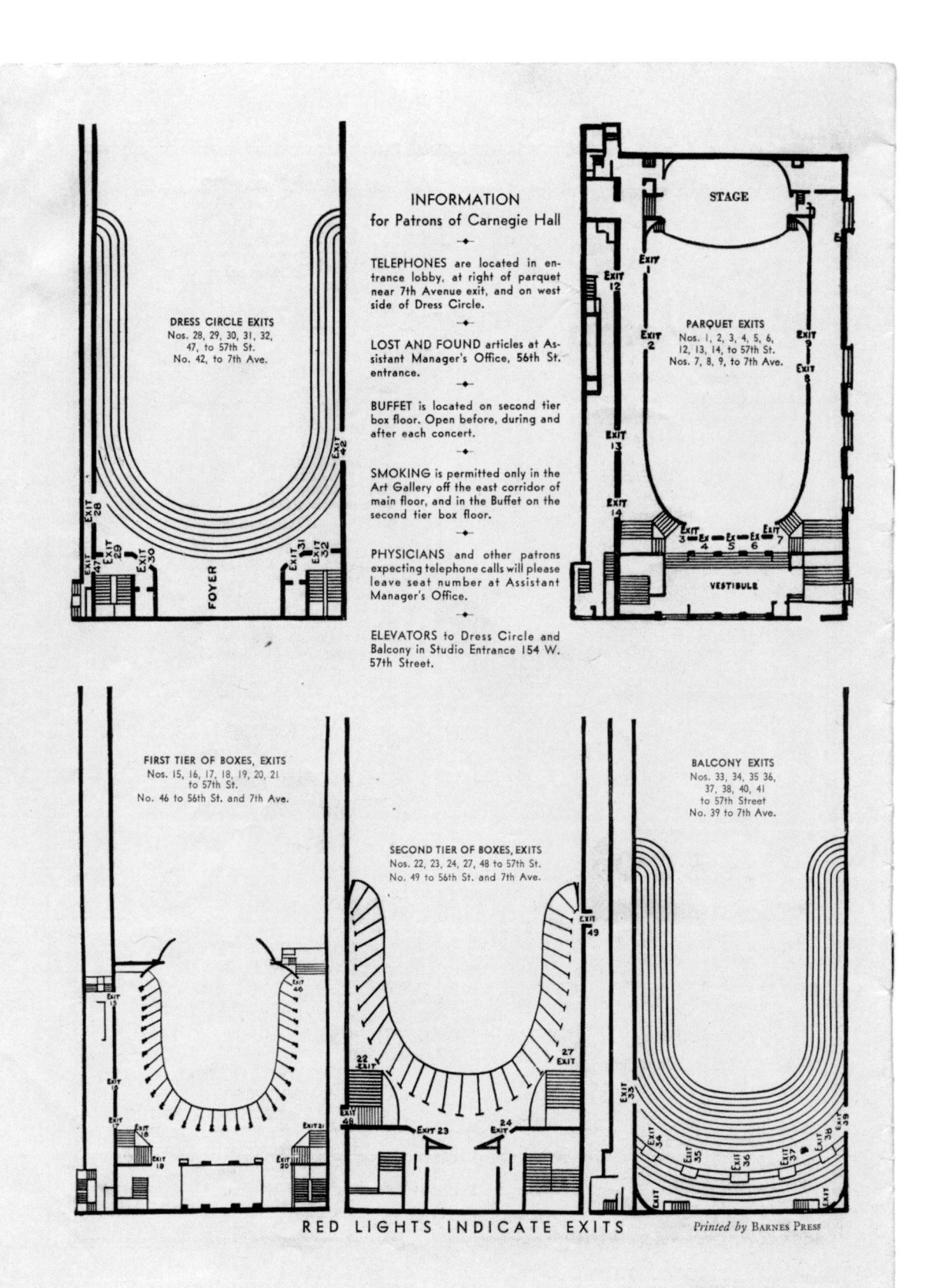

DRESS CIRCLE EXITS
Nos. 28, 29, 30, 31, 32,
47, to 57th St.
No. 42, to 7th Ave.

INFORMATION
for Patrons of Carnegie Hall

TELEPHONES are located in entrance lobby, at right of parquet near 7th Avenue exit, and on west side of Dress Circle.

LOST AND FOUND articles at Assistant Manager's Office, 56th St. entrance.

BUFFET is located on second tier box floor. Open before, during and after each concert.

SMOKING is permitted only in the Art Gallery off the east corridor of main floor, and in the Buffet on the second tier box floor.

PHYSICIANS and other patrons expecting telephone calls will please leave seat number at Assistant Manager's Office.

ELEVATORS to Dress Circle and Balcony in Studio Entrance 154 W. 57th Street.

PARQUET EXITS
Nos. 1, 2, 3, 4, 5, 6,
12, 13, 14, to 57th St.
Nos. 7, 8, 9, to 7th Ave.

FIRST TIER OF BOXES, EXITS
Nos. 15, 16, 17, 18, 19, 20, 21 to 57th St.
No. 46 to 56th St. and 7th Ave.

SECOND TIER OF BOXES, EXITS
Nos. 22, 23, 24, 27, 48 to 57th St.
No. 49 to 56th St. and 7th Ave.

BALCONY EXITS
Nos. 33, 34, 35, 36,
37, 38, 40, 41
to 57th Street
No. 39 to 7th Ave.

RED LIGHTS INDICATE EXITS

Printed by BARNES PRESS

A VIOLINIST OFFSTAGE

The absorbed chess player is Nathan Milstein, distinguished Russian violinist, who on the evening of January 29 will give his only New York recital of the season at Carnegie Hall.

Milstein is as expert at bridge as he is at chess. Indeed, if his violin did not occupy so much of his time he might be a bridge champion. He relates with amusement how at the beginning of his career his manager suggested he might make more money playing bridge than playing the violin.

Numerous other interests round out the rich and varied life of this great violinist. He loves to paint water colors and has a fresh and original way of expressing himself through this medium. However, to the dismay of his friends he will pick up what seems to be an exceptionally fine sample of his work, look at it critically and than calmly tear it up, remarking "I don't like this any more."

Ping pong is another of his hobbies. His proudest boast is that he once beat Heifetz, who is supposed to be champion of this sport among musicians. He likes company and can keep a party entertained for an entire evening, good-naturedly mimicking the mannerisms and gestures of his distinguished colleagues. But often on a long train trip he will go into seclusion in his compartment, talking to no one and spending hours playing Brahms or Bach.

Before returning for his ninth consecutive season in the United States, Milstein spent three months concertizing in South America and three in Europe.

Greetings to Chesterfield Listeners
Lawrence Tibbett

Here's more pleasure for '38...

a happier new year ...and more pleasure for the thousands of new smokers who are finding out about Chesterfield's milder better taste.

Mild ripe tobaccos and pure cigarette paper are the best ingredients a cigarette can have ...these are the things that give *you* more pleasure *in* Chesterfields.

Copyright 1938, LIGGETT & MYERS TOBACCO CO.

Weekly Radio Features
LAWRENCE TIBBETT
ANDRE KOSTELANETZ
PAUL WHITEMAN
DEEMS TAYLOR
PAUL DOUGLAS

CBS

Chesterfield

..you'll find MORE PLEASURE in Chesterfield's milder better taste

— The Concert Program —

Accompanying the program was a lengthy set of notes written by Irving Kolodin who was shortly to collaborate with Benny to write his autobiography and later, the extensive liner notes for the record album. These additional booklets were often added because of the limited space available in the program. Kolodin had just published a book about The Metropolitan Opera and his elaborate notes were aimed at the Carnegie Hall regulars who might be unfamiliar with Swing music. The notes go to great lengths to try and explain what the audience was about to hear by using comparisons with Chopin and Strauss. The principle behind jazz is also laid out with the caveat that 'even the best swing players have moments of stodginess', warning the reader that it is not reasonable to expect that all performances will be white hot with inventiveness and originality! Variety Magazine poked fun at the pretentious nature of the Goodman concert at Carnegie Hall. "This was epitomised", they said, "by the program notes pamphlet... Observers wondered whether swing had ever received such dead-pan attention." Variety took issue with the profound comparisons that were made with 'the great masters' and the erudite way in which the notes were written, in the style of a symphonic program.[94] The complete text from the program notes is included here in Appendix 1.

Tenor Saxophone player, George Koenig has the concert program on his music stand. (See enlargement).

[94] Variety Magazine - January 19 1938

Irving Kolodin's 'Notes on the Program' booklet that accompanied the program.

Notes on the Program

by
Irving Kolodin

BENNY GOODMAN and his ORCHESTRA

Foreword

SWING is to the ballroom type of jazz as brandy is to table wine—a headier, more potent transformation of the same basic stuff. There has been much esoteric pother because swing cannot be summarized or defined in a word or a sentence. But for that matter, neither can *tempo rubato* (which is the essence of Chopin) nor the Viennese style of waltz performance (which is the essence of Johann Strauss's music) be put in the strait-jacket of so many nouns, verbs and adjectives. As in the case of these others, swing is essentially a *style of performance* whose vitality is supplied by a fluctuation of accent between normally weak and strong beats.

To an extent not present in formal music, swing is further a complex of several elements interrelated and interdependent, one not complete without the other. Principal among these is the characteristic improvisation on the theme at hand, almost invariably a communal process in which the ideas initiated by one player are picked up by the others in turn and colored by the force of their own style and personality. But as there is good and bad improvisation, so there are various degrees of impact in the music that might be produced depending on the vitality of the players' imaginations, their technical skill, and, most importantly, the degree of combustion beween them.

Even the best swing players have moments and nights of stodginess when their ideas run to formal figures and cliches, lacking the improvisational flame which is the heart of "hot" jazz. Thus it is not reasonable to expect that all the performances in the space, say, of two hours, will be white hot with inventiveness and originality. Much depends on what swing players like to call "inspiration". But this is merely attributing a mystical quality to the amount of sympathy or kinship generated within a group *as they play*. Lacking this glow and warmth, the same figures and patterns, no matter how faultlessly executed, remain sterile and unaffecting.

So much emphasis has been placed on the performer for the barrenly simple reason that swing *is* performance. Therein lies its principal distinction from all other music, high or low, its strength and probably its most serious limitation. By the standards of the specialized styles of performance noted above, swing is essentially an ephemeral thing, for the daemonic qualities in Chopin's thought, the grace and ardor of Johann

– The Concert Program –

**SUNDAY EVENING
JANUARY 16TH
CARNEGIE HALL
TICKETS NOW AT BOX OFFICE
85¢, $1.10, $1.65, $2.20, $2.75**

CARNEGIE HALL
SUNDAY EVENING, JAN. 16th
S. Hurok presents
BENNY GOODMAN
and his Swing Orchestra
SEATS NOW at CARNEGIE HALL

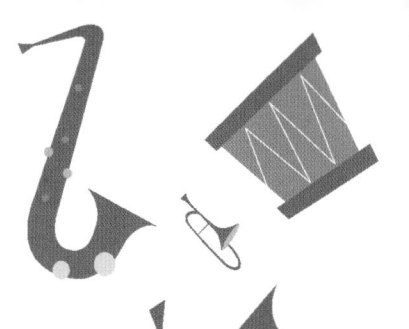

• CHAPTER 9 •

Tickets

The coveted Carnegie Hall tickets were printed by the Globe Ticket Company who are still in business today. The ticket reproduced here is from Benny's archive held at the Yale University Music Library, the name 'Underhill' can be seen written on it. Underhill and Underhill was a photography agency and this ticket was more than likely destined for them, but since the ticket is still uncut and in Benny's possession, it was probably never used. This is likely to be the only surviving whole ticket.

Tickets were put on sale towards the end of December at 85¢, $1.10, $1.65, $2.20 and $2.75. They sold out very quickly, it was reported that almost all of the tickets were sold before the end of 1937.[95] The Carnegie ticket price compares to a $1.50 cover charge at the Hotel Pennsylvania and 35 cents at the Paramount Theatre. The price was high, but not as high as that charged by a young Yehudi Menhuin (21, the same age as Harry James!) who had given a sell-out recital at Carnegie Hall two weeks before. Tickets for his concert were priced at $3.30. It is also worth noting that at Yehudi Menhuin's concert on January 3 1938, 300 extra seats were crammed onto the stage.[96] Managers are always keen to make it look as though their artists are in huge demand, with audience packed in and hanging from the rafters! A quick count of heads on the photographs tells us that there were about 100 extra seats on stage at Benny's concert priced at $2.20 each. (That's $2.00 plus tax!) How those seats were allocated we do not know. Looking at the photos, they do not seem to be the teenage fans that made up the majority of the audience. When the ticket office closed its doors just over a week before the concert, total ticket sales amounted to $4800.[97]

The ticket office at Carnegie Hall was run as a concession and had been controlled by the Heck family since the hall was opened in 1891. Rudolph Heck ran the office in the early days and he passed the responsibility over to his son Walter. Unfortunately, Walter got into difficulties and suspicions were raised about his propriety by the pianist Vladimir Horowitz whom he had over-charged for the use of a piano at one of his concerts. After admitting that he had used the funds inappropriately, Walter Heck was jailed in 1952 for defrauding the government of $147,000 in unpaid admission taxes.[98] This ended a residency at the box office of over sixty years.

95 The Citizen Advertiser, Auburn NY December 20 1937
96 Variety Magazine - January 1938. Also New York Times January 4 1938
97 The Billboard Magazine - January 22 1938
98 New York Times - October 23 1952 – Also. - Storyville Magazine 153. March 1993

Only $2.75 for the best seats! How much would you pay today?

We will probably never know precisely how many tickets were sold for Benny Goodman's concert. Reports vary from as many as 2700 to 3900, but it is really just a matter of estimating how many people were standing. The hall contained 2760 permanent seats plus one hundred on the stage and another hundred or so standing. (Down Beat says one hundred and Variety says two hundred standing.) That makes a total of about 3000. The speculators of Broadway, the 'Scalpers', were, in the main, caught unawares by the overwhelming demand for tickets and failed to buy enough. This had the fortunate result that the audience was largely made up of discerning fans rather than people in the music business, the song pluggers, who would follow the band leaders everywhere in the hope that they might sell one of their tunes to a big name. The 'Daily News' reported "not more than three hundred of those present had reached their thirtieth birthday." When it came to getting tickets for his family, Benny was forced to buy his tickets on the black market from one of the astute dealers who did foresee the potential for a bonanza. Tickets were changing hands at $25.00 a pair, that could be ten times the face value![99] The concert was a sell-out long before the big night and, always the shrewd business man, Sol Hurok tried to book the Goodman band for a repeat performance the following Sunday night at Carnegie Hall.[100] Sadly, he was turned down because of Goodman's prior commitments. The band would be busy preparing for their move from the Hotel Pennsylvania, down Seventh Avenue for another gruelling three week engagement at the Paramount Theatre in Times Square. Starting on January 26, they would play five shows a day between showings of the Mae West film 'Every Day's A Holiday', Louis Armstrong makes a brief appearance in the film too. On opening day at the Paramount Theatre, 25,000 paying customers came through the doors, setting a new box office record.[101] In the end, there was no concert at all at Carnegie on the night of January 23. Benny had been approached many times to go back to Carnegie Hall with a big band to do it again but: "I always nixed the idea."[102]

The Concert ticket, printed by the Globe Ticket Company. This ticket was allocated to 'Underhill' but never used. It remained in Benny's possession until his death.

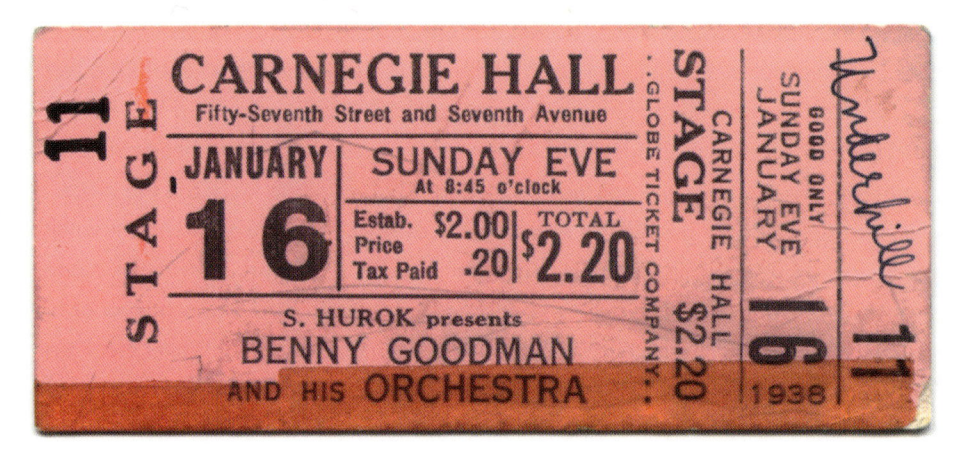

[99] The Citizen Advertiser, Auburn NY – January 20 1938
[100] The Billboard Magazine - January 22 1938. P.16
[101] New York Daily Post – 3 February 1938
[102] Down Beat - February 8 1956 P12

– Tickets –

An advertisement from the New York Times on January 17 1938 – the day after the concert. "For the thousands who were turned away from Carnegie Hall last night"

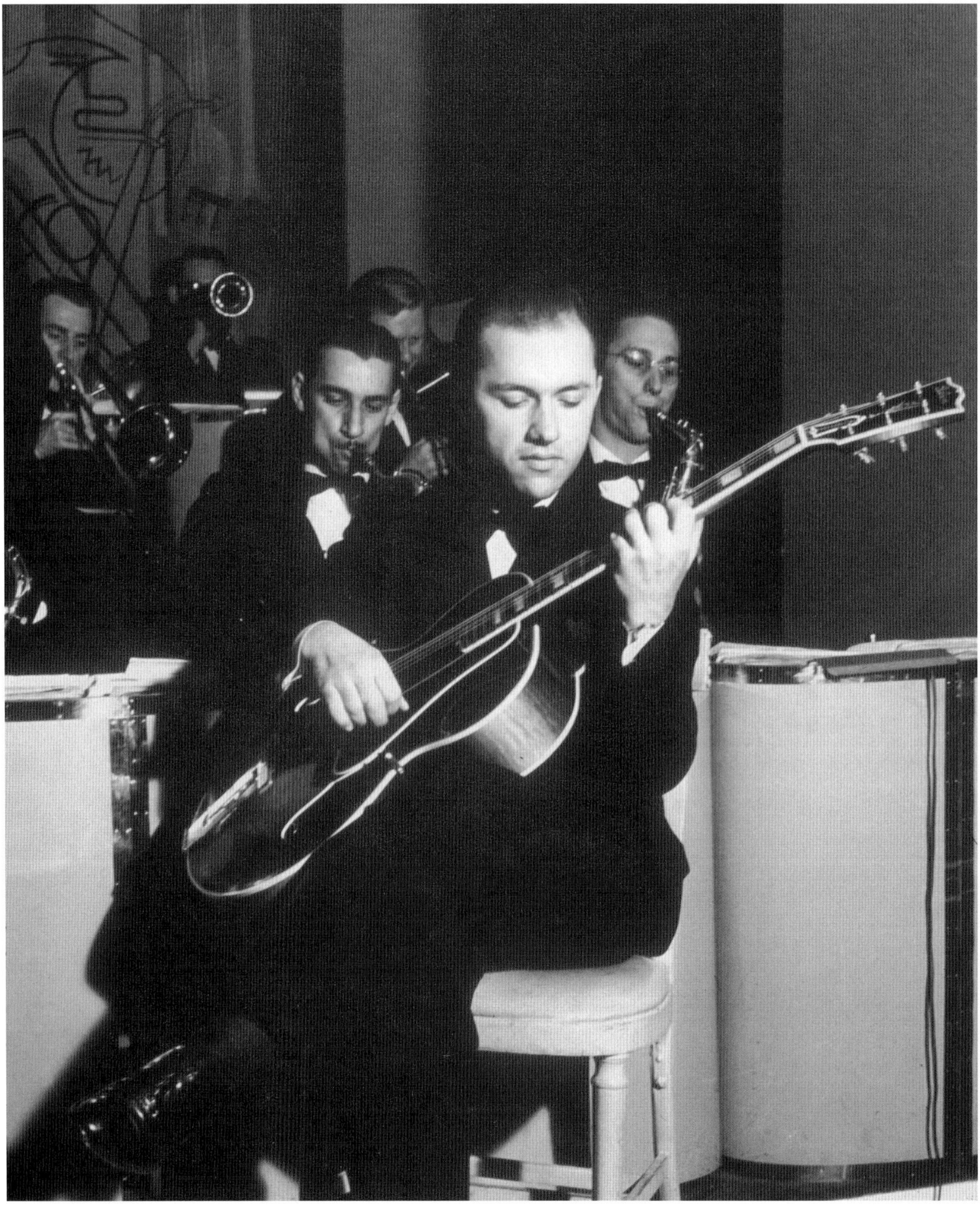

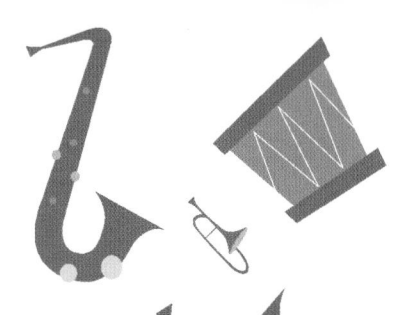

• CHAPTER 10 •

"How long does Mr Toscanini take?"

Classical music was very popular in the 1930s, much more so than it is today. During 1937, NBC broadcast a series of programs called 'Home Symphony'. This was a very successful experiment in mass participation, the program boasted the largest orchestra in the world. The principle was that anybody could join the orchestra from the comfort of their own homes, huge numbers of enthusiastic amateur musicians listened and played along. Coincidentally, after a break for the summer of 1937, the program resumed its Sunday afternoon concerts on the 16th January 1938. By 1938 there were also regular broadcasts of classical music from Carnegie Hall on Saturday nights.

Amongst the celebrated conductors who had stood on the conductor's podium at Carnegie Hall was Arturo Toscanini. Toscanini was an incredibly popular conductor and he had just returned to New York to accept the post as the leader of the NBC Symphony Orchestra, under a blaze of publicity. In October and November he had given concerts with the BBC Orchestra in England which were oversubscribed by thousands, seats had to be allocated by ballot.[103] On his return to the USA from Europe, the fiery Toscanini was involved in a brawl onboard ship with some over-zealous photographers eager to get his picture.[104]

Unlike today, recordings of classical music were the biggest sellers, taking the lion's share of record sales and Toscanini was big news in New York. He had recently been unveiled as the star conductor in a series of ten concerts for NBC with a salary of $4000 per concert,[105] making him the highest-paid conductor ever. He made his first broadcast of this new contract from Radio City with his orchestra on 25th December 1937 before an invited studio audience of 1400, packed with celebrities who treated the conductor with great deference.[106] Toscanini's contract with NBC would not have gone unnoticed by Benny who, with his astute publicity men, was planning his debut at Carnegie Hall a few weeks later. Remember Benny's often quoted remark when he was asked, shortly before the concert, how long an intermission he wanted? "Oh I dunno, how long does Mr Toscanini take?" was his now famous reply.[107]

---

103 The Etude Magazine - February 1938 P.70
104 Down Beat Magazine - January 1938
105 Variety Magazine - January 1939
106 Radio Guide - January 15 1938
107 Rochester Democrat Chronicle - Walter Winchell. January 26 1938

Allan Reuss sits out in front of the band at the Madhattan Room early in 1938.

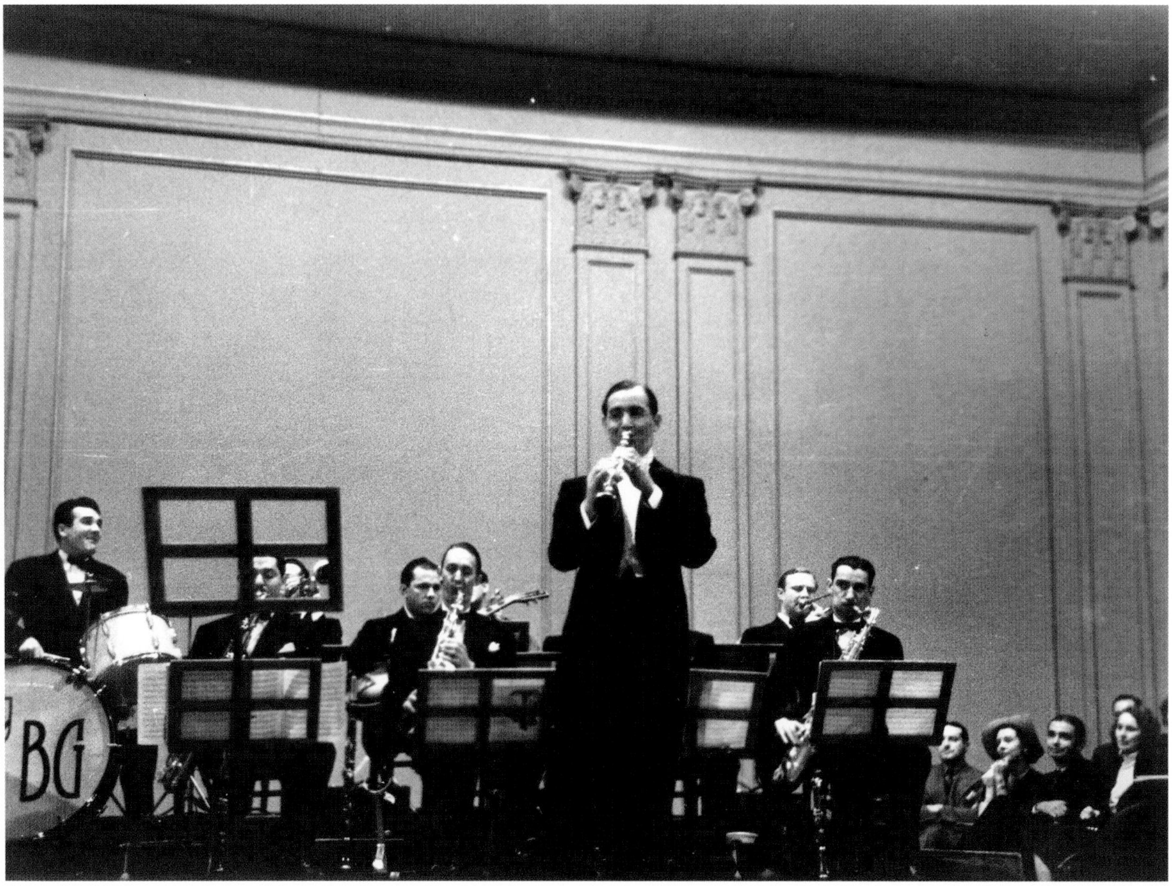
BG

• CHAPTER 11 •

A Cold Evening to Queue

On the morning of Sunday January 16, Duke Ellington, his orchestra and small groups were playing a live radio broadcast from the Criterion Theatre in New York. Benny Goodman's guest soloists from the Ellington Orchestra, Johnny Hodges, Harry Carney and Cootie Williams were all on air for the regular 'Sunday Morning Swing Concert' on WNEW at 11.00am.[108]

Outside Carnegie Hall that same evening large crowds had gathered, restrained by a cordon of police. There was a full moon and the New York Times reported that this was the coldest night of the winter so far, the Hudson River had frozen over at Yonkers and the temperature went down to 16°F (-8°C). Police were posted on the three doors to the hall and insisted on checking tickets, nobody was allowed into the lobby without a ticket.[109] Queues of people had started to form early that afternoon, desperate to get standing tickets or last minute 'no shows'. Bob Inman describes in his scrapbooks how he took the train into Grand Central Station with two friends to try and get a standing ticket at Carnegie Hall. His friends Jim Poe and Bobby Van Schilgan both already had tickets but Bob was unlucky. Rather than hang about, he went straight over to the Savoy Ballroom. There, Bob got tickets for the 'Battle of the Bands' between Count Basie and Chick Webb, which was due to start soon after Goodman's Carnegie concert had finished. In his diary, Bob remarked that the Basie/Webb contest was "One of the most terrific battles of Swing ever put on."[110]

John Hammond's review for Tempo Magazine, noted that around five thousand people were turned away from Carnegie Hall, unable to get tickets.[111] This really was the place to be on that cold Sunday night and anyone who was anybody was there. Sleek cars fought their way through the throng, delivering the celebrities and socialites who came to be seen. The New York World Telegram published a colourful description of the arrival of one group of debutants under the headline 'Socialites at Swing Concert'. This excerpt gives a flavour of the piece:

'Hope Baldwin in a black dress, black fox hip length coat and pink suede hat looked excited as she arrived during the first number. She was accompanied by a sister deb, Nancy Van Vleck, who wore a grey squirrel swagger coat and a black bonnet trimmed with a sweeping black spotted veil. She attracted almost more attention in

Those lucky members of the audience on the right, who managed to get the stage seats, enjoy Benny and the band in full swing.

108 Swing Era Scrapbook - Ken Vail. P.313
109 The Citizen Advertiser – Auburn N.Y - 20 January 1938
110 Swing Era Scrapbook. - Ken Vail. P.314
111 Tempo Magazine - February 1938
112 New York World Telegram - January. 17 1938

her smoked glasses than Ethel Merman, who arrived earlier. They were escorted by two beaus.'[112]

Also outside the hall that night, there was an angry group of pro-Franco protesters, loudly showing their disapproval because Benny had played a 'Night of Stars' benefit concert for the Spanish Loyalists at the Mecca Temple in New York on Sunday December 12, this time with an orchestra led by Alfred Wallenstein.[113] The protestors had picketed the stage door and were chanting and taunting the musicians as they arrived. "Benny Goodman is a red from Spain." Never short of a quip, Ziggy Elman shouted back, "No he isn't, he's a clarinet player from Chicago!"[114] The newsreel footage taken that evening shows brief glimpses of placard-waving protesters parading outside of the hall.[115]

113 The Billboard January 1938. Also New York Times December 14 1938
114 'Oh Jess' - Keith Keller p.84
115 See 'Adventures in the Kingdom of Swing' Sony video

– A Cold Evening to Queue –

This picture was probably taken from the little viewing window next to the stage door.

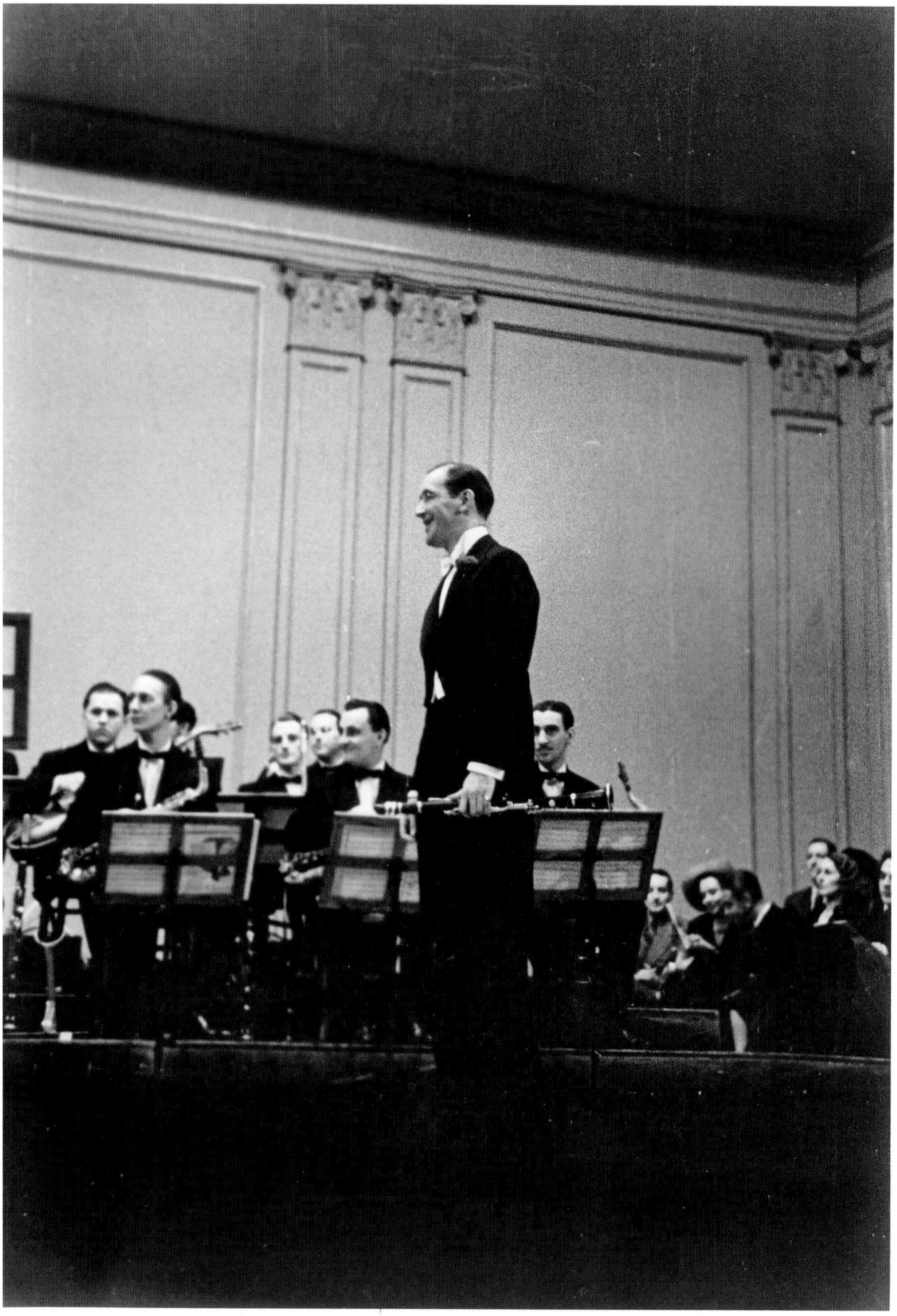

CHAPTER 12

The Concert

The hall was packed, every seat sold, tiered overflow seats were erected on the stage and there was also a large contingent of standees thickly clustered at the back of the auditorium. Most of the lucky people who got tickets were Benny's regular fans but there was a fair number of the Carnegie stalwarts and a small number in 'Soup and Fish' (top hat and tails). Of course the rich and famous were there because that was where you had to be. The audience was well behaved in the early part of the evening, respectful of the hall and full of anticipation. There was a quivering excitement in the air, an almost electrical effect and much laughter,[116] the hall was filled with the sense that something historic was about to happen, an overwhelming air of expectancy. Was the whole thing a monumental mistake? Could Benny's band hold the attention of the audience for a two hour concert without the help of comedians and link men? 3000 expectant New Yorkers were about to find out.

Backstage it was busy. Photographers, journalists, guests and friends had all come to witness, and be part of the occasion. The lucky ticket holders for the stage seats were milling about too. Benny would have been there early, he liked to get himself and his instrument warmed up in plenty of time. Lionel Hampton was the last to arrive but he wasn't due on stage until later. "Sure I'm nervous", said Gene Krupa, "But Gee! I always get nervous - every time we change hotels I get nervous." Duke Ellington's singer Ivie Anderson had come to wish the boys well, "I guess this is the top" she said.[117] Gene Krupa, Teddy Wilson and Ivie, along with a visiting classical violinist[118] were taken on a tour of the back stage rooms reserved for the New York Philharmonic, others were warming up with a jam session in the conductor's chambers. Gene Krupa joked, "Is there anybody in the house?" and grinned. Benny's former singer Helen Ward had dropped by with her six-week-old baby. Her husband Albert Marx was sitting out front in the second row with his brother Lawrence. BG fans will always be indebted to these two: Lawrence took many of the photographs seen in this book. Albert was responsible for having the concert recorded. He had worked closely with sound engineer Harry Smith to record it remotely from Harry's studios. No doubt Albert sat looking at the microphone hanging over the stage wondering to himself, "I wonder if Harry remembered to switch the microphone on?"

116 New York Times - January 18 1938 Olin Downes
117 Down Beat Magazine - February 1938
118 Probably Joseph Szigeti, a friend of John Hammond, who was a keen amateur viola player

Benny and the band look over towards Bobby Hackett as he plays his solo.

Benny, dressed in his elegantly-tailored tails and white tie with a blue carnation in his lapel, was nervous and as white as a sheet. Some papers he was holding were trembling and he was pacing up and down. "I don't think Benny had ever been more nervous", recalled William Esty's Radio Director, Savington Crampton.[119] Everything was ready, it was time to start. Members of the band were crammed together in the small space of the wings. Who would go out first? Gene Krupa had already been out onto the stage to re-tune his drums and was rewarded with a tremendous cheer. (It was Gene Krupa who had persuaded the Slingerland Drum Company to introduce a tuneable Tom Tom.) Benny gave instructions for his guest musicians to prepare to be ushered out on stage at the right moment for the 'Twenty Years of Jazz' and 'jam session' sections of the program. Somebody from the Goodman camp knelt down and gave Benny's shoes a quick buffing-up.

There are conflicting stories about who it was that took the band out on stage, Hymie Schertzer tells of how they had a big discussion about who was going to be the first band member to walk out onto that hallowed stage. Hymie claims that he chaperoned the band out and recalled his early years as a violinist, when his father had hoped that he would turn out to be another Heifetz, "He would have given me such a swift kick for coming out with a saxophone".[120] However, the Down Beat reporter noted that 'Gordon Griffin was finally pushed out first'.[121] In an interview for a TV documentary, Harry Goodman says that he led the band out carrying the bass.[122] Art Rollini tells of how it was Harry James who led the band from the wings.[123]

Pale as a ghost, Benny waited for his band to get settled. At 8.50, with the band in their seats facing an expectant capacity audience, he weaved his way past the ranks of extra seating, out onto the crowded stage. He was greeted by a tremendous cheer from the audience. The 'King of Swing' bowed three times to his subjects, the subjects carried on with their jubilant support. He turned around to face the orchestra and beat off the tempo for the first number, Edgar Sampson's 'Don't Be That Way'. In his autobiography published in 1939, Benny said this about that night: "Personally, it was the thrill of my life to walk out on that stage with the people just hemming the band in, and hear the greeting the boys got. We were playing for 'Bix' and the fellows on the riverboats, in the honky-tonks and ginmills that night."[124]

---

119 Sarasota Herald Tribune - June 24 1986
120 Mort Goode Liner notes - 'The Complete Benny Goodman Volume V'
121 Down Beat - February 1938
122 'Adventures in the Kingdom of Swing' First broadcast on the 'South Bank Show' in the UK July 4 1993
123 Thirty Years with the Big Bands – Art Rollini. P.63
124 The Kingdom of Swing - Benny Goodman & Irving Kolodin. P.233

The Concert

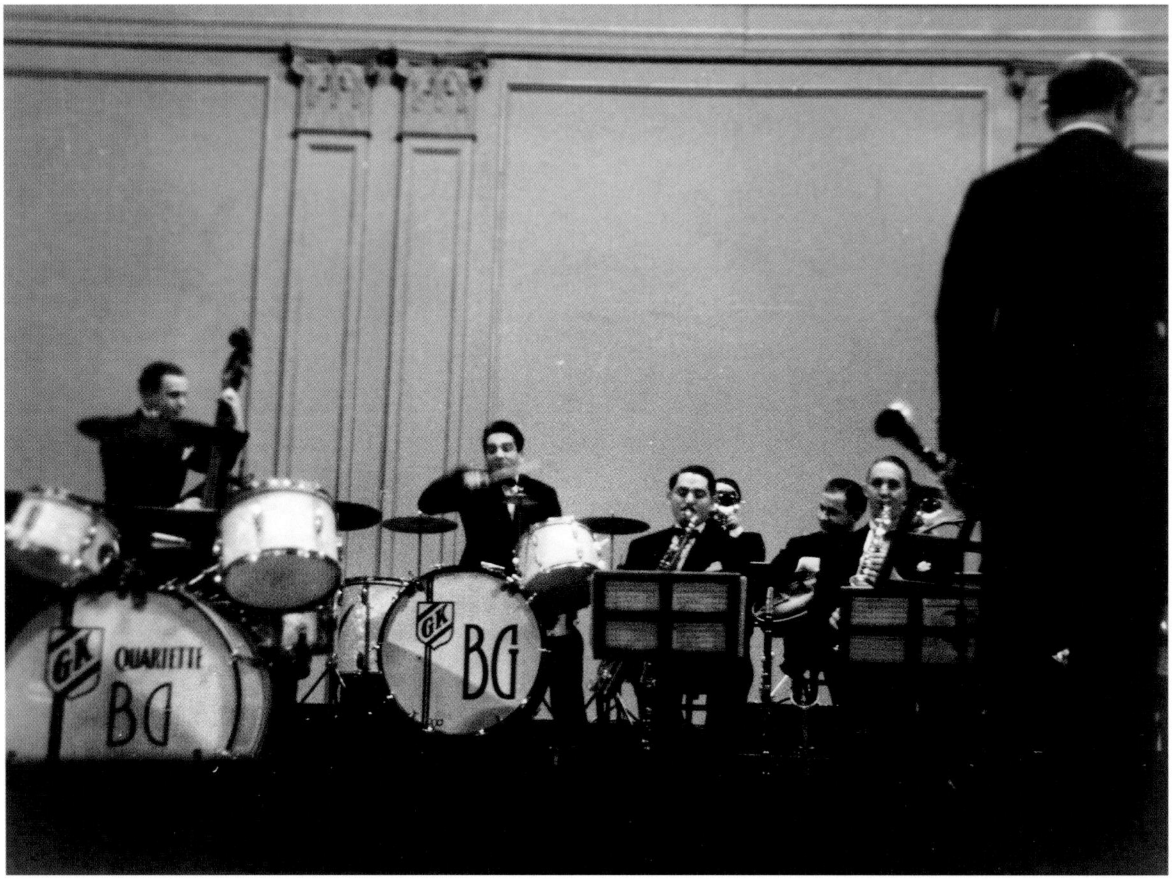
GK
QUARTETTE
BG
GK
BG

• CHAPTER 13 •
The Music

Don't Be That Way

Orchestra:
Benny Goodman (Clarinet). Harry James, Ziggy Elman, Chris Griffin (Trumpets). Vernon Brown, Red Ballard (Trombones). Hymie Schertzer, George Koenig (Alto Sax). Babe Russin, Art Rollini (Tenor Sax). Allan Reuss (Rhythm Guitar). Jess Stacy (Piano). Harry Goodman (Bass). Gene Krupa (Drums).

Interviewed in 1981 for American Heritage Magazine by cornettist and writer, Richard Sudhalter, Benny talked about one potential difficulty of playing in the concert setting: "Playing a job at a place like the Madhattan Room of the Pennsylvania Hotel, where we were then, or most any place, we'd usually start kind of quietly. Play dinner music so to speak. Warm up a little bit. It wouldn't be until later that the band really got rocking. But in a concert you had to hit right from the top, Bang!"[125] One story that is often repeated about this concert is that Benny set the tempo too slow for the first number. Perhaps it was the reviewer's unfamiliarity with this arrangement which led to this impression. They were playing Edgar Sampson's newly arranged version of 'Don't Be That Way' which had only been performed in public twice before at the Camel Caravan broadcasts a few days earlier. Or perhaps it was first night nerves that gave the impression that the band was playing too slowly. If we listen to the Camel Caravan broadcast made just two days later,[126] we can hear that this is taken at an even slower pace and indeed, the RCA studio recording the band made a month later is also played slower than the Carnegie version. Goodman usually played at a slower tempo on studio recordings than in public performances. In Walter Allen's exhaustive Bio-discography of Fletcher Henderson, trumpeter and author John Chilton writes, 'Most musicians would tend to play slower on a recording date, wanting to avoid mistakes in execution, but I wonder if Goodman himself may have set what he considered to be the 'proper' tempo for the 'authorised' or released studio recording'.[127]

Metronome's excellent columnist George Simon (who had been a drummer with the fledgling Glen Miller orchestra in late 1936) reported that Harry Goodman 'looked all white, drawn and scared stiff during the first number'.[128] Harry James got the first

L to R: Harry Goodman, Gene Krupa, Babe Russin, (Harry James), Allan Reuss, George Koenig and Benny with his back to us.

---

125 American Heritage Magazine - October 19 1981
126 Jazz Unlimited CD 2012087
127 Hendersonia - The music of Fletcher Henderson and his Musicians. Walter C Allen. P.506
128 Metronome Magazine - February 1938

big round of applause of the evening when he stood up for his solo and of course Gene Krupa's astonishing machinegun drum break really put everyone at ease, 'Come on guys, it's just another concert' was the message and the guys got the message loud and clear. Quoted in The New Yorker Magazine, WW Nash, who was standing at the back of the hall that night, described the opening number like this: "In fact, I can't remember any other musical event quite like it, unless it was a particular Toscanini concert or Oistrakh's first appearance here. So when 'Don't Be That Way' came rolling out, it was as if a hundred piece band were blasting at you. It was even brassier and louder and more hard-driving than we had dreamed."[129] By the end of 'Don't Be That Way' Harry Goodman had recovered his colour and the guys were relaxed and feeling 'at home' on the Carnegie stage.

Since joining Benny Goodman and establishing the BG quartet, Lionel Hampton had become a popular celebrity and very much in demand. Following on from Teddy Wilson's success at Brunswick with Billie Holiday and others, Eli Oberstein, head of repertory at RCA Victor and the supervisor of Benny's Victor recordings, had invited Hampton to make some recordings under his own name.[130] For four years, before he left Goodman to start up on his own, Lionel had the choice of the star musicians whenever they were in town. Lionel made full use of members of famous bands including Ellington's, Fletcher Henderson's, Stuff Smith's and others, as well as his colleagues from the Goodman band. Two days after the Carnegie concert, Lionel Hampton recorded his own version of 'Don't Be That Way' for RCA Victor with an all-star pick up band that included Edgar Sampson himself on baritone sax along with Carnegie veterans Jess, Cootie, Hodges and Reuss, with Billy Taylor and Sonny Greer.

Sometimes I'm Happy

Orchestra:
Benny Goodman (Clarinet). Harry James, Ziggy Elman, Chris Griffin (Trumpets). Vernon Brown, Red Ballard (Trombones). Hymie Schertzer, George Koenig (Alto Sax). Babe Russin, Art Rollini (Tenor Sax). Allan Reuss (Rhythm Guitar). Jess Stacy (Piano). Harry Goodman (Bass). Gene Krupa (Drums).

The second number played was the lovely Fletcher Henderson arrangement of 'Sometimes I'm Happy'. This was one of the very first Henderson arrangements that Benny ever recorded and had been in the Goodman repertoire since 1935. Fletcher's brother Horace recalled how he used to help Fletcher on occasions when he was under pressure to get work finished on time. Early one morning when he was composing the arrangement of 'Sometimes' Fletcher woke his brother and asked him to help complete the task ready to hand over to Goodman in the morning. Fletcher had written the part for the reeds and had asked Horace to write the corresponding part for the brass.[131]

---

129 The New Yorker - December 26 1977
130 'Hamp' - Lionel Hampton with James Haskins. P.59
131 Swing, Swing, Swing - Ross Firestone. P116

– The Music –

This tune was omitted from the original 1950 Columbia release. The reason was probably not because the recording was too noisy as stated in the liner notes, the sound quality appears to be much the same as the rest of the concert. It was more likely due to the length of the concert being outside the capacity of the two LP format. The 33^1/$_3$ Microgroove was a new innovation in 1950 and it was difficult to fit the whole concert onto four sides of the LP's (although it was not too long before the available time on an LP was extended.) Something had to give and the producers of the records probably opted to drop 'Sometimes' because it was one of the less exciting numbers played.

Admittedly, this is not a 'Killer Diller' but it is a lovely arrangement with some delightful playing by Jess Stacy behind the reed section which gracefully meanders along, slow, relaxed and very self assured. The muted trumpets play 'Henderson Tag' with the reeds and when Harry James is let loose he plays wonderfully. Art Rollini gets his first solo and then suddenly, when the mutes come off the trumpets, Goodman's formidable 'Biting Brass' reveal their teeth! Chris Griffin used to tell the story about Harry Glantz who was a friend of Benny's and a principle trumpet player for the New York Philharmonic. After hearing Goodman's trumpet section for the first time he is said to have remarked, "What the hell do you feed those trumpet players? Raw meat?"[132] Glen Miller had described the Goodman trumpet section as "The marvel of the age."[133]

Short sequences of the concert were captured on film by a newsreel cameraman. It was during one of the softer passages of 'Sometimes I'm Happy' that the cameraman was loudly 'shushed' by the audience for making a noise with his camera.[134] We will discuss the newsreel film in detail later in the book.

Could this be the newsreel camera man standing next to the Carnegie Hall organ at the back of the stage seats? A still from his newsreel footage shows Benny in the same pose.

[132] www.allaboutjazz.com – David French
[133] Trumpet Blues The Life of Harry James - Peter Levinson P.38
[134] Metronome - February 1938

Reflecting on the fact that Benny was more accustomed to playing between film showings at the Paramount Theatre, Down Beat Magazine carried the (probably tongue in cheek) story that, during the second number of the Carnegie concert an elderly latecomer rushed up to an usherette and asked, "What time does the feature film go on?"[135]

'Sometimes I'm Happy' is a classic arrangement and is worth listening to a couple of times just to follow the brilliant section work of the Goodman band. Benny had a great capacity for rehearsal and would go over and over short passages to get them absolutely perfect. He would also rehearse the brass separately without a rhythm section, the thinking being that if they could swing without a rhythm section they would be even better with one.

This recording, along with 'If Dreams Come True' first saw the light of day in 1973 on the bootleg release Sunbeam 127. These were really quite poor transfers and we did not get to hear these two tunes in their proper running order until the full concert was reconstructed in 1999.

One O'Clock Jump

Orchestra:

Benny Goodman (Clarinet). Harry James, Ziggy Elman, Chris Griffin (Trumpets). Vernon Brown, Red Ballard (Trombones). Hymie Schertzer, George Koenig (Alto Sax). Babe Russin, Art Rollini (Tenor Sax). Allan Reuss (Rhythm Guitar). Jess Stacy (Piano). Harry Goodman (Bass). Gene Krupa (Drums).

Next on the program is 'One O'Clock Jump' and who would like to have been in Jess Stacy's shoes as he embarked on this masterpiece? Waiting in the wings was the tune's creator, Count Basie, and just to make things more uncomfortable for Jess, Duke Ellington who attended the concert with Edmund Anderson sat looking over his shoulder from his box just above the stage.[136] To top it all, Benny's other great pianist Teddy Wilson was also waiting back stage for his debut in the Carnegie auditorium. OK Jess, off you go! When asked what it felt like to kick off 'One O'Clock' under Count Basie's scrutiny, Jess remarked "I was playing for him, I was dedicating it to him."[137]

Ellington must have watched the evening's events with a certain amount of envy. A few months earlier he had sat in a box at Carnegie Hall as the personal guest of the renowned conductor, Leopold Stokowski. Stokowski had dropped in unannounced to hear Ellington at the Cotton Club. He was so impressed with what he heard that he invited the Duke back to Carnegie Hall the next night to listen to one of his concerts.[138] This must have whetted Ellington's appetite for his own concert there and the prestige that it would have brought. Ellington's close friend, Edmund Anderson had suggested that he play a concert at Carnegie Hall before Goodman had performed there, but

---

135 Down Beat - February 1938
136 Turk Van Lake talking on NPR's 'First Person Singular' See also Duke Ellington Society Web Site - DEMS
137 IAJRC 1987 Conference audience recording
138 Down Beat - September 1937

Irving Mills the music publisher and business associate of the Duke had blocked the idea on the grounds that an unsuccessful concert would have brought bad publicity.[139] Of course, Ellington went on to perform there many times but as we now know, Goodman's concert became one of the most celebrated concerts in the history of the Hall and it must have irritated Ellington that three of his star musicians will be forever associated with that occasion.

Benny seldom gave Jess Stacy a solo spot on his commercial recordings, so Stacy fans always pay special attention to the vocals on Goodman records because that is where Jess was allowed some freedom to play as he liked. We are really indebted to Albert Marx for his commissioning of these recordings, which are probably the finest examples of Jess playing with the Benny Goodman orchestra. 'One O'clock Jump' is a classic riff-based tune, it repeats a simple phrase over and over to generate the excitement and anticipation that the jitterbuggers loved so much. Down Beat described it as 'the first stick of rhythmic dynamite set off to start the audience into a human wave of rhythmic frenzy'.[140] After the brief introduction from the band, Jess plays his extended tribute to the Count with great confidence and agility. A close listening will reveal that delightful little tremolo that he used as an embellishment at the end of his phrasing. Aficionados will always identify Stacy's work when they hear this little trill.

The new boy in the band, Babe Russin follows and then we are treated to a powerful Vernon Brown trombone solo. Some stabbing interjections by the brass are followed by some more tasteful work by Goodman and Stacy with (at the risk of causing offence to Basie fans) a Basie-like rhythm section. Harry James stands up for another of his stunning and concise contributions, after which the whole thing changes gear and slides into the familiar theme. Melody Maker's correspondent observed: 'Not until the second chorus of 'One O'Clock Jump' did the audience cast off its cloak of sobriety and synchronised itself with the lifting tempi and rollicking riffs'. Towards the end of the number, just before Benny's final solo, the band seems to be running on autopilot set to cruise all night. Benny steps in and brings the whole thing to a brilliant conclusion, although nobody would have minded another seven or eight choruses of the band cruising at altitude. Krupa's little syncopated injections on the cowbell in the last moments are pure Gene-ious! Benny's RCA Victor release of 'One O'clock Jump' recorded in February 1938, became his first record to sell one million copies.[141]

Towards the end of his long career, Benny used to play the Carnegie recording of 'One O'clock' often, just to listen to the interplay between his clarinet and Jess Stacy playing behind him.[142] Benny added this tune to his repertoire in October 1937, about the same time as Basie released his commercial recording and although it was Basie's theme, Benny continued to play it throughout his career whenever he had a big band assembled.

In 1980, musician, writer and Goodman fan, Loren Schoenberg took a job working in Benny's office replacing the noted jazz authority, Frank Driggs. Loren was running

---

139 James Lincoln Collier - Duke Ellington P.217
140 Down Beat - February 1938
141 The Story of Jazz – Marshall Stearns P.215
142 IAJRC 1987 Conference audience recording

his own band then and in 1982, after hearing some of the band's recordings, Benny adopted Loren's entire band as his own. Benny had bequeathed his papers and arrangements to the Irving S. Gilmore Music Library at Yale University, so when Benny died in 1986, Loren was the obvious candidate for the job of cataloguing his arrangements before they were deposited in the Yale archives. At the IAJRC annual conference 1987, Loren told of how he had uncovered an arrangement by Eddie Sauter, entitled 'Jess's Theme'. This is built around Jess Stacy's solo introduction to the Carnegie Hall version of 'One O'clock Jump' scored for a band.[143] If this is an arrangement of the Carnegie Hall version of Stacy's theme, then the question arises of how Eddie Sauter knew what it sounded like. Sauter's arrangement is dated 1943 and the Carnegie Hall concert was not released until 1950.

Twenty Years of Jazz – Sensation Rag

Small Group:
Benny Goodman (Clarinet). Bobby Hackett (Cornet). Vernon Brown (Trombone). Gene Krupa (Drums). Jess Stacy (Piano).

'One O'clock Jump' ended the first section of the concert, which was cleverly divided up to add interest and variety. The 'Twenty years of Jazz' portion gave us a potted history of the genre, starting with a lively version of the Original Dixieland Jazz Band's 'Sensation Rag' (incorrectly entitled 'Dixieland One-Step' on some of the original LP releases). Gene moved to his quartet drum kit towards the front of the stage nestled in front of the piano. He used a slightly different setup for his drums in the small group, without the big floor Tom-Tom and a slightly smaller bass drum. There is some ambiguity as to Bobby Hackett's role in this section of the concert. George Simon says in Metronome that Hackett strode coolly onto the stage, played 'I'm coming Virginia' and strode off again. However, Irving Kolodin writing in the Sun the day after the concert says that Hackett was the cornet soloist on 'Sensation Rag'. Warren Scholl and Al Brackman, reporting for Melody Maker at the time, suggest that he played two numbers: 'Sensation Rag' and 'I'm coming Virginia'.[144] According to Phil Schaap's liner notes for the CD release, it's likely that he also played on 'When my Baby Smiles At Me'.

Benny's interpretation of Larry Shields' clarinet-playing is great fun and Vernon Brown's period trombone-playing is spot on. Benny had acknowledged the fact that the Original Dixieland Jazz Band had had a big influence on him as a youngster in an article in the Christian Science Monitor in 1938: "I was playing jazz on my clarinet when I was eight years old, listening to the records of the Original Dixieland Jazz Band, which made a terrific impression on me...."[145] The Original Dixieland Jazz Band briefly re-formed between the summer of 1936 and January 1938. Benny had obviously enjoyed playing his tribute to them at Carnegie Hall and on February 15 he

---
143 IAJRC Journal Volume 20, No.4 P.23 - MSS 53 Yale Music Library
144 Melody Maker - February 5 1938
145 Christian Science Monitor July 11 1938. (The Story of the ODJB by H O Brunn Sidgwick and Jackson. 1961)

invited Larry Shields, Eddie Edwards and Tony Sbarbaro from the ODJB to join him on the Camel Show. (Nick LaRocca had left the band by then and Bobby Hackett played in his place.) On that occasion they played 'I'm Coming Virginia', 'When My Baby Smiles at Me', 'Dixieland One-Step" and 'Shine'.[146] The noted jazz writer George Frazier described the broadcast as 'a compelling testimony to Larry Shields' clarinet genius'.[147]

I'm Coming Virginia

Small Group:
Benny Goodman (Clarinet). Bobby Hackett (Cornet). Babe Russin (Tenor Sax). Vernon Brown (Trombone). Gene Krupa (Drums). Jess Stacy (Piano). Allan Reuss (Guitar). Harry Goodman (Bass). Possibly others.

Next, Bobby Hackett gave his interpretation of Bix Beiderbecke's two choruses on 'I'm Coming Virginia' which Bix had recorded some ten years earlier. The record had been re-issued on Brunswick, so some of the audience would have been quite familiar with the Beiderbecke version. As a 15-year-old, Goodman had played alongside Bix Beiderbecke on the Lake Michigan excursion steamers so he would be a good judge of Hackett's suitability for the role. There is a nice photograph of Bobby, with his cornet pointed skyward in the Sony 1999 CD release which is incorrectly described as being of Harry James.

Down Beat reported "Bobby appeared to trip up towards the end of the tune."[148] John Hammond noted that Bobby was 'More than a bit nervous in the austere surroundings...The band's accompaniment was a little less than distinguished, which may have accounted for some of Bobby's lack of composure'.[149] Listening today, his performance sounds a little more melancholic than Bix, thoughtful and very pretty. Alan Reuss finishes nicely with Eddie Lang's little guitar break, although we cannot quite hear the touches on the harmonics as in Lang's version.

Bobby was far from happy with his own performance at Carnegie Hall that night. It was a baptism of fire and as Bobby himself put it in 1951, "They wanted someone to impersonate Bix"[150] although he says he never consciously tried to sound like Beiderbecke. (During the Camel Caravan Broadcast of February 15 1938, Benny described Bobby Hackett as: 'The great modern exponent of the Beiderbecke technique.' He went on to say that Bobby never heard Bix play live.)[151] It's a shame we did not get to hear Bobby being himself. Benny had dropped in to jam with Hackett's band whilst he was at the Theatrical Club in Boston a year previously, so they had played together before and Bobby had recently recorded with Babe Russin

---

146 Listen to His Legacy - D. Russell Connor. P.82
147 Down Beat - April 1938
148 Down Beat Magazine - January 1938
149 Tempo Magazine - February 1938
150 Down Beat Magazine - February 9 1951
151 William Esty - "Columbia Broadcasting System. Benny Goodman's Swing School –Program 15." Feb 1938.
http://tobaccodocuments.org/rjr/514563927-3932.html

*(Top) Bobby Hackett plays his solo in 'I'm Coming Virginia'.
This is a photo montage combining two of Lawrence Marx's photographs to produce an image which is very close to the 'Rhythm Magazine' picture below.*

This picture from 'Rhythm Magazine' shows the same scene.

and Vernon Brown[152] so he was amongst friends when he strode on stage at Carnegie.

We can be sure that performing with Benny at Carnegie Hall would not have done Bobby's career any harm (the following month Tempo Music Magazine described Hackett as the 'Guest Star' at Benny's Concert)[153] but Bobby regretted performing that night. "I was a little over my head at that time with guys like BG, I wasn't quite ready."

Bobby and Benny played together frequently in later years and although Benny developed a reputation for being tough with his sidemen, he enjoyed Bobby's company and they became good friends. Bobby told Max Jones: "I make him laugh and don't let him get too serious. He's eccentric, but he's got a lot of good qualities".[154]

Bix had appeared at Carnegie Hall himself. He was part of the orchestra that Paul Whiteman had presented in his experimental music series ten years before. Bix had played his piano composition 'In A Mist' on that very stage. 'The program went off without incident, and when the time came for 'In A Mist', it was a determined Bix who left the brass section and walked forward to where his concert grand had been wheeled out for him. There, in Carnegie Hall, with the eyes of thousands on him, Bix Beiderbecke, self-taught pianist, played a composition he himself had written, with two pianists he deeply admired providing

152 Bobby Hackett and Bio-discography - Harold Jones
153 Tempo Magazine - March 1938
154 Talking Jazz - Max Jones

discreet accompaniment. It is only too possible to speculate on what was in his mind at this supreme moment'.[155]

When My Baby Smiles at Me

Small Group:
Benny Goodman (Clarinet). Bobby Hackett (Cornet). Vernon Brown (Trombone). Gene Krupa (Drums). Jess Stacy (Piano). Harry Goodman (Bass).

At the age of twelve, Benny had performed his caricature of Ted Lewis playing 'When My Baby Smiles at Me' at an amateur jazz night at the Central Park Theatre in Chicago. Charlie Goodman, Benny's brother, found out that there was an amateur jazz night there on Thursdays. The manager of the theatre thought that he might get into trouble for putting a youngster on the stage, so Benny had to stand on the conductor's box in the orchestra pit. Benny didn't win the talent contest but the manager was so impressed with his ability that he was invited back a few weeks later when one of the scheduled acts dropped out. This was his first professional engagement. "The applause was nice, but the five bucks they paid me was even better."[156] Benny reprised his act during the NBC's 'Let's Dance' broadcasts in 1935 when the band performed this parody once more, with Toots Mondello singing and Benny again mimicking Ted Lewis,[157] so when Benny went through his routine at Carnegie Hall it was something at which he was well practiced. Down Beat's correspondent described the performance that night like this "… Benny took off Ted Lewis, even to the angle of his clarinet, with a nuance that said louder than words, that he was playing a caricature."[158]

Shine

Orchestra:
Benny Goodman (Clarinet). Harry James (Trumpet -Armstrong Solo). Ziggy Elman, Chris Griffin (Trumpets). Vernon Brown, Red Ballard (Trombones). Hymie Schertzer, George Koenig (Alto Sax). Babe Russin, Art Rollini (Tenor Sax). Allan Reuss (Rhythm Guitar). Jess Stacy (Piano). Harry Goodman (Bass). Gene Krupa (Drums).

The roots of the 'family tree' of jazz are continually developing and entwining (some might even say that they were 'pot-bound'!), so even a short study of the subject will reveal that everybody seems to have played with everybody else at some stage during their careers. A quick investigation into the work of Louis Armstrong will reveal that Lionel Hampton played drums on Armstrong's original recording of 'Shine' in 1931. So when Harry James stood up and gave us a lightning rendition of the Armstrong

---

[155] Bix: Man and Legend - Richard Sudhalter and Philip Evans. P.256
[156] The Kingdom of Swing. Benny Goodman & Irving Kolodin. P.24
[157] CD Circle CCD-50
[158] Down Beat - February 1938

classic, we can imagine what was going through Lionel's mind as he stood back-stage waiting for the quartet section of the concert to come round. According to Teddy Wilson, Harry James always claimed to be descended from the notorious outlaw Jesse James, 'The Baddest man in the West'![159]

Blue Reverie

Guest ensemble:

Benny Goodman (Clarinet). Johnny Hodges (Soprano Sax). Harry Carney (Baritone Sax). Cootie Williams (Trumpet). Vernon Brown (Trombone). Allan Reuss (Guitar). Jess Stacy (Piano). Harry Goodman (Bass). Gene Krupa (Drums).

Some commentators have suggested that Benny was brave, even foolish to have included members of the Ellington band in the concert. The inference is that they could have easily upstaged the Goodman band. The Goodman group had tried playing Blue Reverie at rehearsals without the Ellington trio, but as Benny noted in his autobiography, "It didn't sound like anything until we asked Hodges, Carney and

[159] Teddy Wilson Talks Jazz – Teddy Wilson. P.44

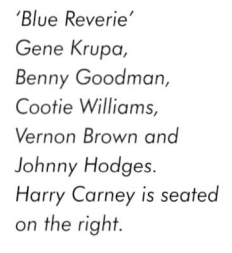

*'Blue Reverie'
Gene Krupa,
Benny Goodman,
Cootie Williams,
Vernon Brown and
Johnny Hodges.
Harry Carney is seated
on the right.*

"Cootie" to sit in and play their original parts."[160] We have already discussed the fact the Benny was not at all confident that he could hold the attention of the audience for the duration of the concert, so perhaps the thought was that he would need all the help he could get. Benny has often said that the Ellington band was his favourite, so this author would prefer to think that the Ellingtonians were invited as honoured guests out of pure admiration. Whatever the rationale behind the inclusion of the Ellington trio, hot on the heels of their concert earlier in the day at the Criterion Theatre, their rendition of 'Blue Reverie' is an absolute gem. Johnny Hodges' playing is simply superb. John Hammond wrote that 'Johnny Hodges was nothing short of stupendous in Duke Ellington's Blue Reverie, in which both Cootie Williams and Harry Carney contributed some of the most exciting music of the evening.'[161] Incidentally, Johnny was playing the soprano saxophone that Sydney Bechet had given him some years before, 'That soprano was given to me in the early twenties, and it's the same one I played right up until the 1940s. I still have it, but I'm about ready to make a lamp out of it now'.[162] Jess Stacy seems to slip up here and plays a slightly short solo (count the bars!).

Another view of 'Blue Reverie' from 'Rhythm Magazine'

By far the most informative contemporary review of the concert was written by George Simon, he wrote of 'Blue Reverie': 'Cootie was cocky, grinning and grumbling into his mute' and Harry Carney, who had the 'most awed expression of the evening', was 'obviously a bit abashed, played well and ran off the stage'.[163] Along with Duke Ellington, Cootie is credited as the composer of this tune. His inclusion here was Cootie's only contribution to Goodman's concert. In a photograph published in Rhythm magazine, we can just make out Benny standing just behind the trio of Cootie, Vernon Brown and Hodges, cradling his clarinet and enjoying the show. Harry's baritone saxophone comes across very well on this recording. 'Blue Reverie' seems to have survived the rigors of the years better than most other tracks on the record. It was one of the six tunes chosen by Columbia to be included on the set of Disc Jockey 78's sent out to radio stations to promote the concert on the air when the album was released in 1950.

Life Goes To A Party

Orchestra:
Benny Goodman (Clarinet). Harry James, Ziggy Elman, Chris Griffin (Trumpets). Vernon Brown, Red Ballard (Trombones). Hymie Schertzer, George Koenig (Alto Sax). Babe Russin, Art Rollini (Tenor Sax). Allan Reuss (Rhythm Guitar). Jess Stacy (Piano). Harry Goodman (Bass). Gene Krupa (Drums).

160 The Kingdom of Swing – Benny Goodman and Irving Kolodin P. 248
161 Tempo Magazine. - February 1938
162 Talking Jazz. - Max Jones. The Macmillan Press. 1987. P60
163 Metronome Magazine - George Simon - February 1938

Duke Ellington's men left the stage briefly and Krupa moved back to his orchestra drum kit for just one number, 'Life Goes to a Party'. This tune was conceived by Harry James and is a tribute to Life Magazine, which published a photo story of the band's stay at the Madhattan Room on November 1 1937. The first recorded example of this Harry James arrangement dates from October 26 1937.[164] Metronome listed Benny's commercial issue of 'Life' on Victor Records as one of the best recordings of 1938. Keen to capitalise on their new star trumpet-player's appearance at Carnegie Hall, Brunswick Records took a half page in the concert program to promote Harry James' and Teddy Wilson's latest record releases. The list included Harry's own recordings of 'Life Goes To A Party' and 'One O'Clock Jump'.

Writing in the liner notes to the 1999 CD release, Phil Schaap discussed the possibility that 'Life Goes to a Party' was intended to be part of the History of Jazz section of the concert. The conclusion reached there, was that 'Blue Reverie' was the last tune played in that section and that 'Life' was not intended to be part of the history lesson. If we look at the program notes reproduced in this book it can be seen that 'Life' is grouped within the history section (at least in a typographical sense). These notes were studiously written as a separate booklet for inclusion within the program by Irving Kolodin. Writing in the New York Sun the day after the concert in his characteristic style, Kolodin said:

'In deference to the fact that this was the first swing concert in formal surroundings, the program included a section entitled "Twenty Years of Jazz," in which the characteristic styles of various jazz personalities were set forth. Included in the progression was the Dixieland Band of hallowed memory ("Sensation Rag"), Leon (Bix) Beiderbecke (with Bobby Hackett as cornet soloist), Ted Lewis (the Goodman clarinet mimicking his "When My Baby Smiles at Me"), Louis Armstrong (Harry James performing a chorus of "Shine"), and Duke Ellington. For "Blue Reverie", by the last of these, Cootie Williams, Johnny Hodges, and Harry Carney of the Ellington orchestra were imported to give authenticity to the proceedings. The series was brought up to date with the Goodman orchestra performing the violent "Life Goes to a Party" by its own Messrs. James and Goodman. Each of the sections was avidly applauded by an audience extremely aware of what was going on'.

It would therefore seem that the intention was to make 'Life' the finale of the 'Twenty Years of Jazz' portion of the program. In his review of the concert in Metronome, George Simon portrayed Harry and Gene as swing warriors at the head of an assault on the hall:

'The entire Goodman group returned to the stage, and almost blasted itself off with Harry James' 'Life Goes to a Party'. Harry himself, as well as Gene, led the devastating attack upon Carnegie walls, which, by the way, held nobly.'

This statement is slightly incorrect in that the orchestra had not left the stage during 'Blue Reverie', they can be seen in their seats enjoying the Ellington boys playing, Harry Carney can be seen sitting alongside, waiting for his solo.

Irving Kolodin was undeniably correct when he said in his album liner notes, 'the band rarely sounded so well again'.

164 D. Russell Connor. - Wrappin' It Up. P.142

Honeysuckle Rose

Guest Ensemble featuring:
Benny Goodman (Clarinet). Buck Clayton, Harry James (Trumpets). Vernon Brown (Trombone). Johnny Hodges (Alto Sax). Harry Carney (Baritone Sax). Lester Young (Tenor Sax). Freddie Green (Guitar). Count Basie (Piano). Walter Page (Bass). Gene Krupa (Drums).

At this point in the concert all but four of the Goodman orchestra left the stage not to return until the second half. In their place came seven men from the Ellington and Basie bands. Johnny Hodges, Cootie Williams and Harry Carney from the Ellington Band and Count Basie himself brought along Freddie Green, Buck Clayton and Lester Young from his band. The Duke Ellington band was certainly a household name in 1938 (Ellington himself was invited to participate in the concert but declined) but the Basie band was not quite as well known. When the stars from these two bands walked on to the stage to join four members of the Goodman band, the audience may not have been aware that up there on the stage, stood a group of musicians who would become some of the most celebrated musicians of the jazz age. It looks like the result of a game of 'Fantasy Jazz Combos' (that well known parlour game!). It goes like this:

With 'Fats' Waller due to appear on CBS' 'Saturday night Swing Club' from Hollywood,[165] who better to play Fats' classic 'Honeysuckle Rose' than his protégée Count Basie? Bring in 'Steady' Freddie Green playing rhythm guitar, bassist Walter Page nicknamed, 'the Big-Un', for his big sound and big stature and the flamboyant Gene Krupa, now we've got a pulse! Add Lester Young playing the tenor sax at his creative best, and Buck Clayton with his lovely lyrical trumpet solos. Let's beef up the brass section with bashful baritone sax player Harry Carney, and we have got an extraordinary band! Since this is just a game, let's include the incomparable alto sax playing of Johnny Hodges with his beautiful tone and inexhaustible supply of ideas. Now bring in Harry James who, by today's Health and Safety laws, would require a fire crew standing by to dampen things down after he plays a trumpet solo, then, just to liven things up a little more, let us augment our line-up with Benny Goodman and trombonist Vernon Brown and here we have summoned up a combination that we can only dream of today.

This is a still from the newsreel film taken during 'Honeysuckle Rose'. We can just make out Harry James, Benny, Johnny Hodges and Buck Clayton.

But this is no fantasy. Here they are, playing for us live for a full sixteen minutes and forty two seconds of pure hypnotic, intoxicating rhythm. Turk Van Lake was absolutely correct when he said that this track alone is worth the price of the entire package.[166] What would we pay to see such a group today?

The concert program gave a tantalising description of the jam session: "Collective improvisation by a group of soloists to be announced. The length of the session is indeterminate, and may include one or more tunes"! When the guest musicians walked

165 Radio Guide - January 22 1938
166 Columbia CD Liner notes C2K 65143

The jam session, L to R: Gene Krupa, Harry James is hidden behind Freddie Green, Johnny Hodges, Lester Young, Benny, Buck Clayton, Vernon Brown and Harry Carney. Note Benny is leading from the rear in this section.

out on stage, there was confusion for a moment as they could not make up their minds where to sit. [167] Benny assumed his role as host and seated the illustrious group ready for the jam session and he seated himself in the back row, 'his professional spectacles gleaming'.[168] According to Teddy Wilson, one of Benny's strengths as a musician was to recognise the qualities of other players. 'He was excellent at running a jam session. He would call out: "You take the next chorus," "Now, we're going out," "Drum solo" or "All right, piano break, four bars"'.[169] The tune chosen to demonstrate the art of the jam session was 'Fats' Waller's 'Honeysuckle Rose' and many people regard this as the high point of the concert. Irving Kolodin's program notes go to great lengths to explain what a jam session is and how to set about creating the sympathetic atmosphere in which the musicians can improvise freely. The audience was asked to accept the jam session in a spirit of experimentation. It obliged willingly and 'pounded its feet in unison. In the best and truest sense, the joint was actually rocking.'[170]

All the musicians get a chance to play a solo except for Vernon Brown and Gene Krupa. We can hear Vernon Brown in the opening and closing choruses but he is difficult to identify anywhere else. It is impossible to tell why Vernon Brown was by-passed, Goodman did signal Freddie Green and Walter Page, both of whom were playing rhythm section instruments not really suited for solo work. Turk Van Lake suggests in the liner notes of Phil Schaap's 1999 version of the concert, that Goodman's decision to signal Freddie Green for a solo was 'startling' and an example of Benny's 'insensitivity'. Yet on page 12 of the concert program Freddie Green is listed as a 'Guest Soloist' not just a 'guest'. It could not have been that much of a surprise to Freddie when he was given the nod by Goodman. Krupa does well sitting in for Jo Jones in Basie's rhythm section but he doesn't really play a solo. According to John

[167] Metronome - February 1938
[168] Time Magazine - January 24 1938
[169] Teddy Wilson Talks Jazz – Teddy Wilson. P.50
[170] Time Magazine - January 24 1938

Hammond writing in Tempo Magazine, Gene Krupa had dominated the other musicians instead of cooperating smoothly. He wrote that audiences have a tendency to intoxicate Gene, with results that occasionally are tremendously exciting but more often upset the balance that is so essential in swing.[171] Listening to the records today, he seems to play quite sympathetically in 'Honeysuckle'.

Reports of the jam session in the Press were mixed, Francis Perkins in the New York Herald Tribune noted that some of the 'more experienced hearers said that this was not amongst the most typical of such sessions'.[172] The World Telegram suggested that 'the inspiration was not altogether flaming'[173] and in a rather sour review in the New York Times, Olin Downes wrote, 'though soloist after soloist of the band tried to contribute something original to the ensemble, little or nothing of the sort materialised'.[174] In response, one irate Goodman fan fired off an indignant letter to the Times Music Editor defending Goodman: "It is unfortunate that a valuable seat at the Swing Concert in Carnegie Hall was wasted on your correspondent."[175] (Olin Downes was the Times' classical correspondent and also wrote a gushing review of the Enesco concert in Carnegie Hall that same afternoon, the Goodman concert would have been a difficult contrast for him to overcome.)

George Simon in Metronome thought the jam session was the weakest part of the program, 'uninspired and uninspiring'.[176] But The New York Post said that 'the Jam Session jelled beyond our wildest dreams'[177] and the New York News declared the 'Jam Session with every harmonist on his own, stirred the crowd unduly, there was such a bobbing and swaying in the audience as to start a great craning of necks and much understated whispering'.[178] Down Beat's Annemarie Ewing explained that the musicians gave 'performances that would surely have been approved by the master improvisers of a hundred years ago...'.[179]

There is a tantalising mention of Count Basie's drummer Jo Jones in The Billboard Magazine, concerning a rumour doing the rounds about Jo's absence from the stage at Benny's Carnegie Concert. Unfortunately, the editor politely declines from giving us the details! We can only guess why Jo Jones was not there, perhaps that was just one too many from Basie's band.

A photograph published in the UK in the April 1938 issue of Rhythm Magazine, is to date, the only shot we have of Count Basie and Walter Page performing with Goodman and the illustrious jammers that night. The picture conveys the atmosphere of the evening well. Johnny Hodges is standing for his solo, with the others all looking on. We can suppose that having the seats on the stage would help create that sympathetic atmosphere Kolodin

Honeysuckle Rose. Here the full band can be seen. Johnny Hodges is standing, this is the only known photograph showing Walter Page and Count Basie. Notice the microphone hanging over the stage.

171 Tempo Magazine – February 1938
172 New York Herald Tribune – 17 January 1938
173 New York World Telegram – 17 January 1938
174 New York Times – 17 January 1938
175 New York Times - January 23 1938
176 Metronome Magazine - George Simon - February 1938
177 New York Post – 17 January 1938
178 New York News – 17 January 1938
179 Down Beat - February 1938

thought might be wanting. Seats on the stage at Carnegie Hall are there at the discretion of the performers, some artists find it rather intimidating, whilst others are enthused by the more relaxed setting. The microphone by which we can re-live the concert today is on view, doing its miraculous work overhead.

In the original 1950 release of the album, Honeysuckle Rose was mistakenly credited to Jimmy Mundy. Somebody at Columbia obviously had it confused with the Mundy arrangement, 'Jam Session'. It is well-known that the original release had an edited version of the Honeysuckle Rose jam session. Benny had suggested in 1963, some 25 years after the concert, that he was happy with the edited version. He was discussing the principle that in some circumstances, 'less is more', noting that everybody had said what they had to say in the solos that were left on the record.[180] Today, for the sake of historical correctness, the trend is to leave nothing out and present things as they were recorded. We are all familiar with the LP's and CD's dedicated to alternative takes and out takes.

Research for this book made a serendipitous find: A complete set of acetate recordings that had once belonged to one of the producers of the concert, Savington Crampton of the William Esty Agency. Crampton had left the William Esty Agency within a few months of the Carnegie concert and took up a job with Fortune Magazine, so it is reasonably safe to assume that he had these dubs made before he left.

The recordings cover 28 sides of 12 inch 78 rpm acetate discs. The labels are plain white with type-written titles, 'Dubbed from an instantaneous recording of Benny Goodman's Carnegie Hall concert'. Since they are undated, we can assume that the labels were typed in the same year as the concert. (Benny played there three times in 1939, if the person typing the labels did it after 1938 they would have to identify the performance and year.) On the back of the labels is the logo which reads: 'Recorded by E V Brinckerhoff & Co Inc. 29 West 57th Street. New York'.

The first playing of these discs revealed the hitherto unheard complete solo of Buck Clayton. Buck's third chorus in 'Honeysuckle' was removed from the original release of the LPs. When Phil Schaap released it in 1999 we found out why. There is a groove skip in his last chorus which probably occurred during the dubbing of the acetates, that Schaap used, from the originals. How the concert was recorded is covered in a later chapter. The Savington Crampton set of discs, although not first-class dubs, obviously pre-dated the dubs used for the 1999 issue because here is Buck Clayton's complete solo, without that annoying skip. Although we have only found another three or four beats, it restores the pace to the music which seemed so badly disrupted by that little click towards the end of his solo. Here for the first time since that day in 1938 we hear the complete jam session.

Savington Crampton's 78 rpm acetate dubs of the concert, this is side 7, the first part of the Jam Session.

180 The World of Swing. - Stanley Dance. P.260

In later years, Buck Clayton remembered the reaction of his mother when he played Carnegie Hall:

"My mother didn't care much for jazz, until years later, when I played Carnegie Hall. Then she says 'Well, if jazz is good enough to go into Carnegie Hall, it must be pretty respectable now.' Because in those early days it wasn't. The only people who liked jazz were prostitutes…and they'd play in those little dives, way down in the basement somewhere… and fights and all that. So my mother didn't want that."[181]

The Trio - Body and Soul

Trio:

Benny Goodman (Clarinet). Teddy Wilson (Piano). Gene Krupa (Drums).

After the jam session the guests plus Harry James and Vernon Brown left the stage and Teddy Wilson walked out for the first time to a 'grand ovation'. By carefully comparing photographs, we can see that the piano lid was adjusted at some stage during the evening. The comparison would suggest that Teddy opened up the piano lid at this point. Gene moved back to his front of stage drum kit and after a little tune up, the trio played 'Body and Soul' the first of the two numbers that it contributed to the evening. Bobby Hackett once said that he loved working with Goodman because it was easy work, every now and then the small group would do a few things and the brass would get a chance to go back stage for a rest and a smoke![182] This was one of the tunes that the trio recorded at their first recording session in 1935, and was really a show piece for Teddy.

During breaks in the touring, studio work and radio shows, some of Benny's sidemen led their own groups for recording purposes. Harry, Jess and Lionel were frequent visitors to the recording studios. Teddy was well established as a recording artist too. He had been very busy in the early part of January 1938. On the 6th he had recorded with Billie Holiday, Lester Young, Buck Clayton, Bennie Morton, Freddie Green, Walter Page and Jo Jones, on the 10th with Mildred Bailey and her orchestra, then on the 11th back with Benny for the Camel Caravan show and on

181 Storyville Magazine No. 128 - December 1 1986 - Chip Deffaa
182 Talking Jazz - Max Jones

These two photographs show that the piano lid was raised at some stage during the evening. The first photograph from Down Beat magazine was taken early in the evening and the second is a still from the newsreel footage. Jess Stacy is at the piano in both shots.

Teddy Wilson and Allan Reuss entertain fans at the Madhattan Room during the intermission.

the 12th January, again with Billie Holiday. All of these recordings have since become classics.

Teddy Wilson only played with the trio and quartet, whilst Jess Stacy did most of the evening's piano work, playing with the orchestra. We could see that Teddy would be keen to get his hands on a piano! It was the same on tour, Jess played with the orchestra whilst Teddy played intermission piano for the diners and dancers. The brilliant jazz writer and critic Otis Ferguson described one such occasion thus:

'Teddy Wilson is as fine an artist at starting late and quitting early as he is at his music, which is the finest. He runs through a few chords. Anyone who wants to hear it a little can move over to the piano. Some do. Just playing to amuse myself is all Teddy says.

Well, how about the Waller tune "Squeeze Me," Teddy; you used to play that pretty nice. Oh that? He says with his fine smile. I believe I forgot that one by now. He feels through the chords with unerring musical sense and listens for the turn of phrase in some backward corner of his mind — like the mind of any good jazz musician, it is a treasury and stuffed catalogue of all the songs the rest of us have thought lovely and then presently put aside for new toys. He finishes, repeats the last phrase. Hm, I knew I didn't have that one rightly any more, he says, shaking his head. But the song is back for us, the song never died at all. He starts the first chords over, and this time his right hand is released from concentration and free on the keyboard,.......'.[183]

In the trio's performance of Body and Soul that night, Benny paid tribute to such a lovely song by playing the melody beautifully and relatively straight, allowing Teddy plenty of space to demonstrate his flawless technique. Without a bass player in the trio, Teddy could make effective use of his left hand and mesh with Gene's bass drum to give the group a little more depth. Gene had had a fairly bombastic evening so far but here he was unobtrusive with his gentle brush work. (After going full tilt for seventeen minutes of 'Honeysuckle Rose' he probably needed a rest!) Benny had once described Teddy as 'the best musician in dance music today, irrespective of instrument' and here we see why.

Avalon

Quartet:
Benny Goodman (Clarinet). Teddy Wilson (Piano). Lionel Hampton (Vibraphone). Gene Krupa (Drums).

Next, one of the three wonders of the swing era, the Benny Goodman quartet. (The other two being: the trumpet section and the full orchestra!) The irrepressible Lionel Hampton, making his first appearance of the evening, gave a big grin as he came out from the wings to join Teddy, Gene and Benny, and almost immediately set his foot tapping for one of the truly great numbers of the Goodman repertoire, the quartet's 'Avalon'. Lionel's charming introduction is immediately recognisable. Gene and Teddy play a lovely duet, then Benny and Lionel come back in for a chorus. Lionel switches to his metallic mallets to give a bit more edge for his solo.[184] (We can see him do this in the quartet number 'I've got a Heartful of Music' they play in 'Hollywood Hotel'.) Gene's seemingly endless supply of fills and rim shots make his modest drum kit seem huge. He and Teddy set up a contagious shuffle allowing plenty of room for Lionel and Benny to play. They cascade their way out to rapturous applause.

By reading the contemporary reports published in the Press the following day, we can get a very good idea of what it must have been like to be in the Carnegie audience that night. Francis Perkins wrote a quite finely detailed report in the New York Herald Tribune on January 17 1938. He described Benny's work with the trio and quartet the night before like this:

'In the usual symphony concert the conductor has the major share of the gesturing, but here Mr Goodman was the calmest in mien, even when he did incredible work on his clarinet, he presided over the sessions of the trio and quartet with an air of paternal benevolence'.

183 New Republic Magazine - December 1936 - Otis Ferguson
184 Melody Maker - February 5.1938

The Man I Love

Quartet:

Benny Goodman (Clarinet). Lionel Hampton (Vibraphone). Teddy Wilson (Piano). Gene Krupa (Drums).

The Goodman quartet first made its recording of George Gershwin's 'The Man I Love' in late July 1937. Tragically, Gershwin died of a brain tumour during that same month. He was only 39. Loren Schoenberg has suggested they recorded this mournful classic as a tribute to this great composer whom both Goodman and Krupa knew well.[185] Metronome readers voted this interpretation of the Gershwin tune one of the best records of 1937. George Simon made note of the fact that Lionel seems to make a false start at the beginning of the Carnegie performance which is masked by the continuing applause from the previous number. The quartet's treatment of this is very much along the lines of the trio's 'Body and Soul'. It is played almost straight, with a great deal of feeling and little embellishment. A master class in ensemble-playing. Often referred to as 'Chamber Jazz', surely the quartet was at its greatest on this wonderful night? This is one of only four pieces from the concert that was ever released commercially as a 78 rpm record.

I Got Rhythm

Quartet:

Benny Goodman, Teddy Wilson (Piano). Lionel Hampton (Vibraphone). Gene Krupa (Drums).

Although 'Avalon' and 'I Got Rhythm' were staple tunes of the BG quartet, they never recorded 'I Got Rhythm' in the studio. 'I Got Rhythm' with its deceptively simple up-and-down theme, was chosen to be the finale of the first half of the concert and the foursome urged each other on like crazy. Teddy and Lionel both took extra choruses. Lionel's sheep noises made some of the more dignified, 'grey-haired gentlemen in the orchestra seats laugh as they have not laughed this side of a smoking car'[186] with the 'dead stops' towards the end catching the audience out both times. George Simon noted that rather than being nervous, the King was now just having himself one 'helluver good time.'[187] In the closing moments of 'I got Rhythm', Gene Krupa was steaming towards the intermission sounding like a run-away train. Like all good concerts, these quartet numbers take the audience to the intermission absolutely breathless. How can they possibly top that in the second half?

Intermission

Gene Krupa appeared to be tired after the gallop through 'I Got Rhythm', he had been working at a phenomenal pace all evening. It was time for a break. Variety Magazine

---

[185] The Complete RCA Victor Small Group Recordings. CD Liner notes
[186] Down Beat - February 1938
[187] Metronome Magazine – February 1938

— The Music —

reported that while the wild-eyed swing addicts were balmy throughout, some of the 'oldsters' in the audience remained puzzled by the whole thing except at the steamy climaxes.[188] A few of them took the opportunity of the intermission to leave!

Writing in February 1939 about the noisy fans at the concert, Benny's recollections sound rather sanguine:

'The Carnegie Hall concert we gave came along about this time and went well despite the highbrows who saw things in the music we never intended putting in – and the hoodlum Jitterbugs, a noisy minority, they blasted out the horns, yelled and stomped a dozen smooth passages of the trio into oblivion, wrecked a few numbers with trick ends completely'.[189]

Warren Scholl writing in Melody Maker about the concert from the human angle, describes the mood of some of the fans in the audience in a similar way:

'Only fault to be found with the concert, strangely enough, was the audience. Those near maniacs who act like they have St. Vitas dance or ants in their pants were very much in evidence, and their stupid habit of whistling and clapping vociferously each time one of the boys took a hot chorus very soon became objectionable'.[190]

This uninvited and over-exuberant audience participation is only testament to the awesome power of the band and the passion that Goodman's music aroused. By all accounts, this phenomenon was in evidence long before Goodman contemplated the Carnegie Hall evening.

He went on to mention intelligent members of the audience who 'shushed' these troublesome fans and described an incident where one chap who was obviously at his wits' end stood up in his seat and shouted, "Shut up, you punks!" each time they started their nonsense.

Almost all reporting of the concert talks about the enthusiastic crowd packed into the hall that night, how hand-clapping whirled through the house, how they vibrated in unison with the Master's clarinet and how they broke out in crashing applause and danced in their seats. Describing behaviour that seems quite mild by today's standards, members of the auditorium staff had never seen an audience that behaved in such a manner: 'Listeners who not only listened but swayed to the music, made sounds and seemed ready to break into some kind of hysterical dance.'

An usher at the concert told the New York Times reporter, 'Young members of the audience who wanted programs were dancing up the aisles to buy them.'[191] One of the Carnegie doormen commented on the frenzy that night: "This is alright for an evening, but give me the symphony orchestras for a longer period of time."[192] Variety Magazine pointed out, however, that 'the enthusiasm was no greater and little noisier than Arturo Toscanini has evoked in the same hall when he has conducted the Philharmonic Symphony'.[193] Giving away the answer to Benny's question, "How long

---

188 Variety Magazine - January 19 1938
189 Collier's Magazine - February 1939
190 Melody Maker - February 5 1938
191 New York Times - January 23 1938
192 Brooklyn Daily Eagle - January 17 1938 P.7
193 Variety Magazine - January 19 1938 P.51

does Mr Toscanini take?", Guy Sykes wrote that the crowd got a fifteen minute let-up for the intermission, it sounds like it was well deserved.[194]

Benny's young fans had some fun during the brief break in the music. According to Melody Maker's New York representative, 'During the interval, the Balcony and Gallery audience went into action with complete disregard for Carnegie Hall etiquette and amused itself by throwing small paper aeroplanes through the hall and, in general, turning the occasion into a Mardi Gras atmosphere'.[195] The reporter for Down Beat remarked that a paper aeroplane launched from the gallery could reach the stage, although there is no evidence of one having successfully made the crossing in the photographs! One newspaper likened the occasion to a Jazz Camp Meeting at which anybody might get religion any moment. 'Mr Goodman accepted the demonstrations with an amused smile as he accepts the antics and enthusiasms of his instrumentalists'.[196]

Ethel Krupa received congratulations on her husband's performance during the break,[197] the World Telegram reported the next day that 'the drummer did everything but skate on the ceiling'! Discussing the visual impact of the concert, Francis Perkins in the Herald Tribune observed that the 'Group's super expert percussionist, whose gestures and facial expressions proved unusually engrossing for those near enough to note them in detail, has talents as an actor as well as an instrumentalist'. Saul Goodman, (no relation to Benny) the legendary timpanist with the New York Philharmonic and later, one of Gene's teachers, burst into the dressing room during the interval, embraced Gene in a bear hug and shouted, "You've done it! You've done it!"[198] During the sojourn

Benny looks down his clarinet at the photographer.

194 Tempo Magazine - February 1938
195 Melody Maker - February 5 1938
196 New York Daily News - 17 January 1938
197 Metronome - February 1938
198 Esquire Magazine - June 1968

backstage, somebody was heard to remark "This was the first audience in Carnegie Hall that ever seemed to enjoy the music it was listening to".[199]

Gene moved between two drum kits during the concert. See the Bobby Hackett photograph page 92.

The second set: Blue Skies

Orchestra:
Benny Goodman (Clarinet). Harry James, Ziggy Elman, Chris Griffin (Trumpets). Vernon Brown, Red Ballard (Trombones). Hymie Schertzer, George Koenig (Alto Sax). Babe Russin, Art Rollini (Tenor Sax). Allan Reuss (Rhythm Guitar). Jess Stacy (Piano). Harry Goodman (Bass). Gene Krupa (Drums).

After the well-earned break, the orchestra returned to the stage for the second half of the concert. Some of them had been backstage since they left to make room for the Jam Session nearly an hour before and they looked nervous again. The rest of the evening belonged to the Goodman Orchestra without the help of star soloists. The tune chosen to trigger the whirlwinds again was Fletcher Henderson's already classic arrangement of Irving Berlin's 'Blue Skies'. Although he was a giant of popular music, Irving Berlin was no fan of jazz or swing, he felt that the jazz treatment spoiled his carefully crafted work. Yes, Henderson's version is far removed from Berlin's original, but it is a marvellous arrangement nevertheless. Listening to Goodman's recording of 'Blue Skies', Berlin became so incensed at the liberties taken with his song that he

199 Metronome February 1938

complained that he had heard only one or two of his original phrases. When Berlin first met Goodman he said, "That is the most incredible playing I've ever heard," and then he immediately added, "Never do that again!"[200]

The Carnegie Hall rendering of this tune was particularly lively and up-beat and, as with all Henderson arrangements, it is fascinating to pick out the layers of instrumentation. It starts off with some rasping, menacing chords of "The storm" as Fletcher called it and moves along very nicely. At one point early on, it sounds as if the audience might have fallen out of time and Gene gave them a broad grin, apparently he liked the spirit anyway, and they soon found their way back to the beat.

Art Rollini had a chance to solo here on tenor sax. Art must have been disappointed to read John Hammond's comment after the concert, that the band had been impressive except the sax section devoid of any exciting soloists.[201] Ziggy Elman's dramatic solo in 'Swingtime in the Rockies' has always attracted a lot of attention but Zig was very exciting here too. Benny's chart for this tune, written in Henderson's own hand and dated 1935, is now in the Yale Music Library as part of the bequest that Benny made to the University shortly before his death.

There is a lovely recording of Fletcher demonstrating the art of the arranger on the Camel Caravan broadcast of September 13 1938.[202] During that show, he asks Benny if he can borrow the band for a moment and uses 'Blue Skies' to illustrate how the saxes and the brass play different parts and how the rhythm section fits in. First, the sections play separately and then in unison, it is not often that we get to hear the sections playing alone like this. It is well worth searching out this Camel show, it is wonderful stuff.

Loch Lomond

Orchestra:

Benny Goodman (Clarinet, Vocal)). Martha Tilton (Vocal). Harry James, Ziggy Elman, Chris Griffin (Trumpets). Vernon Brown, Red Ballard (Trombones). Hymie Schertzer, George Koenig (Alto Sax). Babe Russin, Art Rollini (Tenor Sax). Allan Reuss (Rhythm Guitar). Jess Stacy (Piano). Harry Goodman (Bass). Gene Krupa (Drums).

Petite Californian singer, 'Liltin'' Martha Tilton (she was only 5'2") got an enthusiastic reception as she walked on stage and towards the microphone, accompanied by the band's strangely accurate bagpipe drone. She was wearing a pink ruffled party frock with pink roses in her hair. The first of her two songs, 'Loch Lomond' was a sensational hit in early 1938. It is easy to forget how young the musicians in Benny's band were at the time. Martha was only 22-years-old when she

This is a newsreel film still taken during the second half of the concert and shows the layout of the band as well as Martha's 'house' microphone that failed during the concert.

200 As Thousands Cheer - Laurence Bergreen
201 Tempo Magazine - February 1938
202 LP: Soundcraft 1020. CD: Phontastic NCD 8844

made her debut at Carnegie Hall. Barely five months earlier she was a relatively unknown singer with the Alexander Mayer Chorus in California, now she was the 'Swing Sweetheart' out in front of the top swing band in the country at Carnegie Hall.

'Loch Lomond' was a reworking of Claude Thornhill's 1937 novel hit arrangement for a small group, which featured the singer, Maxine Sullivan. Claude was an old associate of Benny's who had been in one of his very first orchestras in 1934. Goodman's version of this old Scottish tune was prepared for the full orchestra by Jimmy Mundy. [203]

Martha was nervous for her Carnegie debut and unfortunately for her, as soon as she stepped up to the microphone to sing she realised that something was wrong, the house public address system had failed! The worst nightmare for a Carnegie debutant! Speaking about the concert at the 30th anniversary party given by Benny in his New York apartment, Martha explained to William B Williams of radio station WNEW what had happened: "One thing that stands out in my mind so clearly about that concert, even after thirty years, is the fact that I had just gotten started singing Loch Lomond when the microphones all went dead. There was no amplification in the house, so that didn't help the situation at all. I remember I just stepped aside and hollered, what else could I do?"[204] Writing in Metronome Magazine at the time, George Simon also noted that Martha appeared even more nervous than the band and seemed to be singing 'sans microphone'.[205]

The anonymous writer for Down Beat magazine was cruel in his criticism of Martha, noting that it was 'fortunate for Goodman's charming songstress that light travels faster and further than sound, consequently her attractive stage appearance in ruffled gown and her stage presence obvious from her sure delivery, saved her day'.[206] His

Martha Tilton in her 'pink ruffled party frock'.

203 MSS 53 The Benny Goodman Papers in the S Gilmore Music Library, Yale University
204 WNEW LP of Carnegie Party 1968
205 Metronome Magazine - February 1938
206 Down Beat - February 1938

complaint was that it was difficult to hear her version of the tune without it bringing to mind Maxine Sullivan's unforgettable interpretation of the song.

This arrangement was one of the few Goodman tunes in which Benny did not feature as a soloist although he was given a line to sing which he delivered half heartedly, 'his only display of temperament during the evening'.[207] Here is a chance to listen to Jess Stacy making the most of the piano accompaniment behind Martha. The audience responded to Martha's performance with great enthusiasm, rewarding her with the longest ovation of the evening. She took four curtain calls before she was allowed to leave the stage.[208] In order to move things on, Benny was forced to make the impromptu announcement that they weren't prepared for an encore but would bring back Martha a little later. It must have been gratifying for Martha to hear that applause on record for the first time when it was released in its complete form in 1999.

Blue Room

Orchestra:
Benny Goodman (Clarinet). Harry James, Ziggy Elman, Chris Griffin (Trumpets). Vernon Brown, Red Ballard (Trombones). Hymie Schertzer, George Koenig (Alto Sax). Babe Russin, Art Rollini (Tenor Sax). Allan Reuss (Rhythm Guitar). Jess Stacy (Piano). Harry Goodman (Bass). Gene Krupa (Drums).

'Blue Room' was an arrangement of the Rogers and Hart tune that was prepared by Fletcher Henderson especially for the concert. Benny and the band spent time rehearsing the tune in Carnegie Hall on the 10th January. Douglas Gilbert from the New York World-Telegram was at the rehearsal and described how Benny made changes to the score as they ran through it: 'The boys mess around with their sheets and crack a gag here and there but there is no clowning and Benny goes back right where Toscanini stands and they begin again Benny shuts 'em off and he says "what's that – a D-flat?" capping his ears like "gee that's saw' – wait, I'll fix it" and Benny makes a notation on his score and so do the boys on theirs'. 'The saxes jam in and Benny, chortling with the rhythm yells "give it a lotta Umph"'.[209]

They made their first public performance of 'Blue Room' during their Camel show the next day. Unfortunately, no recording of that show has surfaced. 'Blue Room' is a wonderfully typical Henderson arrangement with trumpets layered with the saxes. The reeds come across particularly well on the Carnegie Hall recording of this number, we can really hear that sweet resonance of the hall. Listen for the lovely little harmony they play to introduce Benny's solo. Chris Griffin plays a solo on this number too. Out on the road, the trumpet section would often play each other's parts, just for a change. Here, Griffin's playing is almost indistinguishable from that of Harry James.

Tempo magazine explained that Benny had run up a huge transcontinental telephone bill ordering arrangements for the concert from Fletcher Henderson, who

---
207 Metronome Magazine - February 1938
208 Melody Maker - February 5 1938
209 New York World-Telegram - January 11 1938

According to the World-Telegram, Benny and the boys make small changes to Fletcher Henderson's new arrangement of 'Blue Room' at rehearsals.

was on tour in California at that time.[210] Curiously, Kolodin's program notes state that 'Blue Room' was one of two arrangements that Fletcher had made especially for the Carnegie concert. However, it would seem that there was a late change of plan. There are three Henderson arrangements in the concert and both of the other two arrangements played, were known long before. 'Blue Skies' and 'Sometimes I'm Happy' were both recorded in 1935. If Kolodin was right and Henderson did prepare two new arrangements for the concert, we are entitled to ponder on what the other tune might have been. We know that 'Blue Room' was one, but what was the other? If we look at the new Henderson arrangements that Benny was playing around that time, the most likely candidate for the other chart would be 'Make Believe'. Benny played this tune for the first time on air, just before the concert, on January 12. Perhaps it didn't go down too well? We don't know but it was not included in the concert after all. They didn't record it in the studio until March 1938.

In June 1937, (perhaps in an effort to cut down on his phone bill!) Benny had invited Fletcher to become his full-time staff arranger at a salary of $300 per week!

210 Tempo Magazine - January 1938 P.11 P.23

Fletcher declined the offer and carried on touring with his own band. It wasn't until June 1939 that Fletcher decided to quit being a bandleader to join the Goodman staff permanently as pianist as well as arranger, controversially unseating Jess Stacy in the process. A lot of people were perplexed at Benny's decision to replace Stacy. Although Fletcher Henderson's piano playing is competent and even witty, nobody would suggest that he was anything like the calibre of Jess Stacy.

The Carnegie concert gives us the only recording we have of Gene Krupa playing on 'Blue Room'. Gene left the band in March 1938, before the tune was committed to wax. The studio version, recorded just after Gene's much talked about departure, has Lionel Hampton playing drums, with Lester Young and Freddie Green sitting in.

Swingtime In The Rockies

Orchestra:

Benny Goodman (Clarinet). Harry James, Ziggy Elman, Chris Griffin (Trumpets). Vernon Brown, Red Ballard (Trombones). Hymie Schertzer, George Koenig (Alto Sax). Babe Russin, Art Rollini (Tenor Sax). Allan Reuss (Rhythm Guitar). Jess Stacy (Piano). Harry Goodman (Bass). Gene Krupa (Drums).

Benny's prolific staff arranger Jimmy Mundy supplied this next tune, it had been in Benny's book for about two years. Jimmy was responsible for some of Benny's most successful arrangements including 'Bugle Call Rag', 'Jumpin' at the Woodside', 'Solo Flight', and 'Sing, Sing, Sing'. 'Swingtime in the Rockies' is a marvellous, hard driving 'Killer Diller' in which the brass section is at its cutting best. Here of course was one of the real high points of the evening. Everybody was on top form, Krupa was especially inventive playing 'across' the rhythm toward the end, the biting brass were just astounding and Ziggy Elman's solo was really dirty! In his mock interview recorded late in 1950, Goodman says that this tune was one of the high spots of the program, "Surely Carnegie Hall had never heard the likes of it before".[211] Metronome's George Simon described Ziggy's outburst like this: "All of a sudden, blasting like hell, riding on high out of the ancient alcoves came Ziggy Elman with a trumpet passage that absolutely broke everything up."[212]

The Newspaper The New York Amsterdam News did a feature on the concert focusing on the black performers at the concert, they published a nice photograph of Jimmy Mundy, Johnny Hodges, Cootie Williams and Harry Carney taken that evening.[213] Jimmy Mundy was in the audience for the concert and when asked if he felt anything like George Gershwin, having his music played in Carnegie Hall he replied, "No, I just feel like tapping mah feet!"[214]

Teddy Wilson was of the impression that Jimmy never got the recognition that he deserved for his work with Benny. At one time he was producing something like five

---

211 Columbia Disc Jockey Promotional 78's. XP 45713-1A
212 Metronome Magazine - February 1938
213 The New York Amsterdam News - January 22 1938
214 Down Beat - February 1938

charts a week and they were all excellent.[215] (He is said to have made over 400 arrangements for Goodman.)[216] According to Jimmy, he had originally written 'Swingtime' for Earl Hines' Orchestra and took it over to Benny when he accepted the job as staff arranger in 1936. Benny didn't like the tune's original name 'Take It Easy' and promptly changed it and added his name to the title credits too![217]

Bei Mir Bist Du Shoen

Orchestra:

Benny Goodman (Clarinet). Martha Tilton (Vocal). Harry James, Ziggy Elman, Chris Griffin (Trumpets). Vernon Brown, Red Ballard (Trombones). Hymie Schertzer, George Koenig (Alto Sax). Babe Russin, Art Rollini (Tenor Sax). Allan Reuss (Rhythm Guitar). Jess Stacy (Piano). Harry Goodman (Bass). Gene Krupa (Drums).

Martha Tilton came back and gave a more relaxed and confident performance of the current hit novelty song that was sweeping the nation, Bei Mir Bist Du Schoen. This song started out life in a 1933 Yiddish musical at the Little Parkway Theatre in Brooklyn. Then it was called 'Bei Mir Bistu Shain' – 'By Me You Are Beautiful', written by Jacob Jacobs and Sholom Secunda. After the show closed, Jacobs and Seconda sold the song for $30 to J Kammen, a Brooklyn music publisher who specialised in Jewish songs. Kammen printed a few copies but nobody showed any interest in the song and it lay forgotten for years until the band leader Guy Lombardo stumbled upon it.

Lombardo had a section in his radio broadcasts that featured unknown tunes that he believed would be hits. After it was broadcast, the publishers of 'Bei Mir' were besieged by other orchestra leaders looking for the tune. New lyrics were added by Sammy Cahn and Saul Chaplin, the Yiddish 'Shain' was changed to the German 'Schoen' and the song became a massive hit on the radio and in the theatre.[218] Everybody was singing it, and everybody had their own versions of the title.... 'My Dear Husky Jane' or 'Buy Me A Beer Mr Shane'. At the Black Cat Club in Greenwich Village, a notice was on display that read: 'Bei Mir Bist Du Schoen will be played only at 9.30, 11.30 and 1.30. Please do not ask for it other than at times scheduled'![219]

Variety Magazine took the unusual step of announcing that a show would feature the song and not an actress or an author. The most popular version was probably that of the Andrews Sisters (recorded at the end of November 1937 and featuring Bobby Hackett on cornet) who were responsible for making it the top selling sheet music tune for January 1938. It was also one of the most played songs on the radio late in 1937.

Benny used a fine arrangement of 'Bei Mir' by Jimmy Mundy. We have only one other example of the band playing this arrangement from the period and that was a broadcast from the Madhattan Room on the 18 December 1937. At Carnegie Hall, Gene had a lot

---
215 Teddy Wilson Talks Jazz – Teddy Wilson. P.48
216 Hendersonia - The music of Fletcher Henderson and his Musicians – Walter C Allen. P.510
217 Hep CD Liner notes 'Jimmy Mundy Arrangements'
218 Radio Guide. James Street. - Week ending February 19 1938
219 Rhythm Magazine - March 1938 P.6

to do in this song and set off defiantly kicking beat for beat on his bass drum. The audience recognised the song immediately. When you listen to the recording of the concert, the section work behind Martha is well worth some special attention. Stacy fans will enjoy his inventive playing behind Martha too. During Jess' solo the audience get somewhat out of sync again with their hand-clapping, but the brass soon stamps it out. Benny's Carnegie recording is quite different from his studio version, which he had recorded a few days before the concert. In the studio, he recorded it as a quartet in two parts with Martha, and Ziggy added on the second side. Pop tunes were going in and out of fashion very quickly (as they do today) and by February 1938, Benny had dropped this number from his book.

China Boy

Trio:

Benny Goodman (Clarinet). Teddy Wilson (Piano). Gene Krupa (Drums).

The switching from full orchestra to the trio meant that it was musical chairs on stage again as Gene moved to the front of stage drum kit and Teddy came in on piano. It is not clear whether Jess left the stage or sat in the spare chair parked by the piano, he is not visible in any of the small group photographs so we have to assume that he went back stage. Everybody was very relaxed now and the trio gave a fabulous charge through 'China Boy' taken at a furious pace. All three musicians were in astonishingly good form here. Krupa's solo towards the end of the tune was extraordinary. He laid down a wonderful sizzling beat with his brushes and then suddenly, with what would appear to be an extra pair of arms, he added another layer and started picking out rhythms on his tom-toms too. On the recording, it sounds increasingly impossible with each listening.

In these trio and quartet numbers, Gene's drumming was very relaxed and he seemed to take charge. After all the solos are done, we can hear on the recording Gene call "We're going out." The top prize in this number however, has to go to Teddy Wilson for his brilliant improvisations, the chiming 'Three Blind Mice' chords, the wonderful bass line vamping behind Benny's solos and the characteristic Teddy Wilson downward runs. The quality of the reproduction here makes it difficult to follow the piano sometimes but Teddy's playing was impeccable, as always.

Stompin' At The Savoy

Quartet:

Benny Goodman, Teddy Wilson (Piano). Lionel Hampton (Vibraphone). Gene Krupa (Drums).

Hampton entered and the quartet stumbled into 'Stompin' at the Savoy'. Here is another Goodman classic, one of his early hits for the full orchestra, named of course, after the Savoy Ballroom in Harlem. Several of the first hand reports of the concert mention that during one of the quartet numbers, Gene Krupa knocked a cymbal off its stand, although nobody mentions exactly during which tune this happened. Guy Sykes in Tempo Magazine says, 'Lionel Hampton turned like a flash, replaced the brass disk, and caught it a wallop just on the last beat of the chorus'. He continued, 'a roar of sudden appreciation swelled the hall'.[220] Melody Maker describes the incident like this: 'Here, Hampton displays his adroit showmanship, for, when Krupa hit a cymbal with such force that it fell off the stand, Hampton ran to retrieve it, placed it back on the stand and then engaged in a rhythmic battle with Krupa, both taking alternate shots at the cymbal'[221]. Metronome described it as being like a game of Ping Pong! By listening to the recording, can we identify exactly where this little drama happened? In the closing moments of 'Stompin' at the Savoy' we can hear a sudden wave of excitement and laughter from the audience and then the same again a few beats later, Hampton stops playing and Krupa is delivering some particularly exuberant crashes on the cymbals, with the above descriptions in mind, listen again to the end of 'Stompin', it seems quite possible to believe that it is here that the cymbal incident took place.

Edgar Sampson's compositions were well represented at the Carnegie concert. As well as writing 'Stompin' at the Savoy' he also wrote 'Don't Be That Way' and 'If Dreams Come True'. All three tunes were being played by the Chick Webb band where Sampson had recently vacated his seat as alto sax player, to concentrate on his work as an arranger with Goodman and others.

Dizzy Spells

Quartet:
Benny Goodman (Clarinet). Teddy Wilson (Piano). Lionel Hampton (Vibraphone). Gene Krupa (Drums).

Amongst the pre-publicity for the event was a story in the British Newspaper 'Melody Maker', that Lionel Hampton was writing a Swing Symphony for the concert using the sounds of a newspaper printing works as inspiration.[222] Maybe Lionel was just pulling the leg of a gullible journalist but perhaps he was thinking about using the repetitive rhythms of printing machinery as the foundation for a tune? 'Dizzy Spells' had only been performed in public once, a couple a days before the concert and was written (according to the script of the Camel Caravan Show) during rehearsals on the afternoon of the 11th January. When we listen to this dazzling riff, it is possible to imagine that the main theme of this tune could have been inspired by the rattling machines and conveyor belts of a printing works.

Writing in his book 'The Jazz Years – Eyewitness To An Era' Leonard Feather confirms that this tune was written by Hampton. Feather was a staff writer at Melody Maker during the 1930s and was present in the studio when the Goodman quartet, now with Dave Tough playing drums, recorded Dizzy Spells a few months after the

220 Tempo - February 1938
221 Melody Maker - February 5 1938
222 Melody Maker. - January 1 1938

Here is a wonderful sequence of the quartet hard at work.

Carnegie concert. He recalls what a complex piece this was to play 'which even Goodman, with his limitless technique had some trouble negotiating. He ran over it at least a dozen times before announcing that he was ready for a take'.[223] Perhaps this number was destined to be part of Hampton's Swing Symphony?

The unison playing of Goodman and Hampton in the introduction to 'Dizzy Spells' is electrifying. It is impossible to separate the two instruments. Although the piece is all about Goodman and Hampton, Teddy is ever present playing some lovely figures behind the two front men. His solo has a Fats Waller stride about it. At this stage of the concert, everybody was taking extra choruses and Teddy was instructed to 'take one more'. Gene appeared to call as many of these prompts as Benny. Perhaps this was the cause of some of the friction between the two which led to Gene's departure a

223 The Jazz Years, Eyewitness to an era - Leonard Feather. P.44

– The Music –

couple of months after the concert. The newness and complexity of this tune could explain why Benny and Lionel appeared to get a little lost towards the end of this extended performance. Gene Krupa helped them find their bearings with some slightly exaggerated markers.

Performing at Carnegie Hall the day after Benny, was the great classical Hindu dancer Uday Shan-Kar. Also dancing on stage that night was his young brother Ravi Shan-Kar now known, of course, as the 'Father of the Sitar', not as a dancer. Sol Hurok described Uday's young brother in a performance a few years earlier as "Cavorting engagingly in the role of the Monkey King in the Shiva drama."[224] Gene was passionate about all forms of percussion and never missed a chance to go and listen to anything new or unusual. He attended rehearsals of Uday Shan-Kar's dance troupe and was very interested in the work of Shan-Kar's music director and drummer,

---

224 Impresario. Sol Hurok and Ruth Goode. P.169

Vishnudas Shiraly.[225] It seems that this admiration was mutual, for Shiraly was in the audience for Benny's concert and he had this to say about Gene: "The man has a genius for rhythm. It is quite different from our Indian way of drumming, of course. He beats in multiples of two whereas we think of rhythm in multiples of three. But I am amazed to find that he makes almost a melodic instrument out of the drums. His variations are so intricate that they seem to have an absolute melodic line."[226]

Sing, Sing, Sing.

Orchestra:

Benny Goodman (Clarinet). Harry James, Ziggy Elman, Chris Griffin (Trumpets). Vernon Brown, Red Ballard (Trombones). Hymie Schertzer, George Koenig (Alto Sax). Babe Russin, Art Rollini (Tenor Sax). Allan Reuss (Rhythm Guitar). Jess Stacy (Piano). Harry Goodman (Bass). Gene Krupa (Drums).

By now, the audience must have been used to the heavy traffic on stage, with musicians back and forth all evening. With a remarkable turn of speed, the full orchestra returned to the stage for the finale. Gene moved back to his orchestra drum kit and Lionel and Teddy left the stage for the last time that evening. Benny often described 'Sing, Sing, Sing' as being like the national anthem, it had to be played at every one of his concerts.

The audience in Carnegie were ecstatic at this point and even some of the older, 'penguin-looking' men in the boxes at the side of the hall were dancing.[227] This Louis Prima song had been around for a few years by then. Its original title was 'Sing Bing Sing' and Jimmy Mundy had made an arrangement of the tune for Benny. The first recording we have of it, by the Goodman band, was from a 1936 broadcast with Helen Ward singing. Helen's vocal was dropped after only a short while. Bob Inman's descriptions of performances indicate how the tune seemed to get longer with every playing. The tune quickly developed into the showpiece we know it to be today, with all sorts of things thrown in. Listen out for references to Grieg's 'Hall of the Mountain King', and Chu Berry's 'Christopher Columbus'. In a July 1937 broadcast, Benny is heard to quip as Gene sets to work on the tom-tom, "Look out Krupa, that's how Jam Sessions are born".[228]

As soon as Krupa embarked on the first beats of the tune the audience knew what was coming, or at least, they thought they did. 'Sing, Sing, Sing' had won the Down Beat award for the 1937 Best Arrangement of the Year. The record had been released some six months before covering both sides of a twelve inch 78. 'Sing' had always been a piece in which the musicians could let go a bit. You can hear in these performances, the freshness and vitality of youth. The music is being played by musicians who invented it and who believed in it and there is no sense, in any of these performances, that they were just going through the motions. Almost as if they were trying to emulate the 78

---

225 Gene Krupa by Arnold Shaw. Pin-Up Press Co. 1945
226 Down Beat - February 1938
227 Metronome - February 1938
228 Camel Caravan - June 29 1937 – Un-published recording

record, the concert rendering was split into two halves. 'Sing, Sing, Sing' was a vehicle for Gene and Benny and could have its roots back in the days when Benny was with Ben Pollack. Pollack and Benny used to play long duets at times, just drums and clarinet.[229]

At Carnegie Hall, Gene Krupa was in his element, free to display as much of his unique blend of showmanship and virtuosity as he liked. The audience lapped it up! The trumpet trio were nothing short of sensational. In the recordings we can hear their instruments 'beating' as they play some of the passages together. (It sounds almost like a fast vibrato but it is the effect of the addition and cancellation of wave-forms as they play in unison.) Harry James was a competent drummer and on occasions sat in if Gene was sick. He had written a little drum break for Gene to play to indicate when he was ready to hand over to Harry's trumpet solo. You can hear Harry's cue on this recording. In later years, Benny used to use this break as an audition piece for potential recruits. If they didn't know it, that was the end of the audition![230] Listen, too, for Allan Reuss' rhythm guitar in this recording, he contributes much to the 'jungle atmosphere' of this rendition.

Speaking to virtuoso classical violinist, Joseph Szigeti, after the concert about his solo, Benny confessed this:

Szigeti: "That was C above high C, it's impossible. How did you do it?"

Goodman grinned: "It was an accident."[231]

One of the most memorable things about 'Sing, Sing, Sing', and some people say of the whole concert, was Jess Stacy's solo. The reporter for Time Magazine had mistakenly credited Teddy Wilson with this solo. W.W. Nash, who was in the audience mentioned a 'magical stillness that came down immediately over the audience'.[232] According to Stacy, Benny just pointed to him and said "You take it."[233] At variance to this, Guy Sykes says that it was Krupa who jumped in before Goodman had made up his mind and yelled "Take one Jess." There has been much talk about whether it was a planned solo, and up until quite recently we had thought that this was the first time

229 The Kingdom of Swing. Benny Goodman & Irving Kolodin P.77
230 D Russell Connor
231 The Saturday Evening Post. - May 7 1938
232 The New Yorker magazine - December 26 1977
233 Interview in the Adventures in the Kingdom of Swing Sony video

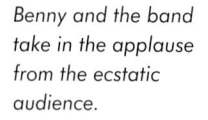

Benny and the band take in the applause from the ecstatic audience.

that Benny had picked Jess for a solo in this tune. Jess said later "If I had known that that solo was coming I would have probably lost the will to live!"[234] 'It was near the end and Jess bends down closer to the piano and digs in. All of a sudden it was loud and clear. The audience was listening without breathing and so quiet'.[235] Al Brackman's dispatch for Melody Maker said that it was one of the most beautiful piano passages of the evening and added that the result did not affect the audience as much as it did the band, which bowed in enthusiastic recognition of the performance.[236]

In his lovely little book about Jess Stacy, Keith Keller tells of how the actor Robert Mitchum would be moved to tears by Jess' solo: "Bob was in the audience of the original Carnegie Hall concert, and every so often he will still dig out the recording and sit listening to it around midnight, and when Stacy's long solo comes, tears will run down his cheeks."[237] Afterwards, Krupa could only repeat, "Just like a symphony, man!"[238] As time goes by, and more recollections of the band's performances come to light, we are coming to realise that Benny had featured Jess as soloist in this piece before. Otis Ferguson mentions Jess soloing prior to the Carnegie Hall date and so too, does Bob Inman. Otis Ferguson quotes Teddy Wilson as saying: "Jess plays one more time like that, I'll never touch the piano again!"[239] If this is true, it must be one of 'the quotes' of the concert!

The Encores

Orchestra:

Benny Goodman (Clarinet). Harry James, Ziggy Elman, Chris Griffin (Trumpets). Vernon Brown, Red Ballard (Trombones). Hymie Schertzer, George Koenig (Alto Sax, Clarinet). Babe Russin, Art Rollini (Tenor Sax, Clarinet). Allan Reuss (Rhythm Guitar). Jess Stacy (Piano). Harry Goodman (Bass). Gene Krupa (Drums).

The audience exploded into applause at the conclusion of 'Sing, Sing, Sing', and there was no question in their collective mind that there had to be an encore. Many commentators have suggested that this was not a good idea, 'Leave them wanting more' is the traditional rule. As the applause died away, the young audience started to call out their requests. On the recording, we can just make out somebody call for 'Stardust'. The band took a breather before they settled on 'If Dreams Come True'.

This is one of the two titles that were excised from the original LP, it was slotted back in here, its rightful place, for the first time by Phil Schaap in his 1999 release. Like 'Sometimes I'm Happy', it was previously available, in rather poor quality on the bootleg LP, Sunbeam 127. Benny had first recorded this Edgar Sampson arrangement

---

234 IAJRC 1987 Conference audience recording
235 Tempo Magazine - February 1938
236 Melody Maker - February 5 1938
237 Oh, Jess. A Jazz Life – Keith Keller. P.132
238 Guy Sykes Tempo Magazine - February 1938
239 The Otis Ferguson Reader. M. Cowley and Otis Ferguson

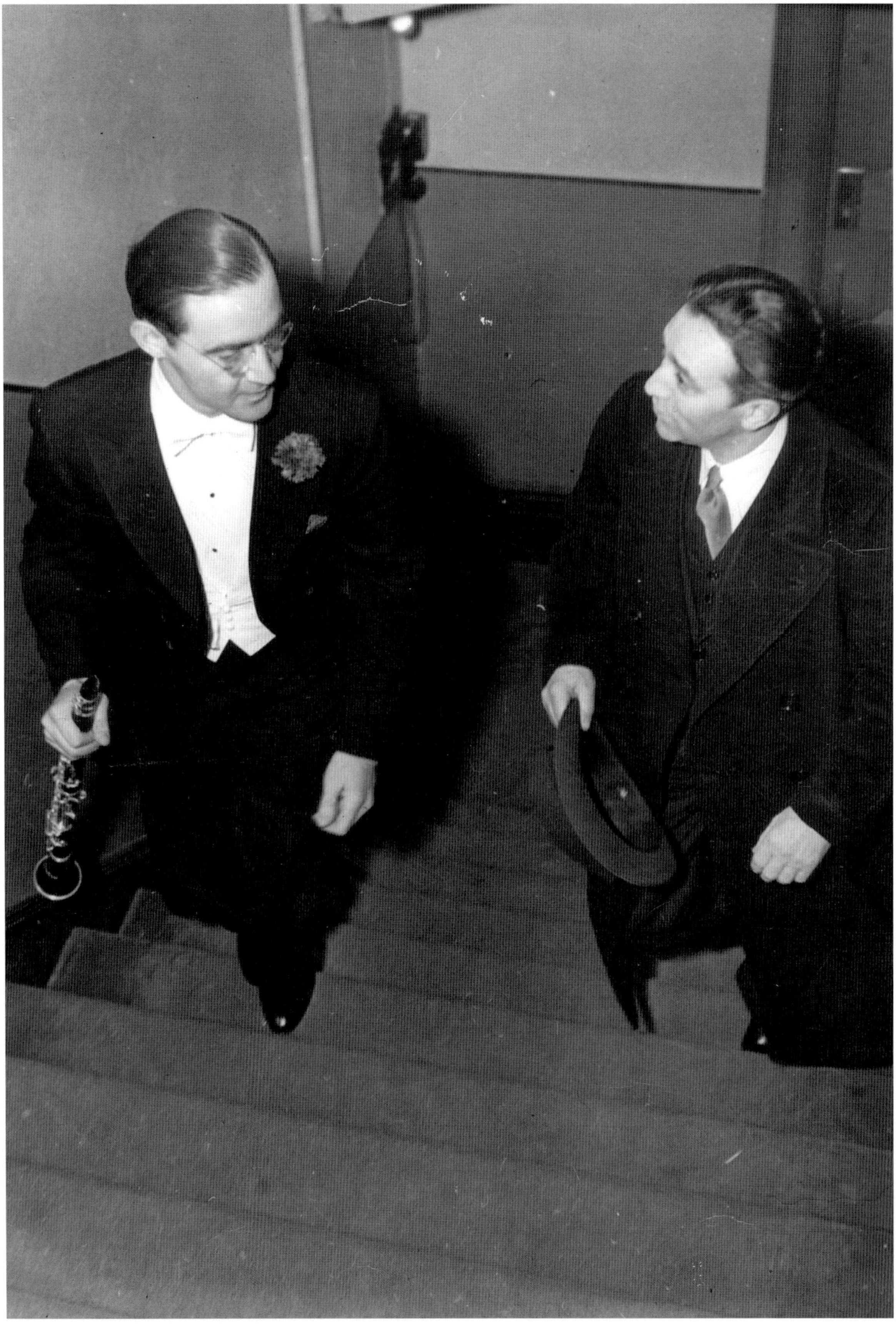

early in December 1937 and the band had played it at least half a dozen times on air that month. This tune had a very short life in Benny's repertoire, only a few months, and it was gone forever. In the first chorus, we can hear one of the few examples of the reed section all playing clarinets, then notice the slick change from clarinets to saxophones. Reviewers agreed that an encore was an anti-climax after the pyrotechnics of 'Sing, Sing, Sing'. Teddy Wilson had recorded this tune with Billie Holiday a few days before the concert along with Benny's Carnegie Hall guests Walter Page, Buck Clayton, Freddie Green and Lester Young.

The second encore, and final number of the concert, was 'Big John Special'. This closing number is a relaxed and punchy rendition that has some beautifully smooth saxophone work and exciting solos from James and Elman. Jess had a great evening and got another chance to play here and he did not disappoint. Vernon Brown and Red Ballard took it up to the climax of the piece which closes the concert in a mellow vein. Big John, nicknamed 'Meatball', was a Harlem restaurant-owner famed for his generous attitude towards serving drinks. 'If you had a buck, OK. If you didn't that was OK too. Everybody loved Big John'.[240] John was the New York musicians' official bartender. Rival clarinet player, Artie Shaw also recorded a tribute to Big John in 1938, 'Shoot The Likker To Me, John Boy'.

After 'Big John Special' and without ceremony, Benny simply walked off the stage followed by his band.[241] Benny is pictured after the concert on the backstage staircase that leads up from the stage looking quite fresh and chatting to an overcoated gentleman, possibly Wynn Nathanson of the Tom Fizdale Agency.

In any group of musicians working at that sort of intensity, the pressure would start to cause problems. Benny's constant drive for perfection and his sometimes insensitive behaviour, coupled with the relentless demands of work, inevitably led to some disharmony in the band. In Mort Goode's wonderfully illuminating liner notes for the RCA series of records 'The Complete Benny Goodman', Herman 'Hymie' Schertzer tells of how Benny was acting very strangely on the night of the concert. "It got so bad that both he and Teddy Wilson gave their notices the next night, though they were both talked out of leaving at that moment."

Benny on the stage stairs after the concert discussing the evening with a friend – possibly Wynn Nathanson of the Tom Fizdale Agency.

240 'The Night People: The Jazz Life of Dicky Wells'' – as told to Stanley Dance
241 New York Sun - January 17 1938

A HISTORY MAKING........BATTLE OF SWING
SUNDAY JAN. 16'
The King of the Drums
The Royalist of the Keyboard
Count BASIE & HIS ORCHESTRA
The Aristocrat of Rhythm
Chick WEBB
VS
& AMERICA'S OUTSTANDING ... SWING BAND
Chick Webb & HIS FAMOUS ORCHESTRA WILL PLAY NIGHTLY AT THE SAVOY
Special Matinee 3 PM
No Increase in Admission
Billie HOLLIDAY FEATURED WITH THE COUNT....
Ella FITZGERALD FEATURED WITH CHICK
THE WORLDS FINEST BALLROOM
SAVOY
LENOX AVE at 140th STREET

After the Concert
attend the
BATTLE OF SWING
between
CHICK WEBB
and his Orchestra
with
Ella Fitzgerald
and
COUNT BASIE
and his Orchestra
with
Billie Holliday
TONIGHT
SAVOY BALLROOM
Lenox Ave. & 140th St.
N. Y. C.

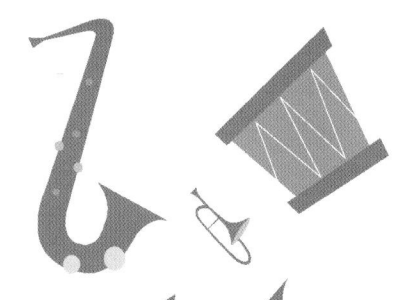

• CHAPTER 14 •

Battle of the Bands

This was the end of a fabulous concert that has gone down in history as one of the greatest concerts ever in Carnegie Hall. However, for the audience, 'the night was but young....'.

Benny's old friend from the Chicago Rhythm Club, Helen Oakley was now working for the Moe Gale Agency and was handling the publicity work for Chick Webb's band.[242] (Moe was Chick Webb's manager and the owner of the Savoy Ballroom.) To make sure that her man did not get overlooked that evening, she placed a quarter page advertisement in Benny's Carnegie Hall program, promoting the 'Battle of the Bands' at the Savoy Ballroom later that evening and inviting all to attend. Obligingly, after the concert, many of the musicians who played with Benny piled into taxi cabs and went to the Savoy to watch the 'Cutting Contest' between the Basie and Chick Webb bands. These Cutting matches or 'Battles' started out in the musicians' 'Cellar Dives' as a way to establish a player's supremacy. When Louis Armstrong first came to New York he 'cut' just about every ranking trumpet player in town to put himself on top.[243]

However, by 1937 the concert promoters got latched onto the idea and Cutting Contests became big box-office attractions, capable of bringing in a lot of paying customers. Metronome's George Simon had used the term to sum up his review of Goodman's concert that night. He said that the Goodman Virile Vipers had 'cut to the core Jack Barbirolli and his Philharmonic Cats'!

In May 1937, Benny's band and Chick Webb had had a cutting match at the Savoy Ballroom. The occasion drew the biggest crowd that the Savoy had ever seen. Teddy Wilson remembered that, "The whole area of Harlem was roped off and the traffic was stopped. All the windows of the Savoy were open and the people in the street were listening to the two bands."[244] Chick Webb was pronounced the winner that evening. Gene famously said that he had never been bested by a better man. In Chicago that June, the Goodman Band had another of these contrived matches, this time they were paired with Roy Eldridge. Press reports indicate that Benny came out on top, Harry James being the star that night.[245]

Helen Oakley's publicity in the Carnegie Hall program had worked a treat and the Basie-Webb battle, after Benny's Carnegie concert, again drew record-breaking

---

242 The Billboard Magazine - November 27 1937
243 The Billboard Magazine - September 25 1937
244 Teddy Wilson Talks Jazz – Teddy Wislon. P.31
245 Down Beat - July 1937

crowds with lines of people blocking the traffic. Hundreds were turned away. It was said that the whole of the Carnegie crowd journeyed 'en masse' to the Savoy. A highlight of the contest was the arrival of Duke Ellington at the Savoy. He was virtually pushed on to the bandstand to play some 'gut-bucket piano'[246] and was swiftly joined by some of Basie's men. At the 'Battle', Chick Webb's band featured Ella Fitzgerald and Basie's band featured Billie Holiday.

What an evening of Jazz that must have been, with Count Basie, Chick Webb, Ella and Billie, Duke Ellington, Jimmy Rushing, most of Benny's band including Benny himself and his family,[247] Red Norvo, Jimmy Mundy, Eddie Duchin and Ivie Anderson. (Forty years later, Russ Connor describes how Benny was tired after the concert and went straight home to bed, at variance with the Metronome report.)[248] Metronome Magazine described Basie as having won the Battle; a re-match was to be scheduled. Lionel Hampton recalled that he was so excited after that evening that he did not sleep for two days.[249] There was a report in the Press that Basie and Chick Webb had a real feud going on. Chick Webb had apparently offered the Count a job in his band, Basie took offence and replied by offering Chick Webb a job in his![250]

---

[246] Melody Maker - February 5 1938
[247] Metronome - February 1938
[248] Carnegie Hall 40th Anniversary Concert. Decca liner notes
[249] 'Hamp an Autobiography' - Lionel Hampton and James Haskins. P.68
[250] Melody Maker - January 29 1938

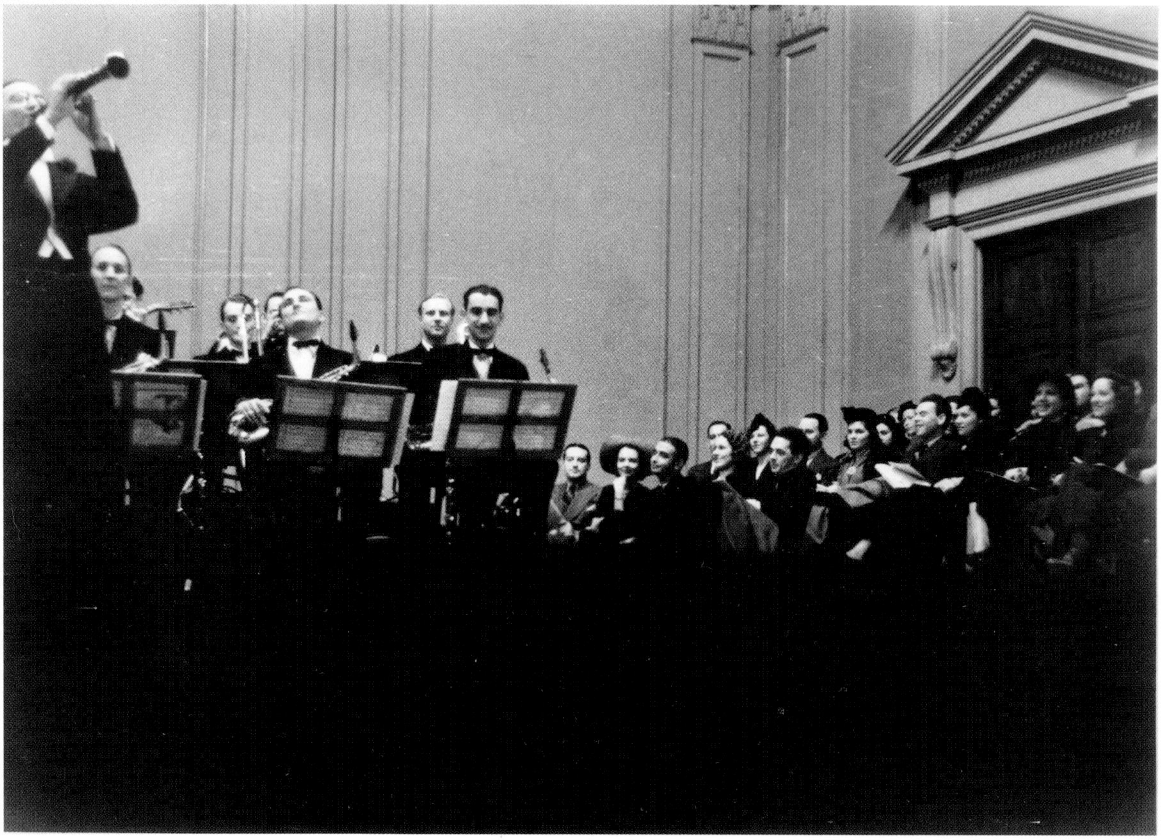

CHAPTER 15

Mozart

At rehearsals a week before the concert, Benny was somewhat defensive when asked about his playing, sounding more like a Chicago gangster than an urbane Chicago classical clarinettist. He announced his plans to go legit thus:

"Listen" says Benny, "Szigeti and a lot of the top men have listened to me and recognised swing as modern and original stuff. They know it's got something. Why, if a lot of the concert stars had Lionel Hampton's rhythm they'd be even greater. And the arrangements I play of Fletcher Henderson's are classics and Jimmy Mundy's too. ... I got a grand idea for the concert, but I'm not going to tell you what it is because maybe we cannot wangle. Anyway, if we do it will be a surprise. ... But I can tell you one stunt I'm going to do, I studied the clarinet seriously, see? I play correct clarinet, and on my sponsored radio program after the concert I'm going to put on say, the Coolidge String Quartet and we'll play the Mozart Quintet for Strings and Clarinet. Fun after the swing session, eh?"[251]

As a 12-year-old, Benny had already made his first professional appearance and it was about then that he started to study classical music under German teacher, Franz Schoepp. Schoepp had worked with members of the Chicago Symphony Orchestra and at the Chicago Musical College. The two years that Benny had with Franz Schoepp had given him a very good grounding in classical techniques.

Anxious to capitalise on his new status as a serious musician, Benny had invited the Coolidge String Quartet to join him on the Camel Caravan show on January 18. At least one member of the quartet, viola player Nicolas Moldavan was at Carnegie Hall for Benny's concert two days earlier and was quoted in Down Beat as saying "I consider Benny Goodman one of the greatest musicians of our time."[252] They played the first movement of Mozart's Quintet for Clarinet and Strings together live on-air, a work that Benny would record a few months later with the Budapest String Quartet. Benny switched effortlessly from playing Swing on the B flat clarinet to Mozart on the A clarinet. The program announcer put it like this:

Dan Seymour: "As you all know, the Professor and the gang moved the swing school into Carnegie Hall last Sunday night and really rocked those hallowed halls with our music. Now, turnabout being fair, we're adding a little Carnegie touch to

---

251 New York World-Telegram - January 11 1938
252 Down Beat - February 1938

Benny reaches for a high note.

the Swing School, with Professor Goodman and the Coolidge String Quartet playing Mozart's Quintet in A major. Professor, tell 'em about it."

Benny: "Well, all I can say is that the Coolidge String Quartet is about the finest in the country. They are sponsored by the Library of Congress and their Chester Music Concerts in Washington D.C. have won international acclaim. We're highly honoured to have them here. I'm going to play with them the first movement of Mozart's Clarinet Quintet in A Major for clarinet and string quartet."[253]

---

[253] R J Reynolds scripts, January 18 1938

Mozart

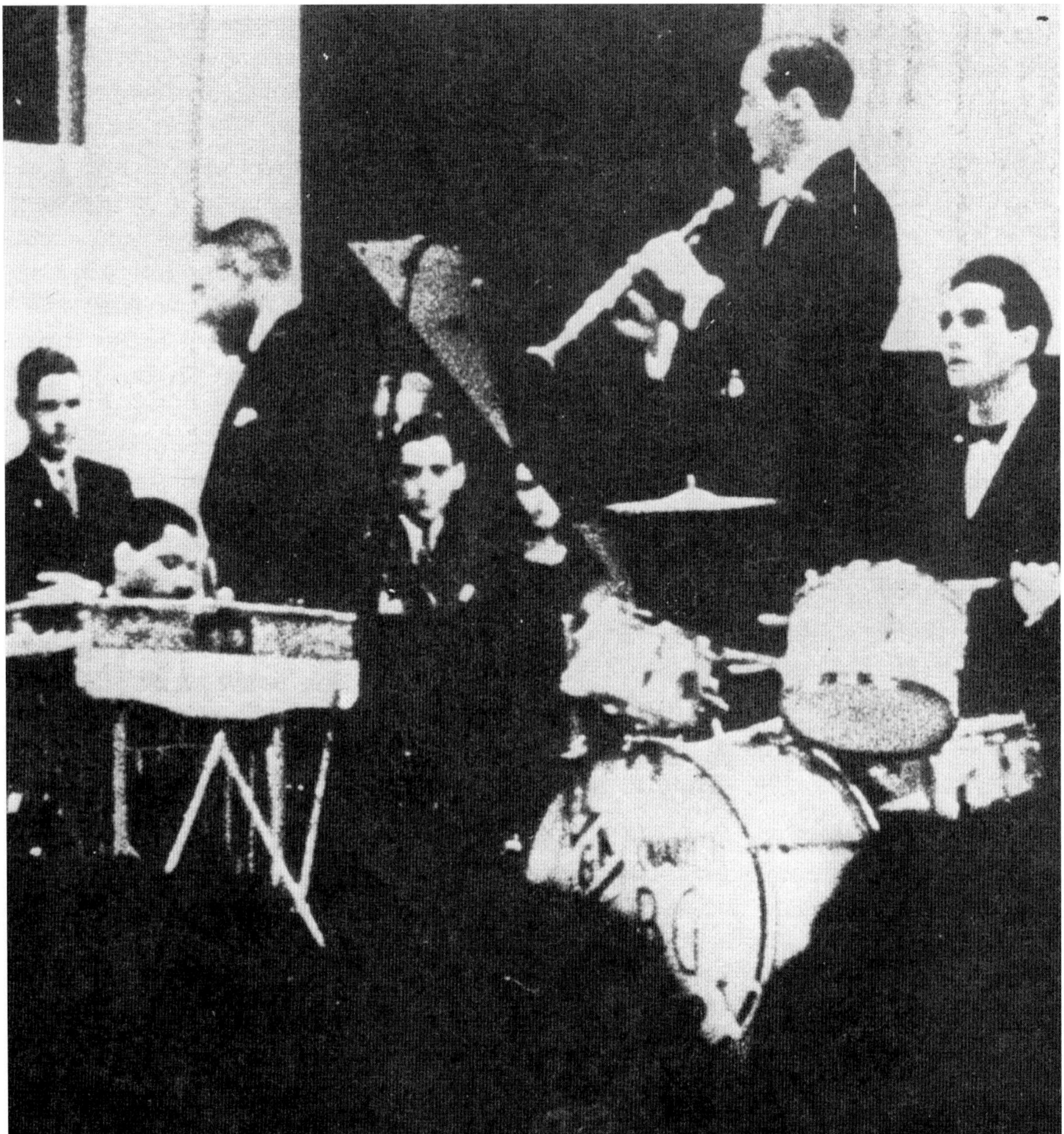

• CHAPTER 16 •

The Photographs

Most of the photos reproduced in this book were taken by Lawrence Marx Jr., Albert's brother. He was sitting in the first few rows and used a Leica camera to capture these 24 shots. All but one of them appears to be fairly sharply focused and nicely composed but in one shot, Lawrence's finger can be seen partially obscuring the lens! Lawrence himself handed the negatives into the Carnegie Hall archives in 1987 along with a few other photographs that he had taken of the Benny Goodman quartet on a different occasion. The pictures have a timeless quality to them. If we didn't know already there is really nothing in them that gives a clue to the date. The band all look resplendent in their bow ties and tuxedos and the pictures that show the audience give nothing away either, they could have been taken quite recently. Five of Lawrence Marx's shots were reproduced in the liner notes for the CBS 1980 release of the album.[254] There, they were credited to 'Foto Files'. The set of photos reproduced in this book came from the estate of Bill Savory, the Columbia engineer who worked on the original record release in 1950.

There are a few other photos from the concert available. There is one very nice photo, taken from the wings and published in the February 1938 Down Beat magazine. There are also several that were published in Metronome in February 1938, taken from the audience and backstage. The negatives for those have long since been lost. Metronome also published a photo in 1951 of the rehearsals.[255] George Simon included a photograph of the rehearsals in his fine book about the Swing Era.[256] The photographs from Rhythm Magazine are interesting. They convey the sense of the occasion well, they are quite grainy but very well exposed.[257] The expanse of the Carnegie Hall stage becomes clear in these pictures too. Sadly, the negatives for these are also long since lost. Esquire Magazine carried a photograph in the June 1968 issue which appears to have been taken from the back of the parquet. The archives at Carnegie Hall have a good photograph taken by a fan from high up in the balcony. The layout of the band and the stage seating is clear here. The Amsterdam News carried a photograph taken at Carnegie Hall of Johnny Hodges, Harry Carney, Cootie Williams and Jimmy Mundy. They also included a shot of Martha Tilton watching over Teddy Wilson and Lionel Hampton at the piano.[258]

Here is the only known picture of Teddy Wilson taken during a quartet number. He can just be seen above Lionel Hampton's vibraphone.

---

254 Benny Goodman 1937-38 Jazz Concerts
255 Metronome Magazine - February 1951
256 'Simon Says – The Sights and Sounds of the Swing Era' George T Simon. P. 388
257 Rhythm Magazine – April 1938
258 New York Amsterdam News – January 22 1938

Readers may be surprised to learn that the background shown in these photographs, the porticos around the doors and the columns around the walls are not real! This is a set, what they called a 'box set'. It is all made of papier maché and wood. The real stage lies behind this theatrical mock-up. There were various sets that could be used at Carnegie Hall depending on the event, these included a 'room set' for small theatrical performances and numerous fabric sets and backdrops. The door shown on the right hand side of the photographs is completely false, musicians entered the stage area through the left hand door. The photograph taken by a fan in the balcony shows the stage right area and the side of the set and the 'real' stage shell behind can be seen. The design of the stage area has changed many times in the last 100 years and it is difficult to say what is original, but we can say that the background that we see in these photographs is just a set.

This interesting photograph was taken by a fan high in the balcony. Here we can see the 'box set' background and the close proximity of the stage seats to the band.

"Take one more Ben!"

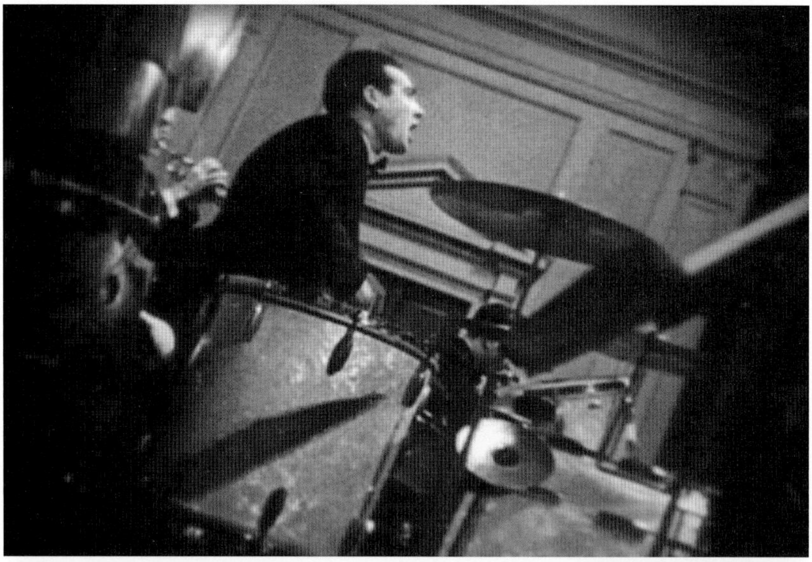
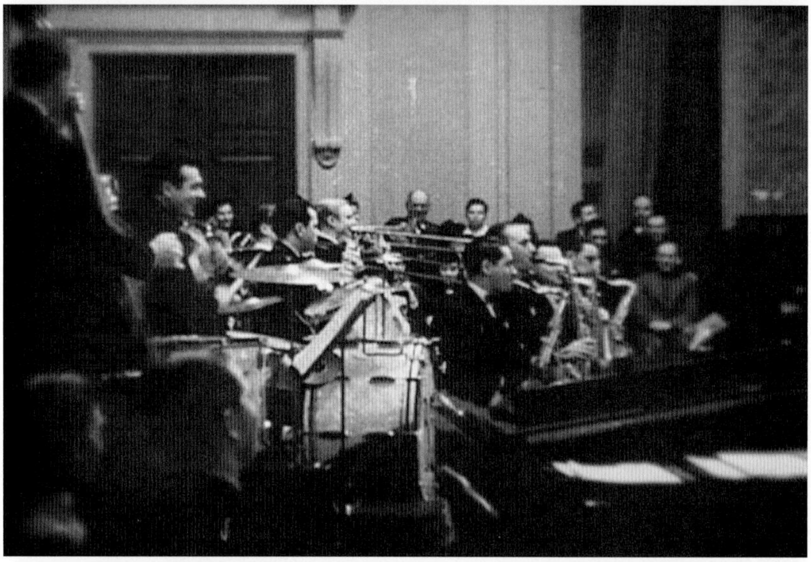
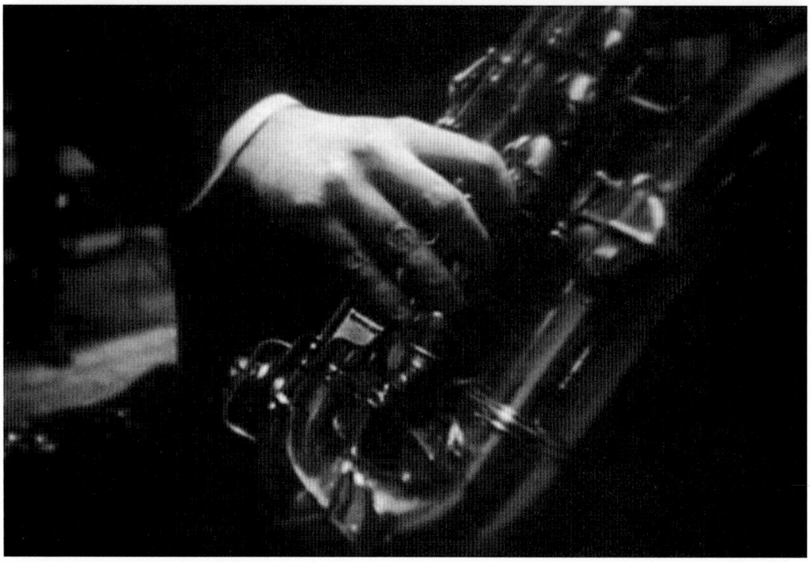

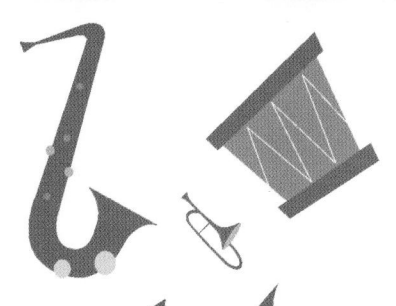

• CHAPTER 17 •
Newsreel Film

In these days of instant communication and 24 hours-a-day news from anywhere in the world, it is difficult for us to imagine a time when news was sent on a roll of newsreel film, by plane if the journey was not too far, or by boat. In 1938, newsreel theatres were relatively few and far between in the US. There were only ten in the whole of America, whereas there were nearly fifty in London alone. However, the American appetite for international news was growing. Graphic film of events like the Hindenburg disaster and the bombing of the USS Panay had brought huge numbers of people into theatres in 1937 and a lot more dedicated newsreel theatres were planned. Film companies like Fox-Movietone and RKO-Pathe were fighting to be first with news. Soon you would be able to go and watch film of college football games shown the same day as the matches were played. Sometimes, the newsreel companies were able to get the top stories onto the screen before the newspapers could be printed. All newsworthy topics were covered, from striking steel workers to the war in Spain and of course Benny Goodman's concert at Carnegie was big news so the newsreel film crew were there!

Newsreel stories were nearly always short, skilfully edited summaries of events in the news. In total only just over one minute of film of the Carnegie concert survives, which is probably all there ever was. Newsreel cameras made a lot of noise in those days and despite being loudly 'Shushed' by the audience, the camera man kept 'grinding away annoyingly for the better part of the concert'.[259] It is easy to understand the audience's annoyance. As we can see from the footage, the camera man was busy all evening shooting from many different locations inside and out of the hall.

Starting with the anti-BG demonstrations outside the hall he moved on to film the queues of fans in the lobby. He even got on to the stage during the concert for a couple of shots, where he must have been clearly visible to the audience crouching down by Gene Krupa's quartet drum kit to film close-up shots of Babe Russin. Careful study of the film does reward us with a little more detail about the evening, things which do not appear on the still photographs taken that night. One of the long shots clearly shows the much talked about microphone hanging over the stage, we can just make out the cables by which it was suspended. If we compare this picture with the RCA technical literature the similarities are obvious. The four tiered rows of lucky people sitting on the right of the stage and their close proximity to the band are clearly visible. Harry

---

259 Metronome Magazine - February 1938

The microphone that Down Beat described as "hanging in austere silence"

Carney's saxophone can be seen positioned on the corner of the stage, ready for the 'Twenty years of Jazz' section of the evening. The whole band is playing, this helps to assign the shot to one of the first three numbers played.

It is very difficult to synchronise the film sequences (which are black and white and silent) with the music, each sequence being so brief. We can easily identify the end of 'Sing, Sing, Sing' because of the drum break and it is possible to synchronise the sound with that short clip. There is a brief glimpse of the jam session shot from behind Gene Krupa in which we can just make out Johnny Hodges, Buck Clayton and Benny. Ziggy Elman and Chris Griffin's chairs are both vacant in this sequence, they were backstage having a smoke! In another shot, Harry Goodman is seen using his bow and the 'biting brass' are standing up in the back row with their mutes in (possibly 'Sometimes I'm Happy'?). The house microphone that Martha Tilton used is clearly visible in a nice shot from one of the balconies and in that sequence we are able to spot the differences in Gene Krupa's two drum kits.

In a comparison of the movie-clips with the still photographs, it can be seen that the lid of the Grand Piano was adjusted at some time during the evening. The lid is shown open wide at the end of the newsreel footage of 'Sing, Sing, Sing' and also in

An illustration from the RCA Victor microphone manual showing the suspension mechanism.

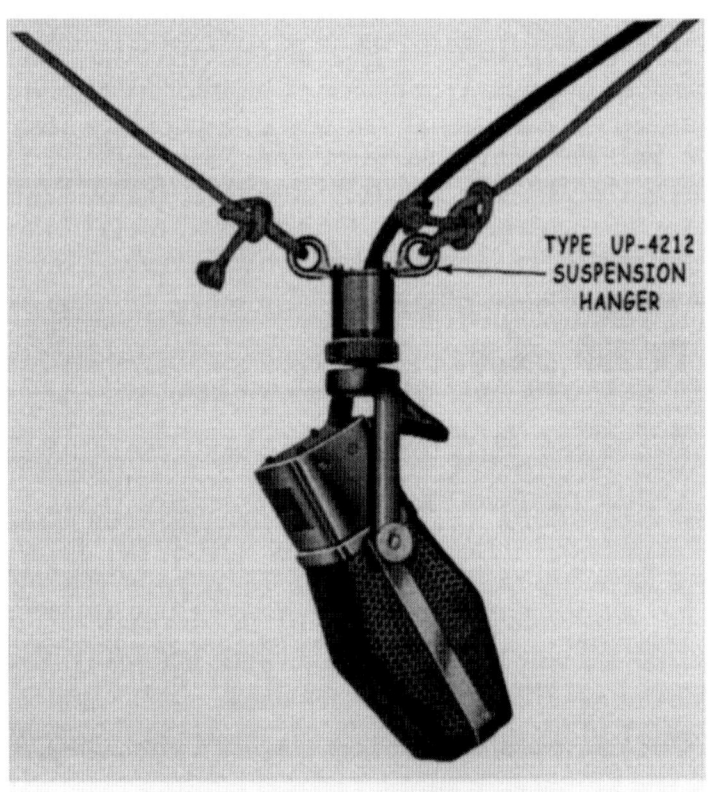

Figure 3—Microphone Suspended

the photograph from Rhythm magazine when the quartet are playing, but it is nearly closed in the photograph published in Down Beat showing Jess Stacy at the piano. The volume of the piano is considerably increased with the lid open, it would seem likely that Teddy Wilson (an exquisitely delicate player) opened it up when he came on stage for the first trio piece.

The newsreel camera man was busy all evening, filming from all parts of the auditorium.

TOM FUQUA
PRESENTS
BILLIE HOLIDAY
WED., APRIL 28 THRU
Mansfield Theatre
The famous 1938 Carnegie Hall Jazz Concert
BENNY GOODMAN
PHILIPS
Benny Goodman
GOODMAN
CARNEGIE HALL JAZZ CONCERT
COLUMBIA
CARNEGIE HALL JAZZ
BENNY GOOD
COLUMBIA JAZZ MASTERPIECES
FAMOUS 1938
CARNEGIE HALL Vol. 2
CONCERT
GOODMAN Featuring
HARRY JAMES
GENE KRUPA
LIONEL HAMPTON
TEDDY WILSON
JOHNNY HODGES
BENNY GOOD
THE FAMOUS 1938 CARNEG
JAZZ CON
BENNY GOODMAN
6 October 1939
LIONEL HAMPTON FLETCHER HENDERSON
CHARLIE CHRISTIAN
SECOND CARNEGIE HALL JAZZ CONCERT
DOWN BEAT
Goodman Came, Saw, And Laid A Golden Egg!
RACHMANINOFF
Serkin
CARNEGIE HALL
SAN FRANCISCO
SYMPHONY ORCHESTRA
PIERRE MONTEUX
CARNEGIE HALL
BOSTON SYMPHONY ORCHESTRA

• CHAPTER 18 •

Carnegie Hall Museum and Archives

Surprising as it may seem, up until recently Carnegie Hall had never held a repository of souvenirs and memorabilia from all of the thousands of famous artists who have appeared there since its opening in 1891. One would naturally assume that the Carnegie basement would be a bulging treasury of programs, autographs and recordings but it was not the case. The hall had gone through a difficult time in the 1950s, and plans were in place to replace the Carnegie Hall with a bright red skyscraper.[260] That idea was eventually dropped and the owner, Robert Simon Jr, tried very hard to save the hall for posterity. Unfortunately, every month he was losing money and that could not go on forever. In the end he decided that he would raze the building to the ground to make way for a car park! During those hard times, many of the documentary records, signed photographs 'To Carnegie Hall' hanging in the corridors and some other artefacts went missing. Virtuoso violinist Isaac Stern formed an action group to save the hall and in April 1960, after a hard fought campaign, the City's Department of Real Estate purchased the hall from its owner, and the non-profit making Carnegie Hall Corporation was formed. The hall had only narrowly missed being demolished.

Over the next twenty years, extensive renovations were undertaken and in 1987 after nearly a year of being closed, a newly-restored Carnegie Hall was open and ready for another hundred years of performing arts. In 1987, as a direct result of a donation by Benny's family of one of his clarinets, the Carnegie Hall Corporation decided that they would build a museum, dedicated to displaying documents, photographs and interesting artefacts for visitors to enjoy. Word was spread that they were looking for interesting material relating to the Hall's exciting history. Over the next couple of years an overwhelming number of fascinating items came pouring in. So much material was gleaned that, in 1991, as part of the one hundredth birthday celebrations, the Carnegie Hall Corporation were able to open a museum within the complex to display some of the more interesting pieces. The inaugural exhibition displayed rare items of memorabilia of Peter Ilyich Tchaikovsky, who had conducted the Symphony Society Orchestra on opening night in 1891, playing one of his own works.

Goodman records on display in the Rose Museum, Carnegie Hall, for the 70th anniversary of the concert.

260 Life Magazine - September 9 1957

Of interest to BG fans will be a set of Gene's drum sticks which came from Brazil and a pair of Lionel Hampton's vibraphone mallets. The clarinet was officially presented to the Corporation on the 50th anniversary of Benny's 1938 concert by his daughter Rachel Edelson. The new museum was also given a page from an autograph book by the son of the legendary house manager in 1938, John Totten. He had collected autographs of almost all of Benny's band and had also persuaded Goodman's road manager Leonard Vannerson and band boy Pee Wee Monte to sign too. All of these items can now be seen in the Rose Museum at Carnegie Hall along with many other items of BG memorabilia.

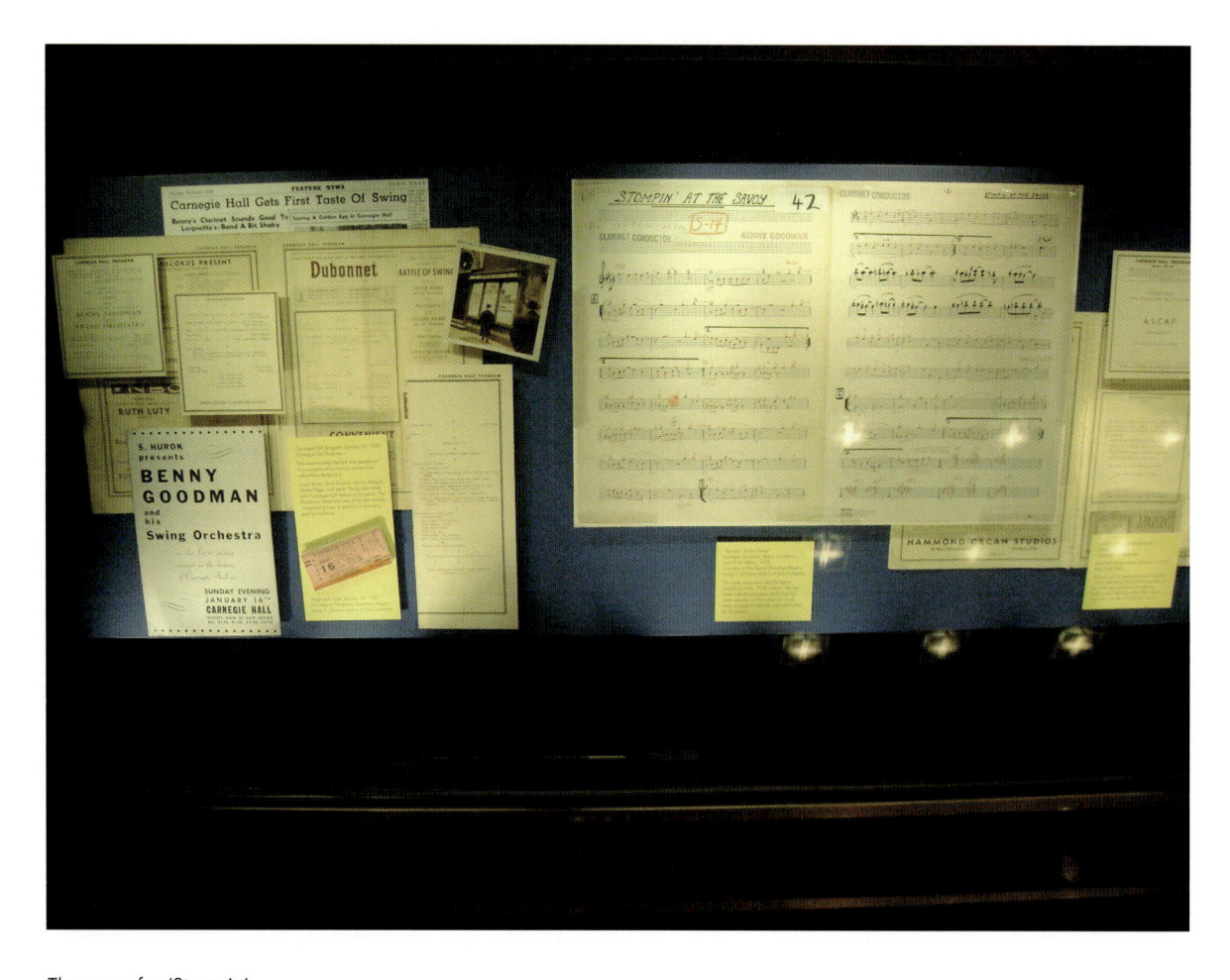

The score for 'Stompin' at the Savoy' and other artefacts on display for the 70th anniversary exhibition in Carnegie Hall's Rose Museum.

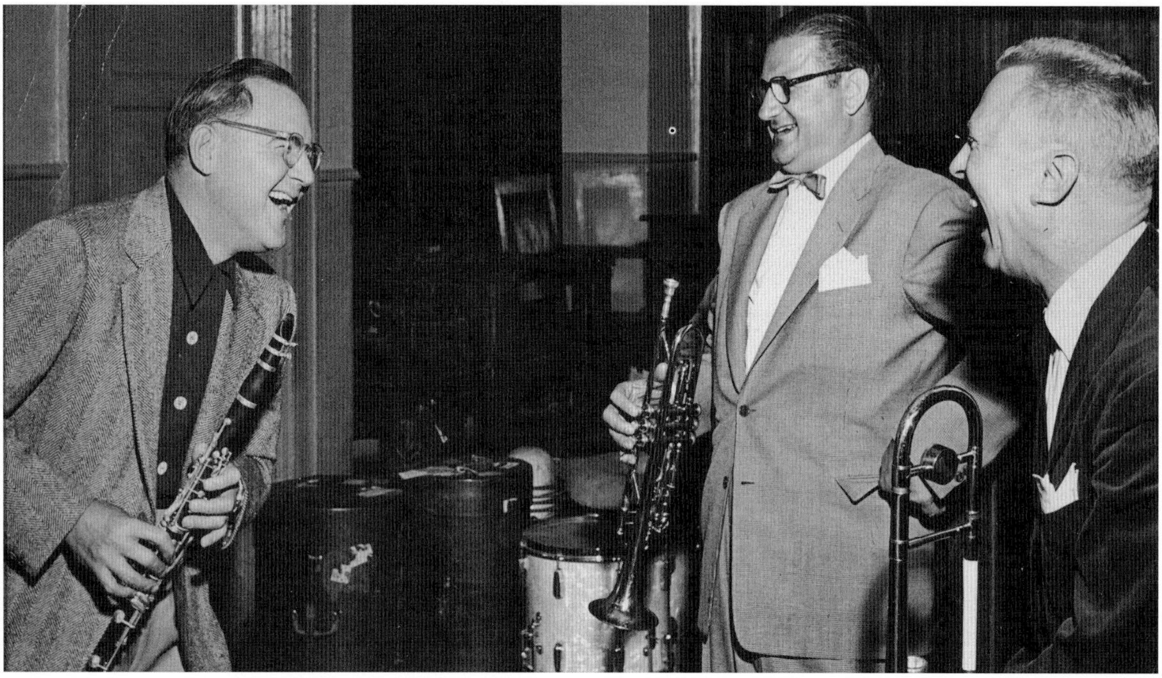

CHAPTER 19

The Recording

Since the day the records were released by Columbia in November 1950, there has been something of a mystery surrounding the recording of what has become the biggest-selling live Jazz record ever. Facts are very thin on the ground. BG's Carnegie Hall concert certainly was not the first live concert to be put onto record, that honour would probably go to Norman Granz with his 'Jazz at the Philharmonic Volume 1'.[261] That concert was recorded in 1944 and released in 1946. Incidentally, for contractual reasons, those JATP recordings featured Gene Krupa under the pseudonym of Chicago Flash! It's difficult for us to imagine now but up until 1950, the issuing of long, live concert recordings was almost inconceivable, partly because of the time limitations of the 78 record but also the intrusive nature of audience hubbub. After all, recording engineers had always worked very hard to avoid extraneous noises. To put out records which included clapping and ambient noise from the audience simply was not acceptable. So perhaps in 1950, Columbia felt it difficult or risky to acknowledge that these were not studio recordings. The early publicity material for the 'Famous Carnegie Hall Jazz Concert' said gently, in small print that it was 'recorded during the actual performance'[262], almost as if the musicians nipped out to make the records during the interval! The ease with which the record-buying public accepted these live recordings surprised everybody. So much so that when Bill Savory told Columbia that he had more of this type of material, they jumped at the chance to release it. Savory's recordings, which he had made from broadcasts during the mid-thirties, were assembled into the awkwardly named and fictitious 'Benny Goodman 1937/1938 Jazz Concert No.2'. The double album was released only two years after the Carnegie Hall recordings. Now they boasted the fact that 'this time the music was accurately balanced for the microphone by radio engineers, for these recordings were made from airchecks of late evening broadcasts'.[263] Airchecks is a name derived from checking microphones prior to broadcast.

In his autobiography published in 1977 and earlier at Benny's 30th anniversary celebration of the concert, John Hammond claimed that the Carnegie concert was recorded by Zeke Frank in his studio on the third floor of Carnegie Hall itself. We now know this not to be the case. The recording of the Carnegie Hall concert was the brainchild of Albert Marx, a young Jazz fan, promoter and entrepreneur. Albert was a

"I told Irving Kolodin that my daughter found the records in a closet"! Benny, Ziggy Elman and Vernon Brown share a joke.

---

261 Oscar Peterson by Gene Lees. P.77
262 Columbia publicity flier
263 George Avakian - Liner notes ML4591 Benny Goodman 1937-38 Jazz Concert No.2

close friend of Benny's in those days and he had recently married Helen Ward who had been Benny's singer, leaving the band in December 1936 to start a family. Up until the Columbia release of the complete concert in 1999, successive releases neglected to mention the fact that it was Albert Marx, who had arranged to have the concert recorded. Albert summed up his feelings about this oversight in 1987 at the International Association of Jazz Record Collectors (IAJRC) conference in California when he said: "All I thought was that my name might be mentioned on the back of the cover or something and it never was and it still isn't to this day."[264] Benny himself did acknowledge that Albert was responsible for the recording in an interview for the Voice of America in 1956: "A friend of mine, by the name of Albert Marx, saw me the next day [after the concert] in New York and asked me if I had an air check of the concert, I said no, I hadn't."[265] However, Albert Marx's part in this story went largely unrecognised until he was belatedly credited as the producer of the original recordings in the liner notes of the 1999 CD release produced by Phil Schaap.[266] Sadly, he didn't live to see his name on the album cover.

In 1987, as a tribute to Goodman who had recently died, the IAJRC dedicated part of their annual convention to Benny Goodman. Invited to attend a question and answer session were Martha Tilton, Jess Stacy and Albert Marx plus other Goodman alumni. Here, the knowledgeable delegates were able to probe the illustrious panel and elicit some fascinating material that, up until that time was virtually unknown. Albert Marx spoke quite passionately about the Carnegie Hall concert and how he remembered the occasion and Jess Stacy, too, was candid in his recollections not only of the concert but also his early days with BG.

The impression is often given that the recordings that were made of the concert were some sort of clandestine amateur effort done as a whim at the last minute. This is far from the case. Albert was familiar with the workings of Carnegie Hall. As a youngster, he had been sent there by his mother on Saturdays to listen to one of the co-founders of Carnegie Hall, the venerable Dr. Walter Damrosch, who gave young people's musical appreciation concerts there.[267] (Alec Templeton's lovely parody of Damrosch's classes 'The Three Little Fishes' is well worth listening to.[268]) It was not unusual at the time to hear music live from Carnegie Hall on the radio. Radio station WOR had made the first broadcasts from Carnegie Hall ten years before in 1928.[269] Indeed, the Sunday afternoon concert on January 16, given by Michele Piastro conducting and Georges Enesco, violin soloist was broadcast live.

The infrastructure for recording and broadcasting at Carnegie Hall was well established and well used. Benny had expressed no interest at all in having the concert recorded: "I've heard all that stuff as often as I want to," was how Albert recalled Benny's reaction to his request for permission to record the concert. Speaking to Whitney Balliett in 1977, Benny reasoned it like this: "In those days, I had airchecks of

264 IAJRC 1987 Conference audience recording
265 Down Beat Magazine - February 8 1956
266 The Famous Carnegie Hall Jazz Concert. Columbia C2K 65143
267 IAJRC 1987 Conference audience recording
268 Flapper CD Past 7075
269 Portrait of Carnegie Hall - Theodore Cron & Burt Goldblatt

the band made all the time - just to hear how new things sounded - and my hotel room was flooded with them. So I thought that I would skip having the concert recorded."[270] Benny had a suite of rooms in the huge Pennsylvania Hotel above the Madhattan Room where they were the resident orchestra. Nevertheless, he agreed to allow Albert to go ahead with his plan to capture the whole concert on record.

Albert Marx commissioned Harry Smith to do the technical work of recording the concert. Harry was one of the most respected independent recording engineers working in New York at the time and had been the head recording engineer at Brunswick, American and Columbia recording companies.[271] Early in 1938, Harry's recording company, 'Artists Recording Services' (sometimes known as 'Composers Recording Services') was busy promoting itself in the pages of the trade magazines. He had published a booklet called 'The Sound of Your Song' to send to prospective clients and his studio had managed to get an editorial piece in Metronome Magazine in February 1938. Since Metronome was the preferred music journal for professional musicians at that time, mention in those pages would have been quite important. According to Metronome, there was hardly an artist in the music game who had not been recorded under Harry's supervision. Metronome listed Bob Crosby, Glen Miller and Tommy Dorsey amongst his clients.[272] He had studios at 156 W44th Street, close to Times Square. Albert had worked with Harry before, at American Records. His long experience in the recording industry made him the obvious choice to record Benny's forthcoming concert.

Harry's 'Artists Recording Services' had built up a very successful business making reference recordings of the type that had littered Benny's hotel room. Band leaders and other musicians wanted to hear themselves to assess how they sounded. Harry Smith had wire feeds back to his studios from the main hotels and some out-of-the-way night spots too. This way, he could capture onto disc new arrangements or different soloists 'live' for evaluation by the band leaders later. The radio stations used these wires too and there was a symbiotic relationship here. The venues with a wire could attract bands to come to places that they would not normally consider and the booking agencies would place bands at these venues to get national radio coverage for the acts that they were promoting. Some of these jobs did not pay so well but the benefit would come through the exposure on the radio. The great lyricist, Johnny Mercer used Harry Smith to make the recordings of his appearances on the 1939 Camel Caravan radio shows with the Benny Goodman Orchestra.[273] They are very good quality recordings, often referred to as 'airchecks' but these were made from a broadcast-quality line feed and not 'off air'.

Harry Smith's recording company 'Composers Recording Service' looking for business in 1937.

---

270 The New Yorker Magazine - December 26 1977
271 Metronome Magazine - February 1938
272 Metronome Magazine - September 1937. P. 83
273 John McDonough on LP GOJ 1030

CRI 459 2M SETS-11-48 H. P.

COLUMBIA TRANSCRIPTIONS
RECORDING ORDER JOB SHEET

JOB N°. H 4149

ORDER TAKEN BY _____
PROGRAM TITLE: DUBBINGS FROM BENNY GOODMAN CARNEGIE HALL CONCERT   R WORK ORDER NO.
SCHEDULED TIME: DAY TUESDAY   DATE 12/19/50   FROM ____ TO ____
CLIENT _____   ATT. OF _____   ORDERED BY WESTON
ADDRESS _____   CUST. ORD. NO. _____   DATE _____
SALESMAN _____

PROGRAM ORIGIN	RECORD SPECIFICATIONS		DISC SIZE	
STUDIO	TO BE PROCESSED	☐	16 x 33 ☐	
C. B. S. LINE	INSTANTANEOUS REFERENCE	☐	12 x 33 ☐	12 x 78
LINE	INSTANTANEOUS REBROADCAST	☐	10 x 33 ☐	10 x 78
AIR	SAFETIES FOR RERECORDING	☐		
RERECORDING	3 records			

SPECIAL INSTRUCTIONS: Dub 2 sets of 10" 78 RPM back to back, the following tunes SOMETIME IN THE ROCKIES, ONE O'CLOCK JUMP, BODY AND SOUL, DON'T BE THAT WAY, BLUE ROOM, CHINA BOY. Be sure to leave applause in. Pls have finished by 4 p.m. and give to Benny Goodman, who will pick them up.

LABEL COPY

SHIPPING INSTRUCTIONS
2-10" D/F
2-10" S/F   Picked up as per
2-12" D/F   instructions 12/19
2-13¼" S/F

TITLES AND NUMBERS		STUDIO HOURS		RERECORDING HOURS STRAIGHT CARRYOVER		RERECORDING HOURS SPOT-SPLICE CARRYOVER		DISCS		16	12
MASTER OR SAFETY NO.	SUB. NO.	FROM	TO	FROM	TO	FROM	TO	SAFETIES	HELD IN FILE		
								MASTERS	TO BRIDGEPORT		
									HELD FOR RELEASE		
								REFERENCE	SHIPPED		
									CLIENTS DISCS RET'D		

ENGINEERS' TIME

NAME	DUTY	REGULAR HOURS	OVERTIME HOURS	TO BE BILLED
Luis P. Valentin	STUDIO ENGINEER			
Ralph Valentin	RECORDING ENGINEER			

PLAYBACK REQUEST: YES   NO   FROM ____ TO ____

BILLING RECAPITULATION

QUANTITY	DESCRIPTION	UNIT PRICE	AMOUNT

• CHAPTER 20 •

How was it recorded?

Harry had decided that in order to be sure to capture the whole concert he needed to use two disc-cutting lathes, one starting three minutes behind the other. That would give him time to set up the next machine ready for the end of the preceding disc. The disc blanks, known as 'acetates' or sometimes 'lacquers', were made of aluminium sprayed or dipped in lacquer. The lathe would cut the groove into the lacquer surface, more often than not from the centre outwards. Whilst their construction makes them virtually unbreakable, they weren't really designed to be played repeatedly. After being played about 20 times the grooves would simply wear away through to the aluminium core. Wooden or sometimes even cactus needles were used to help lengthen the life of the discs. In those days, recordings were made on 12 inch 78 rpm acetates which could only take about three and a half minutes of recorded sound. The Carnegie Hall concert takes up twenty eight sides of acetate discs!

There has been intense debate amongst BG fans about how many microphones Harry used for the recording. How could it be possible to have captured such a detailed recording using just one microphone? Irving Kolodin's original LP liner notes state that it was recorded using a single microphone hanging over the stage. According to Albert Marx, Harry Smith had said that he would use a single microphone. Annemarie Ewing, the correspondent from Down Beat Magazine, reported seeing the microphone hanging in austere silence twenty feet above the first rows of the orchestra. This microphone can be clearly seen on the Movietone Newsreel clips made during the concert[274] and in the photographs published in Rhythm Magazine in 1938.[275] However, there is another microphone in evidence on the photographs and, indeed, in the recordings and that is the public address or soloist microphone used by Martha Tilton. It seems clear that this microphone was part of the recording setup as Martha's vocal is so prominent. If you listen closely you can hear her take a breath before she starts to sing. Would this close-up detail have been picked up by a microphone hanging twenty feet above the stage? During 'Loch Lomond', Benny's singing is 'off mike' for his reluctant refrain giving us proof that Martha's mike was live. As discussed earlier, although the house sound system had failed, Martha's microphone was still working and wired to the CBS mixing desk which was located off stage on the right

Benny placed an order for some duplicate recordings of the concert on December 20th 1950, just after the records were released to the public.

274 Adventures in the Kingdom of Swing video
275 Rhythm Magazine - April 1938

hand side, behind the 'box set'. The signal was then fed back to Harry Smith's studio a few blocks down the street.

If we study the newsreel film shot that evening, we can see that in some scenes the soloist's microphone is on stage and in others it is not there. From this we could conclude that the soloist's microphone was brought onto the stage during the interval for use in the second half of the show. We can also read in Irving Kolodin's album liner notes that during Jess Stacy's solo on 'Sing, Sing, Sing' (after the intermission) 'the laughter in the background was aroused by Goodman's approving expression as he moved the (house) microphone closer to the piano'. That couldn't have been the overhead microphone, it was out of reach. We have to assume that it was Martha's microphone.

Bill Savory was the Columbia engineer who transferred the original 78 rpm acetates to tape for the LP in 1950. Bill later became a close friend of Benny's and was in the audience at the concert that night in 1938 so he was uniquely qualified for the job. He seemed to agree with Benny's long time belief that the concert was recorded using only one microphone[276] but in an interview for Ross Firestone, he suggested that the concert was probably recorded using a setup with the big diamond-shaped RCA type 44-BX hanging over the stage and at least three others.[277] This kind of arrangement was common practice in Carnegie Hall at that time where broadcasts were a regular part of the Carnegie routine, but only the overhead RCA type 44 and one other microphone are on view in the available photographs of the concert.

At this stage it might be worth taking a look at the characteristics of the RCA Velocity, 44 series microphones[278]. The first thing to say is that it could not have been recorded by using the 44 BX, as mentioned by Bill Savory because the 44-BX was not in production until the 1940s. The 44-A was introduced in 1933 and the 44-B in 1938. Since our concert was in mid-January 1938, the most likely candidate would therefore be the type 44-A which was in common use then and was the preferred microphone for broadcasting and studio use. The RCA 44 microphones were revolutionary when they were first introduced and were renowned for their beautifully big rich sound and wide frequency response. They were especially welcomed for their superb response at the lower frequencies.

In some ways the 44 series microphones typified an era. Look at any photograph from the 30's and 40's that included a microphone and it would probably be the 44. Indeed, they are so highly thought of that there are many examples of them still in use

A very nice picture of an RCA Velocity type 44 microphone. Oh yes, that's Martha posing with Benny's clarinet.

276 The Swing Era – Benny Goodman Into The Seventies. Time/Life book
277 Ross Firestone – Swing, Swing, Swing. The Life and Times of Benny Goodman. P.268
278 Instructions for Velocity Microphones Type 44-A with accessories. RCA Victor Company

today. You can even buy a new one now, as copies of this classic are again being manufactured.

The 44 is a bi-directional ribbon microphone. A ribbon microphone works by suspending a small metallic ribbon between the poles of a magnet. Sound waves reaching the ribbon vibrate it within the magnetic field and this vibration induces a minute electrical current which is then amplified to reproduce the sound where it is needed. One quality of this microphone which is important to our story is that it is bi-directional. This type of microphone will pick up sounds from left and right with equal effect but has a 'dead zone' to the back and front. It has a figure of eight footprint of sensitivity. This means that if you hang the microphone over an orchestra you will hear the musicians in the band on either side of the microphone's position but not so much of the audience out front and the reflections off the walls at the back of the stage. Reflections bounced back at a microphone can be particularly insidious because they can produce a lot of interference and distortions.

It is unlikely that Harry Smith hung the microphone over the stage himself, he was probably using a setup from a previous broadcast (that afternoon) but, it is clear that the microphone was quite obviously placed to make full use of its bi-directional qualities. A quick look at the suggested microphone placements in the Velocity instruction manual shows the ideal arrangement for a dance orchestra. The example in the manual is for a 15-piece orchestra and of course Benny's was 14 plus a vocalist. One paragraph in the manual gives us a big clue about how our concert might have

Some suggested microphone placements from the RCA Velocity manual. Figure 9 gives the arrangement for a dance orchestra.

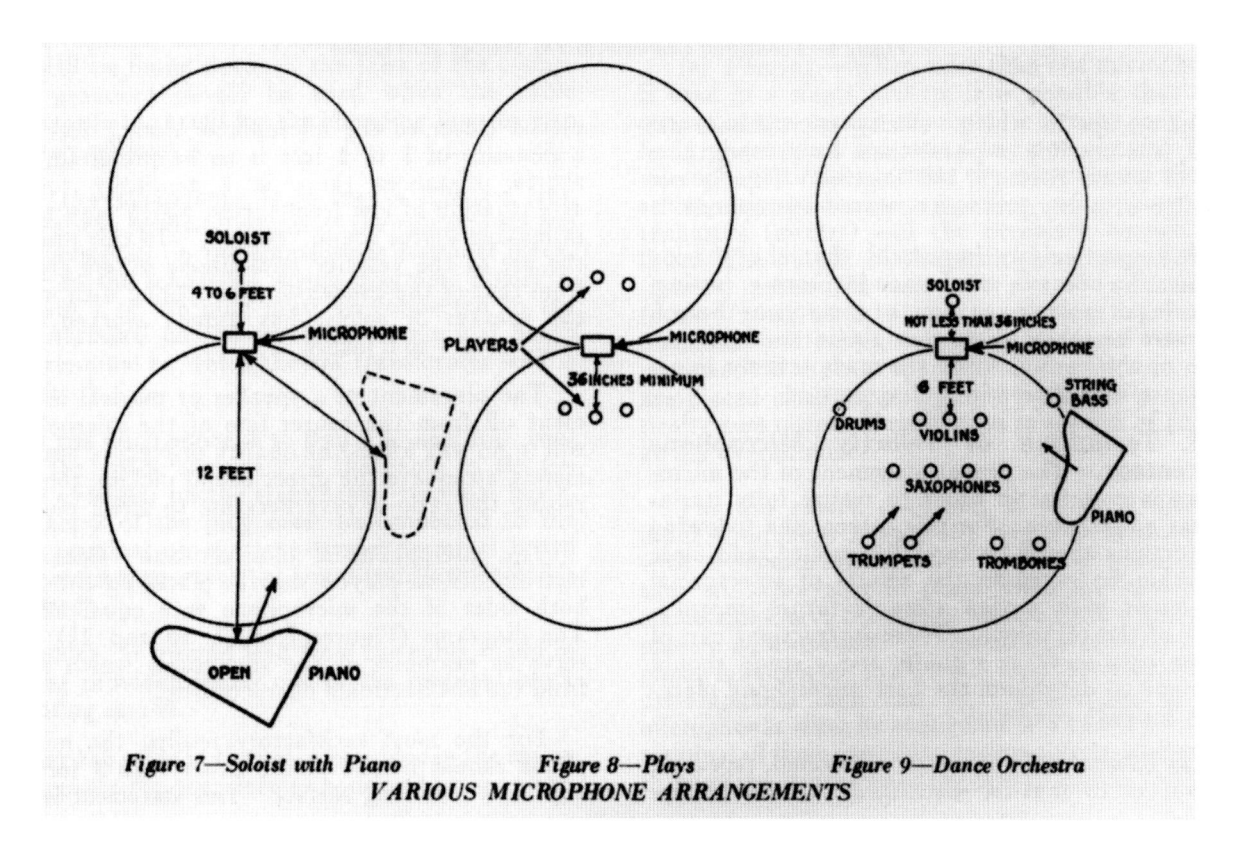

Figure 7—Soloist with Piano   *Figure 8—Plays*   *Figure 9—Dance Orchestra*
VARIOUS MICROPHONE ARRANGEMENTS

been recorded: *'Due to the fact that the artists and the announcers cannot work close to the microphone, [because it is hanging over the stage], some difficulty may be experienced in obtaining the proper balance between the artist [singer] and the orchestra. This difficulty can be overcome quite satisfactorily by using two microphones, one to pick up the orchestra and the other to pick up the artist or announcer'*. This arrangement can quite clearly be seen in stills from the newsreel footage taken that evening and also in the photographs published in Rhythm Magazine in April 1938. The Microphone used by Martha Tilton can be seen quite clearly in Lawrence Marx' photos. The Columbia CBS flag can seen on the photographs and this microphone can easily be identified as the RCA 50-A.

The Velocity instruction manual also states that additional microphones can be used for sound reinforcing. These would be placed in the wings or in the footlights. Since there were banks of seating on either side of the orchestra, if microphones were sited in the wings, they would have that stage seating in between the orchestra and the microphones. This is not an ideal situation for recording. We can just about see the lip of the stage on the photographs and there are no microphones to be seen there either. Our conclusion must be that the concert was recorded using just two microphones! On a recent visit to Carnegie Hall, I sat and listened to a wonderful concert performance given by pianist Andras Schiff. I couldn't help but notice that even today, there was just a single microphone hanging over the stage.

Shortly after the concert, Harry Smith called Albert Marx to tell him his disks were ready for collection and he gave him some wooden needles to play them with so that he would not damage the acetates. A little later, Benny called to ask if he could listen to them, Albert remembered it like this:

'Well, about a week later, I came home from work and my wife said Benny called today and asked if he could listen to the acetates and I didn't know what to say to him. I said that I didn't want anybody to have them because I don't know what will happen. Well anyway we talked about it and finally I called Benny and I said:
"Do you want to listen to the acetates"
and he said
"Yeah, I just need them for a week"
and he said he would let me have them back, well I said
"If I can have them back in a week it's a deal."
So he took the acetates and he kept them. Three months later I still didn't have them back, I had asked for them several times. Well anyway, about four or five months later I got the acetates back and I must say he never thanked me or anything and it was many years later that I discovered that Columbia was going to put them out.'[279]

It is assumed that while Benny had Harry Smith's original acetates he had them copied. Nobody knows how many copies were made but there are at least three, possibly four, sets in circulation. Although Albert Marx made no mention of it at the

[279] IAJRC Conference audience recording

Jess Stacy (left) and Albert Marx discuss the recording of the concert at the IAJRC conference in 1987.

IAJRC conference, Ross Firestone says in his book that an additional set of acetates was made by Raymond Scott, a popular Julliard-trained pianist and talented composer, conductor and electrical engineer!

Raymond Scott had established Universal Recording Inc. in New York and had risen to fame in 1937 with his eclectic quintet.[280] In a very witty and revealing article in the Wall Street Journal in January 2000, John McDonough compares the search for the original acetates for a proposed 1978 re-mastered release of the album, with the search for the 'Holy Grail'. In that article, he explained that the acetates used for the 1950 Columbia release did indeed have Universal labels and not the Harry Smith - ARS label. It could be that Harry had asked Raymond Scott to make an additional set of discs at the same time, using the same wire feed which would have been available to Raymond Scott, who had his Studios in the RCA Building. Alternatively, the Universal set were dub copies made at a later date possibly at the request of Goodman himself. To complicate matters, Benny had also ordered some more dub copies in December 1950 just after the Columbia records were first released.

However it was recorded, we cannot get away from the fact that these recordings have preserved the concert in incredible detail, despite the surface noise from the acetates. They have a great deal of presence and have captured the ambient sound of Carnegie Hall incredibly well. If you listen to other recordings from Carnegie Hall many of them have that same sound. A careful listening to Harry Smith's recordings of this concert on a good quality HiFi system, will reveal a vivid recording with complex subtleties, like the snare on Gene Krupa's drums and the continual chit-chat and banter between the musicians. There is an indefinable quality of presence and this is one of the reasons why listening to this concert is so exciting.

280 The Billboard Magazine - November 27 1937. Page 22

CRI 489 2M SETS-11-48 H.P.	**COLUMBIA TRANSCRIPTIONS**	JOB **N° H 4150**
ORDER TAKEN BY _____	**RECORDING ORDER JOB SHEET**	

PROGRAM TITLE   DUBBING AT 33 1/3 OF BENNY GOODMAN CARNEGIE HALL CONCERT   R.R. ORD.# 18623
SCHEDULED TIME: DAY WEDNESDAY   DATE 12/20/50   FROM   TO
CLIENT   ATT. OF   ORDERED BY WESTON
ADDRESS   CUST. ORD. NO.   DATE
                                                                SALESMAN

PROGRAM ORIGIN	RECORD SPECIFICATIONS		DISC SIZE		
STUDIO _____	TO BE PROCESSED	☐	16 x 33 ☐		
C.B.S. LINE _____	INSTANTANEOUS REFERENCE	☐	12 x 33 ☐	12 x 78	☐
_____ LINE _____	INSTANTANEOUS REBROADCAST	☐	10 x 33 ☐	10 x 78	☐
_____ AIR _____	SAFETIES FOR RERECORDING	☐			
RERECORDING _____					

SPECIAL INSTRUCTIONS: Cut 1 SET 33 1/3 16" transcriptions of the complete Benny Goodman Carnegie Hall Concert album. If it is convenient to cut 2 sets of this please do so. Also if at all possible please have these ready by 10 p.m. this evening.

LABEL COPY   SHIPPING INSTRUCTIONS

                                         PICKED UP BY BENNY GOODMAN

TITLES AND NUMBERS		STUDIO HOURS		RERECORDING HOURS STRAIGHT CARRYOVER		RERECORDING HOURS SPOT-SPLICE CARRYOVER		DISCS	16	12
MASTER OR SAFETY. NO.	SUB. NO.	FROM	TO	FROM	TO	FROM	TO	HELD IN FILE		
								TO BRIDGEPORT		
								HELD FOR RELEASE		
								SHIPPED		
								CLIENTS DISCS RET'D		

ENGINEERS' TIME

NAME	DUTY	REGULAR HOURS	OVERTIME HOURS	TO BE BILLED
LEE MINKLER	RECORDING ENG.			

PLAYBACK REQUEST: YES   NO   FROM   TO
BILLING RECAPITULATION

QUANTITY	DESCRIPTION	UNIT PRICE	AMOUNT

In 1997, the ubiquitous John Hammond was awarded a gold plaque by the National Academy of Arts and Sciences for having produced the Carnegie Hall concert recordings. Although Hammond had a great deal to do with Benny's early success, he had little to do with the production of these records. He had resigned from Columbia in 1946 and didn't rejoin until the early 1960s. By way of acknowledgement to the foresight of his good friend Albert Marx, Hammond passed on the award to him.

Dubbed from Instantaneous Recording of BENNY GOODMAN'S Carnegie Hall Concert

78 RPM - Start Outside
"DON'T BE THAT WAY"

Part 1

Dubbed from Instantaneous Recording of BENNY GOODMAN'S Carnegie Hall Concert

78 RPM - Start Outside
"LOCH LOMAND"

Part 16

Dubbed from Instantaneous Recording of BENNY GOODMAN'S Carnegie Hall Concert

78 RPM - Start Outside
"BLUE ROOM"

Part 17

Dubbed from Instantaneous Recording of BENNY GOODMAN'S Carnegie Hall Concert

78 RPM - Start Outside
FINALE

Part 28

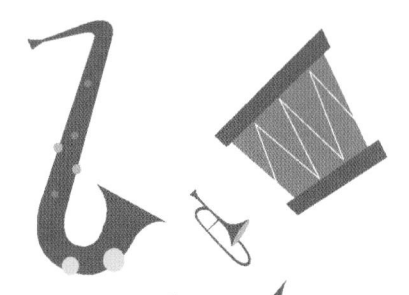

• CHAPTER 21 •

The Acetates are Re-discovered

The story of how the acetates containing the complete Carnegie Hall concert came to light has been told often, although the exact detail of the unearthing of the recordings is described in two different ways. The first version of the story is told on the LP sleeve and also in an article published in Time Magazine in 1950. Sometime in the late winter or early spring of 1950, a seven-year-old Rachael Goodman, rummaging through a closet in her family's Manhattan apartment, came across a dusty tin box of acetate records and said, "What are these Daddy?"[281] We now know this not to be true, probably the result of a mix-up with names and the PR man's love of a good story. The authentic version of their discovery was published a few years later, as part of the revival of interest in BG that came with the release of the movie 'The Benny Goodman Story'. Benny gave an extensive interview to disc jockey Willis Conover, who hosted a regular Jazz show on the 'Voice of America'. Benny told this story of how the discs re-surfaced in the interview which was broadcast on the 27th January 1958:

"You know I never knew where they were; they used to show up at the office and then at the apartment, or if I moved they would show up in the place I moved to. So about 12 years later I moved out of a place we lived in New York on 92nd St., and my sister-in-law, Mrs. Rachel Speiden, [John Hammond's elder sister. Later, re-married to become Rachel Breck] who was going to take the apartment over after I left, called me and again told me that these records were at her apartment and unless I came over to take 'em, her son, Dougie, would get ahold of them and that would be the end of the records. (LAUGHS). So I went to the apartment and collected the records and called a couple of friends of mine and asked them to go over and listen to these records. I thought it might be fun - they might be funny, after 12 years, or amusing or something. Well, we got quite a shock!"[282]

According to Benny's biographer Ross Firestone, Benny was very excited by what he heard on the fragile acetate discs and started to play them around the house. Goodman had a reputation of being rather ham-fisted with technical equipment, so his long time friend, Bill Savory suggested that he get them transferred to tape as soon as possible before they became damaged. Benny, the columnist Frank Coniff, John Hammond and Rachel Breck[283] together took the discs to Reeves Sound Studios in

Just four of the 28 sides of acetate 78's that made up the complete concert. These were commissioned by radio producer, Savington Crampton.

---
281 Time Magazine - December 4 1950. P 62
282 See Voice of America interview in Down Beat Feb 8 1956
283 Rachel Goodman-Edelson (Benny's Daughter, speech at 50th anniversary concert in Carnegie Hall 16 January 1988)

– 157 –

New York to have magnetic tape copies made.[284] Benny then used these tapes to sell the idea of issuing the concert to Columbia Records.

Reeves Studios was one of the most advanced in the city at that time, and in fact, some say its founder, Hazard 'Buzz' Reeves had invented the acetate record before the Second World War[285] When Ted Wallerstein, the President of Columbia, heard the tapes in the summer of 1950, he was struck by how good the 1938 Goodman orchestra sounded after nearly twelve years and how much the wild applause added to the atmosphere of the recordings.[286] He immediately set to work on securing the rights to the music. Wallerstein was of course very familiar with Goodman's music, he had recruited Goodman to the Victor label late in 1934 whilst he was Victor's president.[287] The legendary Columbia producer, George Avakian, was given the job of negotiating a deal with Goodman for the rights to the recordings. Avakian knew Goodman well and a deal was agreed in a very short time.

---

[284] New Yorker Magazine - December 26 1977
[285] Reading Jazz by Robert Gottlieb p235
[286] Benny Goodman / Louis Armstrong concert tour program 1953
[287] John Hammond on Record John Hammond & Irving Townsend. P.144

– The Acetates are Re-discovered –

COLUMBIA RECORDS INC.

SEVENTH AVENUE • NEW YORK 19, N. Y., U. S. A.   A SUBSIDIARY OF THE COLUMBIA BROADCASTING SYSTEM, INC.

August 1, 1950

Mr. Benny Goodman
1155 Park Ave

Dear Mr. Goodman:

The following, when signed by you and by us, will constitute a complete and binding contract between us.

You have furnished us with record matrices in the form of tape recordings of your 1938 CARNEGIE HALL JAZZ CONCERT containing sufficient recorded material to constitute two 12-inch Long Playing (LP) Microgroove records (4 sides).

You warrant and represent that you are the sole and exclusive owner of such matrices and of all matrices (disk, tape, or other) containing the same recorded performance. If requested by us, you will furnish us with any other matrices which may be outstanding.

You have paid or will pay any fees or compensation necessary to clear such matrices for use in the manufacture and sale of phonograph records.

If these matrices and the recordings contained therein meet our engineering standards and are satisfactory for the manufacture and sale of phonograph records, (1) such matrices shall become our entire property and we will manufacture and release for sale phonograph records made therefrom, and (2) you will neither manufacture nor sell phonograph records derived from such matrices nor allow anyone else to do so. In the event the matrices are not satisfactory to us they will be promptly returned to you with no further liability on our part.

We will pay you in respect of records made from such matrices a royalty of 10% of the retail list price in the country of manufacture, of 90% of all records sold embodying performances hereunder on both sides thereof, and one-half the amount of such royalty for 90% of all records sold embodying performances hereunder on only one side thereof; provided, however, that for records sold in Europe we may, from time to time, at our election, base the percentages either upon the retail list prices in the country of manufacture, or the retail list prices in England. Royalties for records sold outside of the United States are to be computed in the national currency of the country where the retail list prices above mentioned apply, and are to be payable only when such royalties

Manufacturers COLUMBIA MASTERWORKS and COLUMBIA POPULAR RECORDS

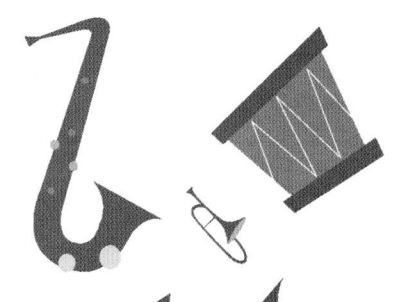

• CHAPTER 22 •

The Records

News that Benny had a set of recordings of the concert reached the public in the summer of 1950. Goodman had used the Carnegie tapes made at Reeves to help persuade Columbia to invite him back to the fold after a three year stay with Capital Records. Benny signed a new three year contract with Columbia on the 1st August and it was announced to the Press that he had returned to Columbia to record "Longhair as well as Jazz sides" and that he had brought with him the long lost Carnegie Hall recordings. The deal included the recording of 24 sides a year and the rights to issue the Carnegie Hall concert, which they released on two LP microgroove records later in the year.[288]

At the time that Albert Marx commissioned the recording of the concert, Benny Goodman was contracted to Victor and they were not happy with letting Columbia release the recordings, understandably feeling that the records should bear the Victor label. The situation could only be resolved with a court case, which went in Columbia's favour, ruling that Benny's contract with Victor only covered studio recordings and of course, Carnegie Hall was a 'live' recording.[289] Columbia had pioneered the new Long Playing format and the lengthy Carnegie concert, with its concert atmosphere and extended performances, suited this new medium perfectly.

By 1950, the concert had achieved legendary status even though the only people to have heard it were the 3000 members of the audience. With the release of the album, its legendary status would be put to the test, everyone would have a chance to form an opinion. The way was almost clear for Columbia to unleash the double album. The only thing left to resolve now was how to apportion payment to the musicians who played that night. Russell Connor provides us with the answer to that gritty problem. The artists would be paid according to how many bars that they played at the concert. Since he accompanied just about every bar of music on the program, Gene Krupa was apparently in full agreement with this method of calculation.[290]

Staff producer, Howard Scott, and research engineer, Bill Savory, were given the job of transferring the recordings from the original lacquer acetates on to tape so that the music could be cleaned up and edited. Howard Scott was a very experienced producer and had worked on Columbia's classical catalogue for their prestigious 'Masterworks' label. Howard was also an accomplished pianist who had studied at the famous

---

288 Down Beat Magazine - August 23 1950. Also: Billboard Magazine - January 27 1951 P.3
289 The Complete Benny Goodman Vol III - Liner notes by Mort Goode
290 Listen To His Legacy. D Russell Connor. P.80

Benny's contract with Columbia Records for release of the Carnegie concert, dated 1 August 1950. Signed by Benny and Ted Wallerstein, Columbia's President.

Mr. Benny Goodman   -2-

are received by us in the United States and in the dollar equivalent, at the rate of exchange at the time we receive payment.

If such matrices are satisfactory and are used, we will pay you promptly after determining that fact, the sum of $10,000.00 and such payment shall be charged against your royalties when earned. We will render an accounting to you within forty-five days after June 30th and after December 31st of each year during which records made hereunder are sold.

It is understood and agreed that we shall not be subject to any other costs, fees, charges or royalties whatever on account of the manufacture and sale of records from the above described matrices, except for the royalty specifically provided herein, and except for copyright royalties if applicable to the selections included in such matrices.

You indemnify us against claims of any kind by persons performing in the recordings contained in such matrices, and against any other claims arising out of our use of such matrices, except for copyright royalties if subject to copyright.

                                                 Very truly yours,

                                                 COLUMBIA RECORDS INC.

                                                 By _____
                                                              Executive Vice President

ACCEPTED:

_____
BENNY GOODMAN

R I D E R

This contract is subject to the approval of the American Federation of Musicians. After it is approved we will select, within sixty days, the material that we will use on the Long Playing (LP) Microgroove record. Within four months after selecting such material we will release same.

Julliard Music School in Manhattan.[291] Savory was a multi-talented physics graduate, who had studied at Harvard, he was also a musician and a close friend of Benny Goodman. In the 1930s, Bill had worked for many of the independent recording studios where he had privately recorded many other live Goodman performances that we have all come to know and love. Both Bill and Howard were part of the team that developed the Long-Playing microgroove record launched by Columbia in 1948.

Some of the difficulties Bill Savory faced in assembling the acetates into a contiguous record were explained in Ross Firestone's biography of Goodman. Savory commented about the lack of bass on the recordings and said that if he tried to lift Harry's bass, all he got was Gene's foot on the bass drum.[292] Ross Firestone also tells us that the process of cleaning up the recordings took six weeks of hard work.[293] A Press release issued by Columbia in 1999, states that the recordings were re-mastered on the 25th October 1950. If this was the date on which the job was completed, that only leaves just over two weeks for the manufacture and distribution before the LP was released on the 13th November![294]

291 New York Times - June 21 1998
292 Ross firestone
293 Swing, Swing, Swing - Ross Firestone. P.369
294 Columbia/ Legacy Press Release September 21 1999

Bill Savory, seen here fooling around in the recording studios, made the original masters of the concert for Columbia.

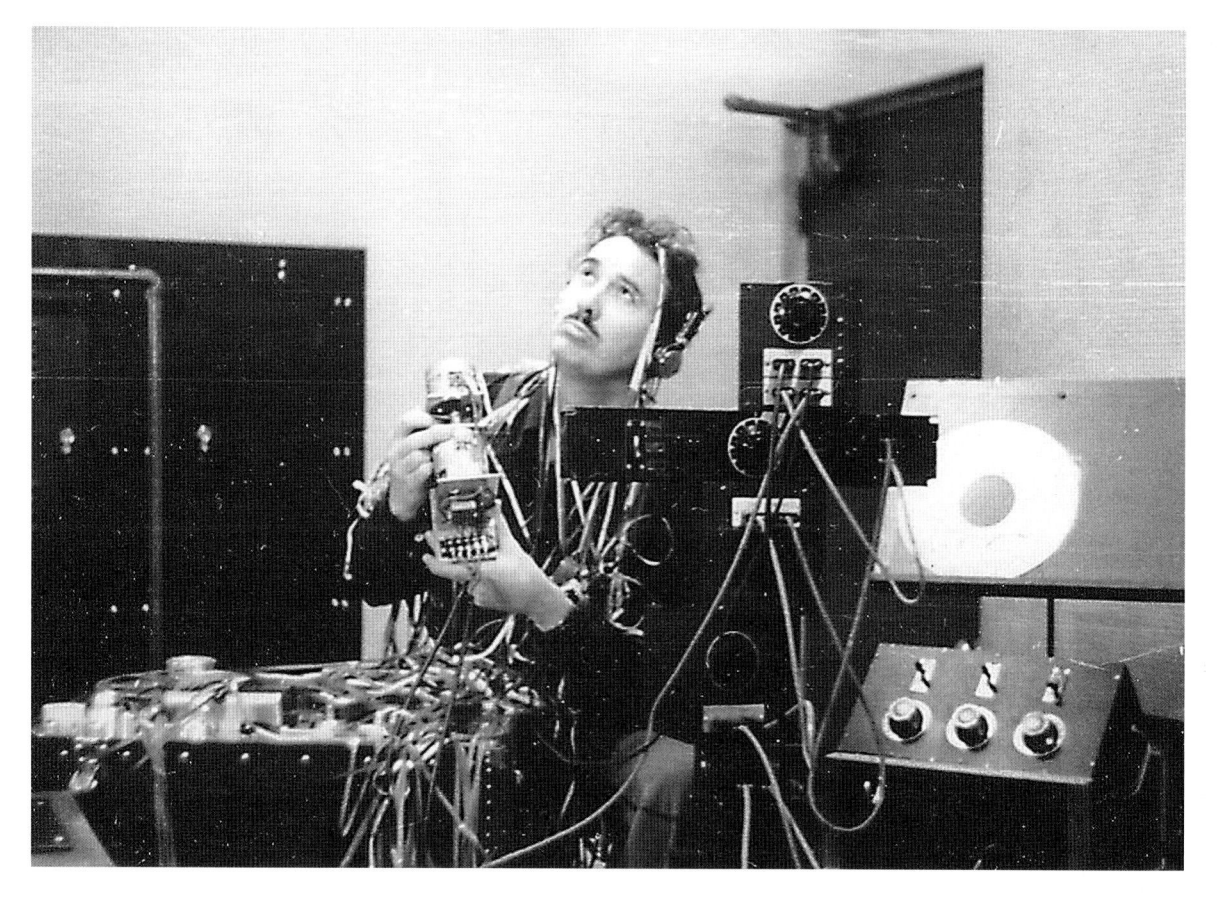

SET SL 160

BENNY GOODMAN

WITH

HARRY JAMES
COUNT BASIE
TEDDY WILSON
GENE KRUPA
LIONEL HAMPTON
COOTIE WILLIAMS
BOBBY HACKETT

AND MANY
OTHER GREAT
JAZZ ARTISTS

DON'T BE THAT WAY
ONE O'CLOCK JUMP
DIXIELAND ONE-STEP
I'M COMING VIRGINIA
WHEN MY BABY SMILES AT ME
SHINE
BLUE REVERIE
LIFE GOES TO A PARTY
STOMPIN' AT THE SAVOY
DIZZY SPELLS
SING SING SING
BIG JOHN'S SPECIAL
JAM SESSION
BODY AND SOUL
AVALON
THE MAN I LOVE
I GOT RHYTHM
BLUE SKIES
LOCH LOMOND
BLUE ROOM
SWINGTIME IN THE ROCKIES
BEI MIR BIST DU SCHON
CHINA BOY

The Famous 1938
CARNEGIE HALL *Jazz* CONCERT

LONG PLAYING — lp — MICROGROOVE **COLUMBIA** NONBREAKABLE RECORDS

• CHAPTER 23 •

The Album Design

A lot had been going on in the record industry in the intervening years between the recording of the concert in 1938 and the release of the Carnegie album in 1950. There had been a union recording ban in the USA which started in 1942 and lasted over two years and, of course, there was a world war, neither of which did much to help the record industry!

Back in December 1938, CBS Radio bought up 'American Records' who then owned the name 'Columbia Records'. William Paley at CBS put Ted Wallerstein in place as Columbia's new company president. Columbia was struggling to stay in business when Wallerstien took over and he had to make some dramatic changes to the business to keep it afloat.[295] Within a few months he had signed Goodman to the Columbia label, his name would certainly improve sales, and Benny stayed with Columbia for the next seven years. He restructured the pricing of the records, dramatically reducing the price and amongst other things, he set up a new graphics department. Wallerstein hired a young designer named Alex Steinweiss to run the art department where he was in charge of logos, letterheads and promotional material. Steinweiss and Pat Dolan, the advertising manager, came up with the idea of putting original designs on record sleeves rather than the plain generic format that all records had in those days and the record album as we know it, complete with unique eye-catching design work, was born.[296]

This simple idea worked well and improved record sales enormously. In 1942, Jim Flora was hired to share the work-load and the two designers split the work between them, Steinweiss taking the classical music side which he loved and Flora working on the jazz designs. Flora's designs are now highly regarded works of art and some of his album covers are prized by collectors regardless of the records they contain. After the war, George Avakian accepted a job on the production staff at Columbia and resumed work on the project that he had started on a part-time basis in 1940, to release some of the classic jazz recordings from a decade or so earlier. There are some classic Flora designs for record albums like 'Louis Armstrong's Hot Five' and 'Bix and Tram'. When the brief for a design for the Carnegie Hall concert came along in 1950, Jim Flora had left Columbia for a short time to live and work in Mexico, so the design work for Benny's album was done by staff designer Jim Amos whom Flora had hired in 1947.[297]

---

295 John Hammond on Record – John Hammond and Irving Townsend. P. 212
296 Irwin Cushid's interview with Jim Flora in 1998
297 Irwin Cushid's interview with Jim Flora in 1998

James Amos' well known LP cover design.

We can see Amos' signature on the album cover, but it is clear that the album design is heavily influenced by Flora's work. The stylised instruments in the background and the curly lettering are very similar to the output of Jim Flora in that period. The album designs differed from country to country. The design for the Canadian release of the Columbia album is totally different, likewise with the South American issue.

In 1953, Columbia (USA) decided not to renew its links with Columbia (UK), its affiliate in Britain, and agreed a mutual deal with the Dutch electronics giant Philips, who would handle the distribution of their records in Europe and Australia, whilst Columbia would do the same for Philips' records in the USA under the new 'Epic' label.[298] Philips' design for the Carnegie Hall LP set was re-worked for the European market although they had very similar elements: stylised cartoon instruments and a close-up photograph of Benny holding a clarinet (printed back-to-front on the British issue!) The Philips Australian release was different again, adopting a more traditional design. And so it goes on to this day, each region having its own ideas of what will make the album sell, the variations are never ending.

[298] New York Times - April 28 1953

James Amos' signature on the LP.

– The Album Design –

BENNY GOODMAN'S
"CARNEGIE HALL CONCERT"
ON
COLUMBIA RECORDS

OSL 160

Available at Your Favorite Record Shop

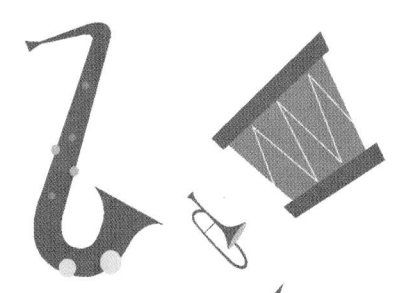

• CHAPTER 24 •

The Record is Released

The release of the album was met with somewhat indifferent reviews in the music Press. Whilst Metronome was reasonably positive, Down Beat, who had always been a strong supporter of Benny, was decidedly negative: "Too much of what has been captured on these sides are the crowd-pleasing devices, not the music which made Goodman the talk of musicians as well as musicdom." The records did get a lot of air-time on radio. Michael Levine of Down Beat quoted one disc jockey as saying "It is the greatest Jazz ever put on records."[299] In what was to be the first of a multitude of different permutations, Columbia released it on the Masterworks label as a double album SL-160, or two single albums ML 4358/9.[300]

Sales of the Carnegie Hall records went surprisingly well in the first few years, so well, that Columbia decided to release another set of live recordings, the so-called 'concert No. 2' set. Columbia, notionally celebrating BG's 25 years as a recording artist, re-issued the Carnegie Concert album in 1956, re-edited and re-mastered onto three single LP's, offering a supposedly improved sound. It was also re-packaged in a trendy double album boxed set with a photograph of Benny playing in front of a mural by the American artist Attilio Salemme. In conjunction with all of this, came a flurry of numerous selections from the concert on 7 inch singles and Extended Play 45's, some of these have well-informed liner notes written by Columbia's George Avakian. Along with the Long Playing album, Philips chose to release 'Blue Skies' and 'Swingtime in the Rockies' in Germany on a ten inch 78. This and a couple of Japanese issues of 'Sensation Rag' and 'The Man I Love' were the only commercial releases on the old 78 format.

Shortly after the record was released in November 1950, Columbia put together a set of promotional 12 inch 78's that contained six tracks from the album and spoken commentaries by BG along with a script. These short reflections on the concert were intended to be spliced into a conversation with a disc jockey, so that it would appear that they were interviewing Benny in person during a half hour program. These pre-recorded commentaries were included in Phil Schaap's 1999 'complete' CD release.

In 1956, riding a tidal wave of popularity generated by the Universal movie 'The Benny Goodman Story', RCA Victor and Columbia both reissued a plethora of

299 Down Beat Magazine - January 1951
300 Metronome Magazine - February 1951

recordings from their Goodman back catalogues. RCA Victor still had the rights to the Goodman band's recordings for that extraordinary 1937/38 period, although not the Carnegie concert itself or the 'Live' recordings. The soundtrack of the 'Benny Goodman Story' was issued on the Decca label through their association with Universal International. Capital Records had an album out too, 'BG in HiFi'. Music publishers and instrument manufactures all had their BG merchandise on display in the music magazines. These were boom times again for Benny Goodman.

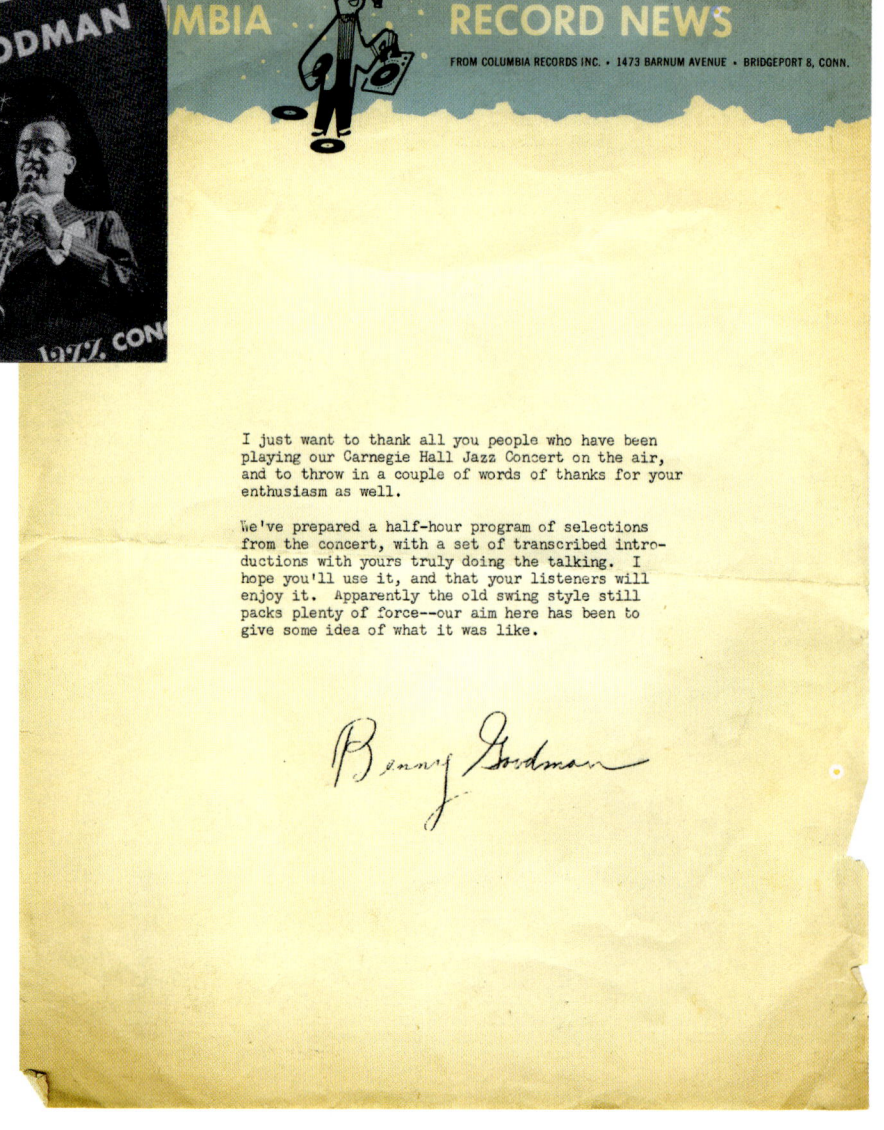

(Right) An open letter from Benny to the disc jockeys that had been playing his records. Included was a set of 78rpm records and a commentary by Goodman.

(Above) A publicity flier for the records.

I just want to thank all you people who have been playing our Carnegie Hall Jazz Concert on the air, and to throw in a couple of words of thanks for your enthusiasm as well.

We've prepared a half-hour program of selections from the concert, with a set of transcribed introductions with yours truly doing the talking. I hope you'll use it, and that your listeners will enjoy it. Apparently the old swing style still packs plenty of force—our aim here has been to give some idea of what it was like.

Benny Goodman

– The Record is Released –

(Top) The promotional 78s issued to disc jockeys along with a script used to simulate an interview with Benny.

COLUMBIA
LEGACY

FOR IMMEDIATE RELEASE   SEPTEMBER 21, 1999

BENNY GOODMAN AT CARNEGIE HALL - 1938: COMPLETE
RESTORES "THE MOST HISTORICALLY SIGNIFICANT CONCERT IN JAZZ HISTORY," WITH ORCHESTRA, TRIO, QUARTET AND JAMS WITH BASIE AND ELLINGTON BAND MEMBERS

Full-length *real-time* program is reconstructed from long lost 78 rpm acetates, now includes "Sometimes I'm Happy" (with Harry James and Art Rollini), "If Dreams Come True," and *complete* "Honeysuckle Rose" with full solos by Harry Carney, Freddie Green and Buck Clayton

Latest edition in Columbia/Legacy Jazz Masterpiece series set for November 2nd in-store date

> "The greatest truth, however, is the magical music performed that Sunday night at Carnegie Hall. Here, there are many heroes. The musicians that night defended jazz's honor as art and secured for it a permanent place in the concert hall. Had they bombed, the music might have become a lost art after jazz lost its hold in the pop field after the Swing era. Bravo BG & Company. And thank you."
> -- from the liner notes by reissue producer Phil Schaap

The night of January 16, 1938, regarded for decades as a singular turning point in the fate of jazz, is chronicled on ***BENNY GOODMAN AT CARNEGIE HALL - 1938: COMPLETE***, in which the "King Of Swing" not only broke the sound barrier at New York's venerable old concert hall but also, for the first time in history, presented racially integrated lineups of musicians in orchestra, trio and quartet settings, including guests from the **Duke Ellington** and **Count Basie** bands. First issued in truncated form on LP in 1950, the discovery of the true, original 78 rpm acetate recordings from 1938 has finally enabled the concert to be restored to its full-length *real-time* running order. This new deluxe double-CD edition, analog and digitally remastered at Sony Music Studios in New York, and with a 40-page booklet graced by rare photos and fascinating essays, is set for Novermber 2nd in-store date as part of the Jazz Masterpieces series of Columbia/Legacy, a division of Sony Music.

Today's advanced digital sound technology alone makes this edition a worthwhile investment, as well as an enlightening experience for anyone who has owned the various LP versions or even the first generation CD. Topping these sonic improvements, however, there are three

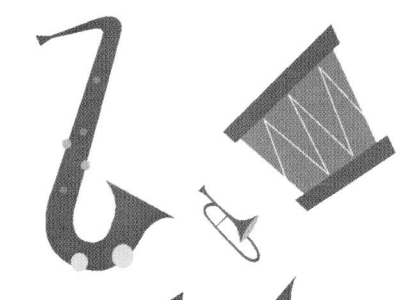

• CHAPTER 25 •

The Complete Concert for the First Time

In November 1997, the Columbia LP achieved the coveted 'Gold' status and a presentation disk was awarded by the **Recording Industry Association of America**, the RIAA. It was around this time that record producer and radio host, Phil Schaap, started work on releasing a new 'complete' version of the album. Schaap had spent a lot of time on the trail of the original acetates which had apparently gone missing from the Columbia archives. After a long search, Schaap had tracked down a folio of discs which at first, seemed to be a precious first generation set. Sadly, they turned out to be rather poor quality dubs, offering no improvement over the already issued Columbia LPs. Eventually, after the intervention of George Avakian, the original set used by Columbia in 1950 was located in the possession of Howard Scott, the producer of the Columbia LP. Goodman had given the discs to him as a gift for his outstanding work on the album.[301]

Schaap took an archaeological approach and decided to do as little as possible in the way of restoration other than removing some of the more obtrusive clicks and pops. One of the big problems in working to restore acetates discs is that they are very difficult, if not impossible, to clean. Traditional solvents used in cleaning shellac records will simply dissolve the lacquer of the acetate record. Just about the only thing that can be done to remove the debris that collects in the grooves is to wipe them with a damp cloth. Schaap had the acetates transferred to a digital format using a specially customised moving-coil cartridge and stylus, designed and custom-made for these acetates.

In preparing the recordings for release, he was also very careful to leave as much of the background crackle intact, for fear of stripping out any of the recorded ambiance. Something like 16,000 individual 'ticks' were accessed and about half of them were judged to be removable without interfering with the music's essence. This was seen by many as the wrong way to go about the process and when the much-heralded re-mastered CD was released, it was greeted with consternation in some quarters.

The other task was to set the correct pitch for each disc. The fact that the original acetates were cut on two different machines, means that the playback speeds would

The Columbia/Legacy press release announcing the forthcoming 'complete' concert re-mastered by Phil Schaap.

301 Wall Street Journal - John McDonough – 12 January 2000

be slightly different and this would change the pitch of the music if it were played back at a different speed from the original. Each of Harry Smith's two recording machines has a distinctive sound too, so when the sequence of discs was assembled into a continuous recording by Bill Savory in 1950, the difference between the two machines was very apparent. One of the recorders seems to have a more rounded sound than the other and so the set of acetates are alternately not so good. In some places there is a distinct lurch between the discs where they are spliced together. It also appears that each of the recorded discs was attenuated just after they start. We can sometimes hear a change in volume just after each new disc begins. Yet another complication was that nearly all of the tunes played at the concert were longer than one side of an acetate disc. The result was that most of the tunes span more than one disc. Schaap's team had the difficult job of making all of these transitions seamless and in spite of all these obstacles have produced a very consistent sound throughout the CD.

The most wonderful thing about Schaap's restoration however, is that now, for the first time, we were able hear the whole concert in 'real time' exactly as it happened. This can be verified by comparing Phil Schaap's version to the Savington Crampton early dubs (see the description in the 'Honeysuckle Rose' section) where the gaps between tunes are the same length. The only differences are that the Crampton set has an extra few notes of Buck Clayton's solo in the jam session and at the start of the concert, where the Crampton set has a slightly longer section of audience 'hub-bub' before the band starts to play 'Don't Be That Way'.

Schaap and his team had re-edited the whole concert, removing some of the slightly clumsy and abrupt transitions between tracks and including all of the applause and audience ambiance that was excised from the original 1950 release. Many people have now used the Schaap re-issue to produce their own 'cleaned up' versions of the concert and there are now a variety of so-called restored issues to choose from, many claiming sometimes rather ambiguously, to be new versions.

In archaeological conservation and historical sound renovation, much damage has been done in the name of 'restoration'. We have all heard 'restored' vintage recordings which have a horrible treacly veiled quality achieved with the over-use of computerised aids. It is said by some that the original Columbia LP release, engineered by Howard Scott and Bill Savory has a greater dynamic range and more bass than the CD issue. Maybe the acetates had deteriorated over the intervening years or maybe the more extended range in the upper region has overpowered the same amount of the bass that was present on the earlier issues. It is a tribute to Benny's band that the concert sounds as good as it does on these recordings. The best bands are always well balanced, the better the band the easier it is to record. We must acknowledge here the fine work that Phil Schaap has done on his 1999 CD re-issue of the complete concert.

– The Complete Concert for the First Time –

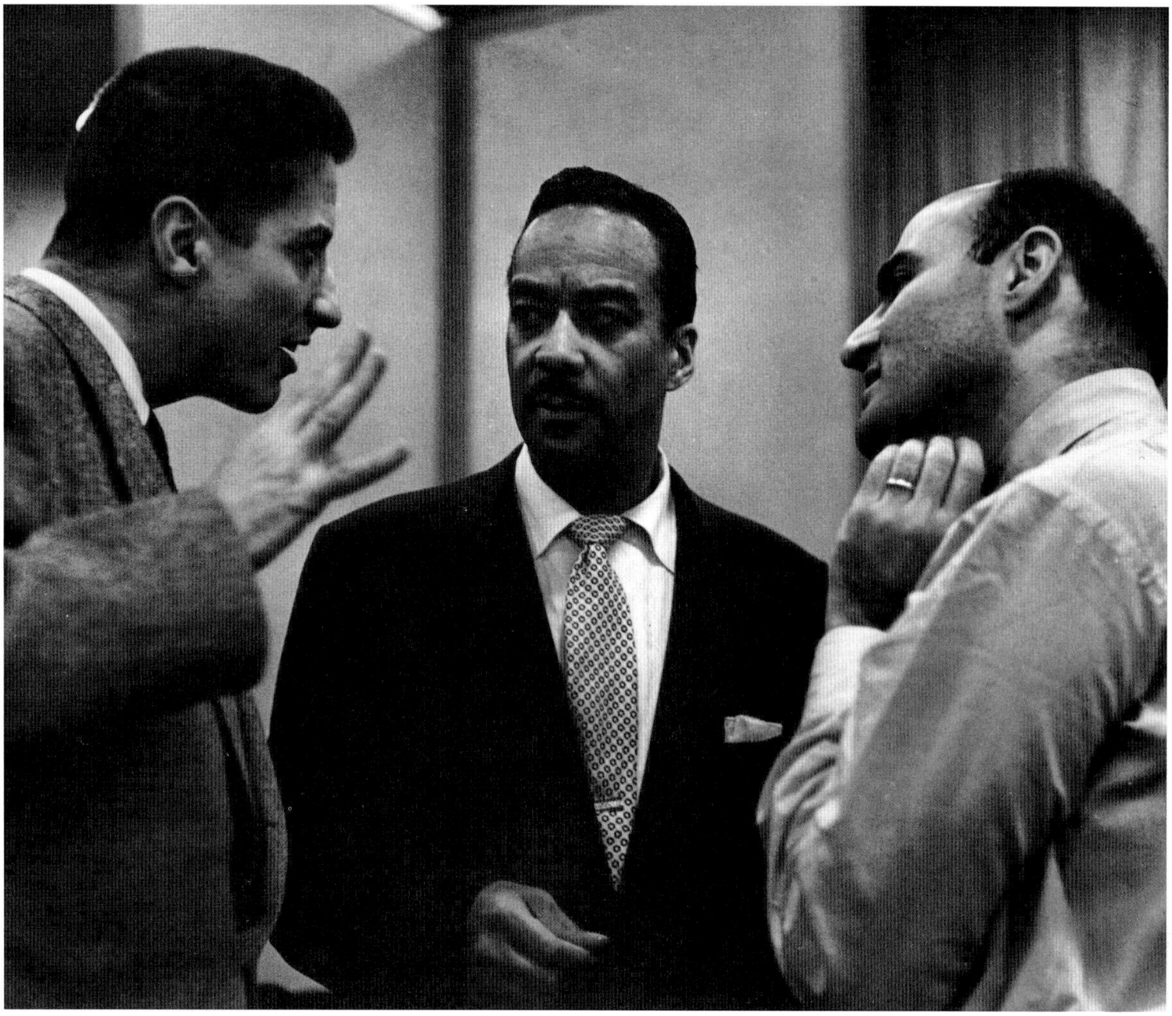

• CHAPTER 26 •

What Next?

That is the story of the 'The Famous 1938 Carnegie Hall Jazz Concert', a remarkable concert that we can all relive, thanks to the foresight of Albert Marx and the technical skill and ingenuity of Harry Smith. It was clear in 1938 that the concert was a big success. The band was riding high but where do you go after Carnegie Hall? For the next couple of months they stayed in the New York area and seemed to carry on in the same routine, we cannot help feeling that this must have been an anticlimax for all of them. Some of the success of the Carnegie Hall concert must be attributed to the guest musicians and not solely to the BG band. Those guest stars were only there for that one evening and had long since gone back to their own bands.

Benny always considered his Carnegie band to be his greatest, but the pressure of touring started to take its toll on them. It is difficult to believe that they were only together in that exact permutation for three months and they had only managed to record three sides together in the studio: 'Bie Mir Bist Du Shoen', 'Don't Be That Way' and 'One O'Clock Jump'. Fortunately, there are quite a few live recordings available of the 'Carnegie band'.

After some very public bickering on stage at the Earle Theatre in Philadelphia, on March 3, Gene Krupa left the band, a move that was widely rumoured. This resulted in an avalanche of lurid headlines and Press speculation about the reasons for the split and the relationship between Goodman, the consummate musician and Krupa, the exuberant showman! Gene quickly assembled a new band and was immediately signed to Brunswick Records. Within a few days, two more long serving members of BG's Carnegie orchestra, George Koenig and Allan Reuss also decided to call it a day. Benny brought in Bud Freeman on tenor saxophone, Dave Tough on drums and guitarist, Ben Heller.

A change of direction for Benny came in April 1938 when he made his first classical recording. John Hammond was a keen amateur viola-player and close friend of Alexander Schneider, a violinist with the Budapest String quartet, and it was Hammond who persuaded them to join forces with BG and make their first American recording. On April 25 1938, Benny recorded Mozart's Clarinet Quintet with the Budapest String Quartet, the same piece that he had played live on air two days after the Carnegie concert with the Coolidge String Quartet.

A couple of days later, Benny tried to recapture the magic of Carnegie Hall with a concert at the Symphony Hall in Boston, with disastrous results. The choice of music

Benny Goodman's brother-in-law, John Hammond with trumpeter Buck Clayton and record producer George Avakian, photographed in 1953 at the Columbia studios. All three contributed to the success of the Carnegie Hall album.

was very much the same as the Carnegie Hall program.[302] Bobby Hackett was on hand again and according to George Frazier he played very well, but it is not clear whether Benny had any other guests that night.[303] The big problem in Boston was not the band, but the audience. They were so rowdy that the noise made it impossible for the band to hear themselves play. On a couple of occasions, Benny had to stop the performance and plead with the audience to quieten down.[304]

On July 13 1938, Benny set sail for England for a 3-week vacation, his first for 3 years. Leaving his band behind, his intention was to find more music for himself and the Budapest String quartet to perform, on record and in concert. On his last Camel Caravan show before he left, Benny said the he would be listening-in while he was away. Whilst in England, he met up with the virtuoso violinist, Joseph Szigeti.[305] Szigeti and Goodman knew each other well and it was Szigeti who suggested the he commission Béla Bartók to write a piece especially for the three of them. Benny Goodman underwrote the project financially and Bartók completed the work 'Contrasts' by the end of September.[306] It was reported in Melody Maker that Szigeti was due to perform at Carnegie Hall that winter and Goodman would probably join him there.[307]

On August 3, the day after he got back to New York, Goodman had another go at a Carnegie-type concert in Chicago's Rayinia Park, with indifferent results.[308] In his continuing attempt to go 'up-market', in November 1938, Goodman and the band started an 8-week gig at the auspicious Empire Room at the Waldorf Astoria Hotel in New York. There is an unusual photograph in Collier's Magazine in February 1939. It is a relatively rare colour shot of the Goodman orchestra at the New Year's Eve party there. The suave guests looked very different from the usual young jitterbug crowd. An article under Benny's name appeared in Stage Magazine in November claiming this was the first time a Swing Band had had an engagement in Park Avenue.[309]

To start 1939 off in a similar manner to 1938, the day after Goodman finished at the Waldorf, he played at Carnegie Hall with Joseph Szigeti, playing a world premier of Béla Bartók's new work, 'Contrasts'. On that occasion Endri Petri played piano although Goodman and Szigeti did record the piece together with Bartók in 1940.

Where do you go after Carnegie Hall? You go back to Carnegie Hall of course! Benny played Carnegie Hall three times in 1939, and over his long career he walked out on to that famous stage 25 times in all. Appendix 2 lists all of Benny's concerts there.

---

302 IAJRC Journal – Audience recording
303 Down Beat Magazine - June 1938. P.4
304 Collier's Magazine - February 25 1939
305 Melody Maker - September 24 1938
306 Joseph Szigeti - With Strings Attached. P.127
307 Melody Maker - September 24 1938
308 D. Russell Conner - Listen to His Legacy. P.89
309 Stage Magazine - November 1938

When Benny moved into The Victor Hugo restaurant in Beverly Hills, they used his Carnegie Hall appearance as proof of his status. It was at the Victor Hugo that Benny first played with Charlie Christian in 1939.

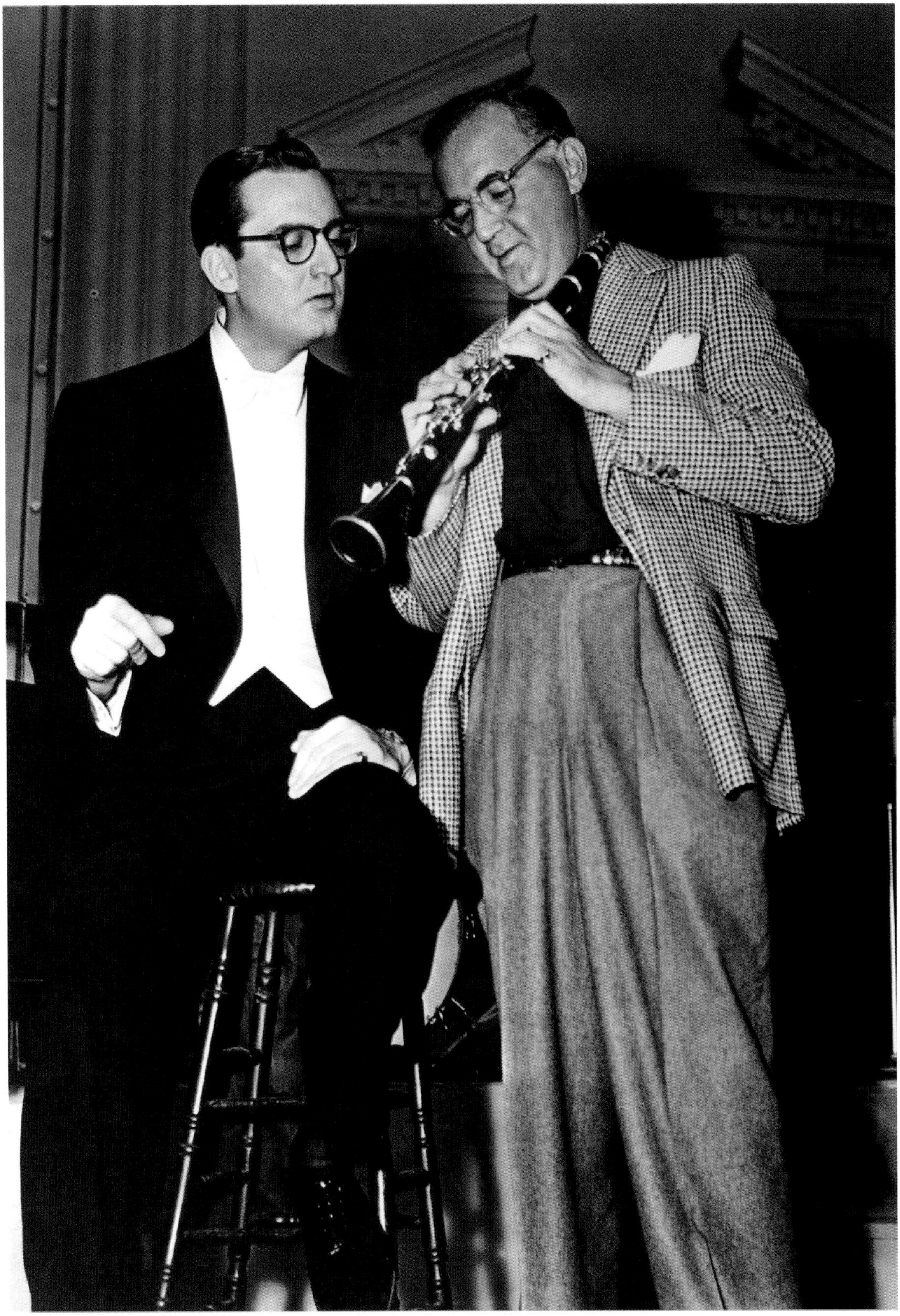

• CHAPTER 27 •

The Anniversaries

1948 Ten years have passed and the concert has yet to be released on record, Benny's appearances on the Camel Caravan shows, the antics of the young fans and the 'Killer Dillers' are all just a distant memory. Russ Connor says in his discography that little is known of Benny's movements for early 1948, we do know that he was in California in February where he met the young Swedish clarinettist Stan Hasselgard. In April 1948, Metronome ran a story saying that Benny had itchy fingers and was planning to get back into the band business. The article reported that he was out to prove that he could still play the clarinet and that he was not as old fashioned as some people thought… On May 10th 1948, Benny took a new 'Bop' septet into Carnegie Hall for a concert: Stan Hasselgard, Clarinet; Wardell Gray, Tenor Saxophone; Teddy Wilson, Piano; Joe Bushkin, Piano; Jonah Jones, Trumpet; Morey Feld, Drums; Fred Robbins, Host.[310] Unfortunately, no recording of the concert has come to light.

1958 Twenty years have now elapsed and Benny's landmark debut at Carnegie Hall was now well established as part of the swing era folklore, due in the main to the overwhelming popularity of the recordings. Plans were made to celebrate the twentieth anniversary with a concert which was to be televised. Benny wanted to bring Harry James back to his band for the night but Harry was unsure. Harry was now a big star with his own band and reluctant to rekindle his relationship with Benny unless it was financially worth his while. The two of them were unable to reach an agreement and the concert was called off.[311] Benny did however give a short interview to William B Williams of radio station WNEW in which he recalls his attempts to buy tickets on the black market for his family. He also re-tells the story of how the acetates were found in his sister-in-law's apartment.

1968 Thirty years, and nostalgia for the concert is building! Benny decides to throw a party in his Manhattan apartment on January 16 and invites as many of the old gang as he can muster, most of the band respond positively along with Sol Hurok and John Hammond.[312] William B Williams was on hand again and interviewed many of the guests for his radio program a few days later. Portions of his conversations were put onto an LP issued privately by WNEW. Russell Connor was there with his tape recorder

"You stick your fingers in these holes and blow in the pointed end and jazz comes out here"! Benny gives Steve Allen a clarinet lesson on the 'Carnegie Hall' set for the Hollywood film 'The Benny Goodman Story'.

---

310 Carnegie Hall Archives
311 Trumpet Blues:- The Life of Harry James - Peter Levinson. P.207
312 Down Beat Magazine. - March 7 1968 - John McDonough

and taped Benny, Jess, Gene, Lionel and Ruby Braff jamming together, portions of that session were filmed too. From an historical point of view, Williams' tapes do not contain much new information. Nevertheless, it is interesting to hear Martha's recollections of her faulty microphone and Sol Hurok's thick accent!

1978 Benny plays a concert at Carnegie to celebrate the fortieth anniversary which, by all accounts was poorly received. The band were not properly rehearsed and ill-prepared, they lacked the experience gained through long months on the road. Although there were absolutely top class musicians on hand, they did not get a real chance to play in a relaxed way. The performance was also dogged by sound problems. It is suggested that Benny was more interested in the fact that the concert was to be recorded for an LP release and neglected the audience in Carnegie Hall that night.[313]

1988 Benny Goodman died in 1986. The honour of celebrating the 50th fell to talented clarinet and soprano sax player Bob Wilber who presented a re-creation of the concert at Carnegie Hall. Bob was a member of Benny's orchestra in the late fifties and had made arrangements for Benny too. During the concert, Benny's daughter Rachel Goodman-Edelson, came on stage and presented Isaac Stern with one of her father's clarinets which would be given a permanent home in the Carnegie Hall museum. (Stern was the driving force behind the 'rescue' of Carnegie Hall when it was threatened with demolition in the late fifties.) Rachel also told the true story of how the set of acetates was rediscovered by her auntie, Rachel Breck. Rachel Breck was the sister of John Hammond and Alice, Benny's wife. She was close to her sister, in fact she was the only guest at Alice and Benny's wedding in 1942.[314] She was at the concert in 1938 and also at the 1988 anniversary concert. Benny's brother, bass-player Harry Goodman had come over from England to be in the audience for the concert in 1988.[315] On stage were Lionel Hampton, Martha Tilton and several other musicians who had played in Goodman's bands over the years: Doc Cheatham, Al Grey, Buddy Tate, John Bunch and Panama Francis.

1998 On January 16, 1998 a re-creation of the concert was performed at the Ellington School of the Arts in Washington, DC by the New Columbia Swing Orchestra under the direction of Burnett Thompson.

2008 Canadian clarinettist, Bob DeAngelis along with a 40 piece orchestra came to Carnegie Hall and performed their tribute to Benny Goodman's concert 70 years before, 'Coronation of a King'. Also at Carnegie Hall in 2008, archivist Gino Francesconi exhibited a collection of artefacts associated with Goodman's various performances at the Hall.

---

313 Down Beat Magazine - June 1 1978
314 The producer John Hammond and the Soul of American Music. - Dunstan Prial. P.161
315 IAJRC - John McDonough - Jan 2007

only on Columbia 33⅓ (Lp) Records the famous

Benny Goodman

Carnegie Hall Jazz Concert

Recorded During the Actual Performance—January 16, 1938
23 classic selections featuring a veritable Who's Who of American Jazz!

VOLUME I

Don't Be That Way • One O'Clock Jump • Dixieland One-Step • I'm Coming Virginia • When My Baby Smiles At Me • Shine • Blue Reverie • Life Goes To A Party • Jam Session • Body and Soul • Avalon • The Man I Love

Columbia LP Record ML 4358

VOLUME II

I Got Rhythm • Blue Skies • Loch Lomond • Blue Room • Swingtime In The Rockies • Bei Mir Bist Du Schön • China Boy • Stompin' At The Savoy • Dizzy Spells • Sing Sing Sing (With a Swing) • (Parts I and II) • Big John's Special

Columbia LP Record ML 4359

Both Volumes—Set SL-160

Benny Goodman and his Orchestra with Harry James, Ziggy Elman, Jess Stacy, Gene Krupa, Count Basie, Teddy Wilson, Lionel Hampton, Bobby Hackett, Johnny Hodges, Harry Carney, Cootie Williams, Freddy Green, Walter Page, Lester Young, Buck Clayton, Martha Tilton and many, many other celebrated stars.

ORDER TODAY!

Columbia Records

First, Finest, Foremost in Recorded Music

Bibliography

A Different Era. (1950, December 4). Time Magazine , pp. 62-63.

Alkyer, F. (1995). Down Beat: 60 Years of Jazz. Milwaukee: Hal Leonard.

Allen, W. C. (1973). Hendersonia: The Music of Fletcher Henderson and his Muscians. Highland Park N.J: Walter C Allen.

Avakian, G. (1955?). Jam Session on 'Honeysuckle Rose' Liner notes. Columbia 45 EP A-1788 .

Avakian, G. (1955?). Sing Sing Sing. Liner notes. Columbia 45 EP A-1677 .

Balliett, W. (1977, December 26). Our Local Correspondents. The New Yorker , pp. 33-41.

Baron, S. (1979). Benny, King of Swing. London: Thames and Hudson.

Basie, C. M. (1986). Good Morning Blues. London: William Heinemann.

Bergreen, L. (1990). As Thousands Cheer - The Life Of Irving Berlin. London: Hodder and Stoughton.

Brun, H. O. (1961). The Story of The Original Dixieland Jazz Band. London: Sigwick and Jackson.

Chusid, I., & Economon, B. (2007). The Curiously Sinister Art of Jim Flora. Seatle: Fantagraphics Books.

Clayton, B. (1986). Buck Clayton's Jazz World. London: The Macmillon Press.

Coller, D. (1997). Jess Stacy, The Quiet Man Of Jazz. New Orleans: Jazzology Press.

Collier, J. L. (1989). Benny Goodman and the Swing Era. New York: Oxford University Press.

Collier, J. L. (1987). Duke Ellington: The Life and Times of the Restless Genius of Jazz. Michel Joseph Limited.

Condon, E. (1947). We Called it Music. New York: H Holt.

Connor, D. R. (1988). Benny Goodman, Listen to his Legacy. Lanham, Maryland: Scaercrow Books.

Connor, D. R. (1996). Benny Goodman, Wrappin' It Up. Lanham, Maryland: Scarecrow books.

Connor, D. R. (1958). BG - Off The Rocord. Fairless Hills, Pennsylvannia: Gaildonna Publishers.

Convention Report. (1987, October). IAJRC Journal .

Cron, T. O., & Goldblatt, B. (1966). Portrait Of Carnegie Hall. New York: The Macmillan Company.

Columbia records announces the release of the double album in Down Beat magazine in 1951.

Crowther, B. (1988). Benny Goodman. London: Apollo Press Limited.

Dance, S. (1971). The Night People: The Jazz Life of Dicky Wells. Washington: Smithsonian Institution Press.

Dance, S. (1980). The World of Count Basie. New York: C Scribner's Sons.

Dance, S. (1970). The World of Duke Ellington. De Capo Press.

Dance, S. (1974). The World of Swing. New York: C. Scribner's Sons.

Farrell, B. (1972). The Swing Era - Benny Goodman Into the 70's. New York: Time-Life Records.

Feather, L. (1988). The Jazz Years: Eyewitness to an Era. London: Pan Books.

Ferguson, O., & Cowley, M. (1997). In The Spirit of Jazz - The Otis Ferguson Reader. De Capo Press Inc.

Firestone, R. (1993). Swing, Swing, Swing. London: Hodder and Stoughton.

Frazier, G. (1968, June). Take Thirty. Esquire Magazine , pp. 97-99.

Goodman, B. (1938, September 27). Give Swing a Chance. Look Magazine , pp. 27-31.

Goodman, B. (1938, May). Jam Session. Pictorial Review , pp. 15, 59.

Goodman, B. (1939, February 25). Now Take The Jitterbug. Collier's Magazine , pp. 11-13 60.

Goodman, B. (1938, November). Swing It, Mrs Vanastor, Swing It! Stage Magazine , pp. 26-27.

Goodman, B. (1938, May 14). What Swing Really Does To People. Liberty Magazine, pp. 6-7.

Goodman, B., & Gehman, R. (1956, January 20). That Old Gang of Mine. Esquire Magazine , pp. 26-31.

Goodman, B., & Kolodin, I. (1939). The Kingdom of Swing. The Stackpole Company.

Gottlieb, R. (1997). Reading Jazz. London: Bloomsbury Publishing Plc.

Hammond, J., & Townsend, I. (1977). John Hammond on Record. Ridge Press/Summit Books.

Hampton, L., & Haskins, J. (1989). Hamp: An Autobiography. London: Robson Books.

Hardy, R. (1937, November 1). Life Goes To A Party. Life Magazine , pp. 120-124.

Hurok, S., & Goode, R. (1946). Impressario. New York: Random House.

Joint Rocked. (1938, January 24). Time Magazine , pp. 58-59.

Jones, H. (1999). Bobby Hackett - A Bio-Discography. Greenood Press.

Jones, M. (1987). Talking Jazz. London: Macmillan Press.

Kappler, F. K., & Simon, G. T. (1979). Benny Goodman. Alexandria, Virginia: Time-Life Records.

Keller, K. (1989). Oh, Jess! A Jazz Life. New York: Mayan Music Corporation.

Lees, G. (1988). Oscar Peterson: The Will to Swing. Toronto: Lester & Orpen Dennys Limited.

Levinson, P. J. (1999). Trumpet Blues; The Life of Harry James. New York: Oxford University Press.

Libby, T. W. (1994). Carnegie Hall. New York: Carnegie Hall Corporation.

MacCarthy, A. (1974). Big Band Jazz. London: Barrie & Jenkins Limited.

Bibliography

Magee, J. (2005). The Uncrowned King of Swing: Fletcher Henderson and Big Band Jazz. New York: Oxford University Press.

Marmonstein, G. (2007). The Lable; The Story of Columbia Records. New York: Avalon Publishing Inc.

McCalla, J. (1982). Jazz: A Listener's Guide. Prentice-Hall Inc.

McDonough, J. (2006, December). Benny Goodman at Carnegie. IAJRC Journal , pp. 29-40.

Norris, F. (1938, May 7). Killer-Diller: The Life and Four-Four Times of Benny Goodman. Saturday Evening Post .

Prial, D. (2006). The Producer: John Hammond and the Soul of Amercian Music. New York: Farrar, Staus and Giroux.

Robinson, H. (1994). The Last Impresario: The Life, Times and Lagacy of Sol Hurok. New York: Viking.

Rollini, A. (1987). Thirty Years With The Big Bands. London: The Macmillon Press.

Schickel, R. (1987). Carnegie Hall - The First 100 Years. New York: Harry N Abrams Inc.

Schickel, R. (1961). The World of Carnegie Hall. Greenwood Press.

Scholl, W. W. (1939, March). Goodman's Three Survivors. Rhythm , pp. 105 - 113.

Schuller, G. (1989). The Swing Era. New York: Oxford University Press.

Shapiro, N., & Hentoff, N. (1955). Hear Mr Talkin' to Ya. New York: Holt, Rinehart & Wilson Inc.

Shaw, A. (1945). Gene Krupa. New York: Pin-Up Press.

Sheridan, C. (1986). Count Basie - A Bio-Discography. New York: Greenwood Press.

Simon, G. T. (1971). Simon Says: The Sights and Sound of the Swing Era 1935 - 1955. New York: Galahad Books.

Simon, G. (1968). The Big Bands. Macmillon.

Singer, B. (2001, April). How Did Benny Goodman Get to Carnegie Hall. American History , pp. 22-28.

Stearns, M. W. (1956). the History of Jazz. New York: Oxford University Press.

Steinweiss, A., & McKnight-Trontz, J. (2000). For The Record - The Life and Work of Alex Steinweiss. New York: Princeton Architectural Press.

Sudhalter, R. M. (1981, October/November). American Hertage Magazine , pp. 5-13.

Sudhalter, R. M. (1999). Lost Chords. New York: Oxford University Press.

Szigeti, J. (1949). With Strings Attached. London: Cassel & Co.

Tracy, S. (1995). Bands, Booze and Broads. Edinburgh: Mainstream Publishing Company.

Vache, W. W. (2005). Sittin' In with Chris Griffin. Lanham, Maryland: Scarecrow Press.

Vail, K. (2005). Swing Era Scrap Book. The Teenage Diaries & Radio Logs of Bob Inman. Lanham, Maryland: Scarecrow Books.

Ward, G. C., & Burns, K. (2000). Jazz: A history of America's Music. New York: Alfred A Knopf.

William Savory - In Memoriam. (December 2004). Journal of Audio Engineering , 1297.

Wilson, T., Ligthart, A., & Van Loo, H. (1996). Teddy Wilson Talks Jazz. New York: Bayou Press.

Various issues of the following magazines and journals as cited in the text:

American Heritage Magazine
American History Magazine
Collier's Magazine
Down Beat Magazine
Dream World – Love and Romance Magazine
Esquire Magazine
Harpers Magazine
IAJRC Journal
Jazz Rambler
Liberty Magazine
Life Magazine
Look Magazine
Melody Maker
Metronome Magazine
Pictorial Review
Rhythm Magazine
Saturday Evening Post
Stage Magazine
Storyville Magazine
Tempo – The Modern Music Magazine
The Billboard Magazine
The Etude
The New Yorker
The Radio Guide
Radio Mirror
The Ray
Time Magazine
Variety Magazine
The New Republic Magazine

Newspapers:

Amsterdam Daily News
Brooklyn Daily Eagle
New York Herald Tribune
New York Mirror
New York Daily Post
New York Times
New York WorldTelegram
Sarasota Herald-Tribune

The Daily News
The New York Sun
Wall Street Journal
The Citizen Advertiser, Auburn NY
Palladium Times

Other sources:
Yale University Music Library Archival Collection. MSS 53
Legacy Press Release - 21 September 1999.
Legacy DVD – Benny Goodman: Adventures in the Kingdom of Swing.
Columbia Records Inc. Contract with Goodman for the rights to the music, 1st August 1950. Courtesy of the Estate of Benny Goodman.
Columbia Records Inc. Promotional flier 1950. 'The Most Exciting Record Event of the Year'.
Columbia Records Inc. Promotional 78 records and radio scripts.
Columbia Records Inc. Benny Goodman's 25th anniversary booklet.
Operating Instructions for the RCA Velocity Microphone (1938).
The Art of recording the big band. - Robert Auld
R J Reynolds – Swing School radio scripts. www.tobaccodocuments.org
R J Reynolds – Promotional booklet 'This Thing Called Swing'.
16mm Newsreel film of Carnegie Hall Concert. From the author's collection.
Warner Brothers DVD - Hollywood Hotel

The following liner notes were referred to in the text:

Title	Label	Catalogue No.	Date
Bach Goes To Town – The Genius of Alec Templeton	Flapper	Past CD 7057	1995
Benny Goodman - Honeysuckle Rose (Notes by G Avakian)	Columbia	A-1788	1955?
Benny Goodman – Clarinet Classics	Pearl	Gem 0057	1999
Benny Goodman – Sing, Sing, Sing. (Notes by G Avakian)	Columbia	A-1677	1955?
Benny Goodman – The Complete RCA Victor Small Group Recordings	RCA / BMG	09026 687642	1997
Benny Goodman 1937-38 Jazz Concerts	CBS	CBS 66420	1980
Benny Goodman and His Orchestra From The Famous "Let's Dance" Broadcasts	Circle	CCD-50	1998
Benny Goodman and His Orchestra Camel Caravan Broadcasts. September 13th/20th 1938.	Soundcraft	LP-1020	
Benny Goodman Live at Carnegie Hall 40th Anniversary Concert.	Decca	DBC 3-4	1978
Benny Goodman On The Air – Original 1935-36-38 Broadcasts	Jazz Unlimited	201 2087	2003
Benny Goodman Plays Jimmy Mundy	Hep	Hep CD 1039	1993
One More Time! – WNEW LP William B Williams	WNEW		1968
The Benny Goodman Caravans. Ciribiribin	Giants of Jazz	GOJ 1030	1983
The Complete Benny Goodman Volume VIII	RCA – Bluebird	AMX2-5568	1980
The Complete Benny Goodman. Volume V	RCA – Bluebird	AXM2-5557	1978
The Complete Madhattan Broadcasts Volume 1	Viper's Nest	VN-171	1995
The Famous 1938 Carnegie Hall Concert	Columbia	SL 160	1950
The Famous 1938 Carnegie Hall Concert	Columbia/Legacy	C2K 65143	1999

Bibliography

SWINGTIME IN THE ROCKIES .... *J. Mundy*

Mundy is the present staff arranger for the Goodman orchestra. Previously he did similar work for the orchestra of the Negro pianist Earl Hines. So far as the title is concerned, it has no other meaning than a mild play on words, and the fact that it is distinctive. Since the library of jazz includes such sequences of words, in titles, as "Humpty Dumpty", "Skip the Gutter", "Prince of Wails", "Duck Wucky" and "Diga Diga Doo", it may be seen that "Swingtime in the Rockies" is in an estimable tradition.

The piece begins immediately with its most characteristic phrase, a rhythmic figure which comprises both the first sixteen measures of the tune and its last eight. The middle section provides a more melodic phrase and a harmonic change. Both the first and second occurrences are for the ensemble, with only brief solos. However, the trombones have the lead in the third chorus, spelled briefly by the clarinet. The latter then has a solo chorus, followed by one for the trumpet. The ending is much the same as the beginning. (Mundy Arrangement).

BEI MIR BIST DU SCHOEN .... *Jacobs-Secunda-Cahn-Chaplin*

As these words are written, the name of Sholom Secunda and the tune he wrote a year ago for a Yiddish musical comedy of Second Avenue are in the ears of millions of Americans. Whether they will still be a week or a month hence, is a question no man can answer, the vogue of a jazz tune being as brief as it familiarly is. However, its adaptability for swing treatment suggests that it might be added to the list of the songs to which jazz players revert over the years.

The arrangement follows a progression of: ensemble for the first chorus, a vocal refrain for the second, a clarinet solo for the third, with the piano heard in the middle section, succeeded by the ensemble for the last eight measures. What follows is Jewish dance music in its purest form (scholars of such matters refer to it as a "froelich") warmly treated by the Messrs. Elman, Krupa, and Goodman. The last sixteen measures of vocal refrain are added as conclusion. (Jim Mundy Arrangement).

SING, SING, SING .... *Louis Prima*

The elaboration of this tune in several ways sums up the procedures, the spirit, and the technical devices that have been incorporated into practically every one of the interpretations heard on this program. If one prefers orthodox musical terminology, it is a free fantasy, based on two themes, with an indeterminate number of solos (depending, as has been said before, on the mood of the performers). The first of these is the tune which gives the work its name; the second is Fletcher Henderson's "Christopher Columbus", utilized because its pace parallels the tempo of the name tune, and because its characteristic phrase provides an appropriate contrast. "Sing, Sing, Sing" began, so far as the Goodman interpretation is concerned, during an engagement at the Palomar Ballroom in Los Angeles, in the summer of 1936. It was taken up again and extended for a tour of movie houses initiated at the Paramount Theatre in New York last February. The original arrangement by Jim Mundy covered scarcely a third of its present length, the rest being built up by the players in innumerable performances.

Throughout the piece, the tom-tom is used instead of the more conventional snare-drum and bass, and it is this instrument which provides the initial impetus with a solo. An extensive introduction follows, appropriate to the length of the piece of a whole. "Sing, Sing, Sing" is then heard from the saxophones, virtually in its original form. A clarinet variant follows, leading to a tom-tom bridge, which arrives at "Christopher Columbus", pronounced by the brass. Another tom-tom solo prefaces a brass chorus on "Sing, Sing, Sing". The development then reverts to "Christopher Columbus", much altered. When the ensemble has finished another dissection of "Sing, Sing, Sing", the tenor has the lead in the first of a group of solos, followed by the clarinet (over a growling brass background), trumpet, and piano. By now both tunes have been reduced to their rhythmic outline, with little to indicate whether one or the other is momentarily under consideration. The drum tapers down to a faint patter. Then the ensemble bursts forth in one exuberant transformation of "Sing, Sing, Sing", bringing the piece to a close. (The order of the solos may be altered as the occasion suggests.) (Mundy Arrangement)

These notes would not be complete without an acknowledgement to John Hammond, whose suggestions have been of substantial value; and to Hugues Panassie, whose "Hot Jazz" (M. Witmark and Sons, New York, 1936) is an invaluable guide.

CONCERT DIRECTION
(By arrangement Music Corporation of America)
HUROK ATTRACTIONS, INC.
30 ROCKEFELLER PLAZA, N. Y. C.

• APPENDIX 1 •

Notes on the Program

by
Irving Kolodin

BENNY GOODMAN and his ORCHESTRA

Foreword

SWING is to the ballroom type of jazz as brandy is to table wine — a headier, more potent transformation of the same basic stuff. There has been much esoteric pother because swing cannot be summarized or defined in a word or a sentence. But for that matter, neither can tempo rubato (which is the essence of Chopin) nor the Viennese style of waltz performance (which is the essence of Johann Strauss's music) be put in the strait-jacket of so many nouns, verbs and adjectives. As in the case of these others, swing is essentially a style of performance whose vitality is supplied by a fluctuation of accent between normally weak and strong beats.

To an extent not present in formal music, swing is further a complex of several elements interrelated and interdependent, one not complete without the other. Principal among these is the characteristic improvisation on the theme at hand, almost invariably a communal process in which the ideas initiated by one player are picked up by the others in turn and colored by the force of their own style and personality. But as there is good and bad improvisation, so there are various degrees of impact in the music that might be produced depending on the vitality of the players' imaginations, their technical skill, and, most importantly, the degree of combustion between them.

Even the best swing players have moments and nights of stodginess when their ideas run to formal figures and clichés, lacking the improvisational flame which is the heart of "hot" jazz. Thus it is not reasonable to expect that all the performances in the space, say, of two hours, will be white hot with inventiveness and originality. Much depends on what swing players like to call "inspiration." But this is merely attributing a mystical quality to the amount of sympathy or kinship generated within a group as they play. Lacking this glow and warmth, the same figures and patterns, no matter how faultlessly executed, remain sterile and unaffecting.

So much emphasis has been placed on the performer for the barrenly simple reason that swing is performance. Therein lies its principal distinction from all other

The back page of Irving Kolodin's notes on the program.

music, high or low, its strength and probably its most serious limitation. By the standards of the specialized styles of performance noted above, swing is essentially an ephemeral thing, for the daemonic qualities in Chopin's thought, the grace and ardor of Johann Strauss' inventions are a feast for the eye on paper, or to the mind if less than consummately played. But jazz has produced no composers to match the talents of the performers it has spawned, with the result that the unbounded inventiveness, the taste and the energy of the best players have created their own kind of music: what used to be called "hot" jazz and in its present incarnation has been dubbed swing. If a parallel exists, it is in the gypsy music of Hungary which is likewise largely improvised.

Since these remarks are addressed to those whose knowledge of swing is limited it may be well to emphasize the importance of the arranger in contemporary swing. He is the liaison man between the composer and the performer. A small combination, such as the trio and the quartet to be heard on this program, or the seven or eight players to be heard in the jam session, intuitively understand each other's intentions and can cooperate effectively without written guidance. But the playing of the larger group of fourteen takes its direction and discipline from the routine indicated in the score made by the arranger.

Almost all swing playing reflects an effort to escape from the most confining element in present day jazz, the prison whose bars are the thirty-two measures of the average tune. Since the first sixteen and the last eight measures are almost invariably similar, the amount of repetition in a merely straight playing of six or seven choruses would be deadening. To aid the improvisation by the solo players, the arranger creates a framework on which the variations may be hung. If he is a skillful arranger, the framework will be congruous and symmetrical in itself, making of the six or seven repetitions of the tune a consecutive whole generally building to a climax in the sixth or seventh. He provides an introduction which establishes the basic tempo and atmosphere, a harmonization of the tune (almost invariably more ingenious than the composer's own), modulations from chorus to chorus (for variety), and also indicates the points where the various soloists take their solos.

In some instances a type of solo or variation is sketched out, with a careful accompanying pattern, thoughtfully orchestrated, to eliminate messiness in the sound and to give a better background for the known type of figuration favored by a certain player. Once an arrangement has been broken in, however, and has been memorized by the players, there is apt to be a great deal of variety in the performance heard, say, at a week's interval. In the heat of playing new solos will be improvised, a figure devised by a soloist will be worked into an accompanying pattern for a new variation, eventually extending the arrangement by as much as twice its original length. The prime example of such extension is "Sing, Sing, Sing", of which only a small portion was originally arranged, and which bas now extended itself — by what one might call a species of musical parthenogenesis — to a structure often minutes' length or more, depending on the mood of the players.

The best arranger, of course, is the man whose temperament is itself that of the hot musician, who can create a harmonic structure that is interesting without impeding elaboration, who can devise variations of a tune that will stimulate the soloists to actual creative efforts of their own. By common agreement, the celebrated Negro pianist and band leader Fletcher Henderson is at present without equal in creating swing arrangements; and several examples of his highly individual skill are included on this program.

DON'T BE THAT WAY .... **Edgar Sampson**
"Don't Be That Way" is a new arrangement and thus virtually a new work by Edgar Sampson, whose "Stompin' at the Savoy" was one of the first tunes to be associated with the Goodman Orchestra (it will be heard in a quartet version later in the program). The composer-arranger is also well-known as a saxophone player, and has been a member of several prominent Negro orchestras, particularly that of Chick Webb.

The arrangement features a graceful legato phrase, first heard from the saxophone section immediately after the introduction, punctuated by a rhythmic figure for the brass. The brass has the lead in the middle section of the thirty-two measure tune, thereafter reverting to the first pattern again. For the second chorus the solo shifts to the clarinet, who is also heard in the last eight measures, and also leads in the third variant of the opening tune. By this time, the rhythm has grown more aggressive, with off-beats from the drum. The piano has the middle section of this chorus, the alto resuming thereafter. The climax is reached in the fourth strain, which builds to an interesting alternation of trombone and clarinet solos, and a final series of crescendo effects at the close. (Sampson Arrangement).

SOMETIMES I'M HAPPY (Hit the Deck) .... **Vincent Youmans**
This fine tune by Vincent Youmans, now a dozen years old, was first heard in "Hit the Deck", and is one among a limited quantity of Broadway popular music adaptable for swing playing. For it Fletcher Henderson provided an arrangement that is a masterpiece of its kind, for the abundant imagination and supreme good musical taste that dominates its length. Though the elaboration is kept within earshot of the tune almost throughout, it begins to swing with the first bars of the introduction. As Edgar Jackson of the English magazine, The Gramophone, has said of another Henderson arrangement – "Many of the phrases are of a type which no band with any feel of rhythm could resist swinging. It only needs a few such bars to infect, as it were, the whole arrangement..."

The first chorus is principally a tasteful orchestration of the melody with the muted trumpet leading above a background of saxophones resourcefully harmonized. However, a new accent is given to the tune with a powerful trumpet solo against off-beats in the drums and cymbals at the outset of the second chorus, succeeded by a tenor saxophone solo in a somewhat quieter vein for the second half of the chorus. Another of the fine transitional phrases which are a particular feature of this arrangement leads to the third chorus where the saxophone choir has a charming ensemble figuration colored by a bit of discreet solo in the piano. This scheme is carried through the chorus, then dissipated by a blast from the trumpets who dominate the scene in a warmer style for the fourth chorus, supported by a rhythmic pattern that piles up the accents at the end of the chorus. A clarinet solo leads to the fifth variation, derived from the last figure of the preceding chorus which balances reeds and brass with a clearer statement of the basic tune, in conclusion, to remind us what all this has been based on. (Henderson Arrangement)

ONE O'CLOCK JUMP .... William (Count) Basie

Prominent among the "royal family" of Negro band leaders (which has included such nobility as King Oliver, and Duke Ellington) is Count Basic, pianist and composer, who will be heard in the jam session later in the program. The title "One O'clock Jump" needs no explanation among musicians, especially to those who have played in traveling bands, and know the pangs of one-night stands and long "jumps" to the next engagement. For others it may be said that the connotations are those of bus rides, jolting roads, tired muscles and little sleep.

The phrase on which the piece is based is one that Basic often used as a pianist in Bennie Moten's Kansas City band, and eventually elaborated into its present form. It is first heard (after the usual formal introduction) from the piano, which takes the first twenty-four measures against a rhythm background. This is followed by a series of other solos, of which the first may be from the tenor saxophone, then the clarinet or the trombone. Since this particular arrangement is not of the strictest kind, an indefinite number of solos follow, depending on how the band is swinging. Finally the saxophones work out a short insistent figure, against trombone slurs and trumpet accents, which pushes itself on and on to the conclusion.

TWENTY YEARS OF JAZZ
SENSATION RAG (Dixieland) .... E. B. Edwards

There has always been, in jazz, a species of musician who was moved by the material with which he was concerned to improvise his own variations and alterations of a basic tune. The first celebrated white band to specialize in this type of performance (in emulation of the Negro bands of New Orleans) was the Original Dixieland Jazz Band which was well-known in the South as early as 1913. The five players eventually reached New York in 1917 and enjoyed a tremendous success at Riesenweber's, extending their popularity to London after the war. In certain respects their playing represented pre-war rag-time in full bloom; in other respects it looked ahead to the higher skill and closer integration of hot jazz.

By some divine ordination, the Dixieland players favoured a five-piece combination of piano, clarinet, cornet, trombone and drums on which they produced enormously spirited music. Among the most characteristic of their numbers were "Tiger Rag" and "Clarinet Marmalade", both written by members of the band (LaRocca and Shields respectively). Moreover, both of them remain in the repertory of every true jazz band today, since both are apt material for hot improvisation. As the authentic reproduction of "Sensation" (also written by a Dixieland player) indicates, jazz was still in its earliest phase of development. Here may be heard the simple patterns, the unvarying rhythmic scheme, the generally unsophisticated formula of breaks, the lack of modulation, which are synonymous with Dixieland. Trombone smears and "fancy" clarinet runs were then the hallmark of jazz and they occur copiously in every chorus. Nevertheless, the Dixieland style had sufficient vitality to retain its exponents to the present time, with several orchestras of today utilizing it, modified and refined, in their repertory.

I'M COMIN' VIRGINIA ("Bix" Beiderbecke) .... Cook-Heywood
One of the few white musicians to approximate the feeling as well as the style of the best Negro musicians, Leon "Bix" Beiderbecke is reverenced even today by jazz players though he died in 1931 at the age of twenty-six. His public career included scarcely more than seven or eight years of playing with musicians of a caliber approaching his own — and a good part of this time was dissipated in the usual commercial activities — but he nevertheless left a considerable legacy of recorded music of a remarkably high average quality. The sincerity and fervor which were his particular characteristics even extended to a preference for the cornet instead of the trumpet. Despite the grosser implications of the lowlier instrument, its freer and warmer tone suited his ardent style more intimately than the more brilliant trumpet, with its exhibitionistic possibilities.

Though he was noted for the passion and intensity of his improvisation in fast tempo, the quintessence of "Bix" is to be found in his variations on such a slow tune as "I'm Comin' Virginia", in which his imagination and depth of feeling were permitted an unlimited range of expression. Bobby Hackett, who plays this simulation of the "Bix" manner, has modeled his entire style on the precepts of his great predecessor and perfected to a remarkable degree the intonations and phrasings of Beiderbecke. As well as being an inimitable performer on his own instrument, "Bix" had considerable gift for composition. Despite his limited musical background he left a series of brief pieces which are strongly individual in harmonic color and rhythmic life. It is such expressions as these which strengthen one's feeling that the best of America's musical talent has found its outlet in the exceptional jazz musicians whose principal resources have not been technic or formulae, but pure musicality and feeling.

WHEN MY BABY SMILES AT ME (Ted Lewis) .... Munro-Sterling-Lewis
Ted Lewis, self-styled "high-hatted tragedian of jazz" represents, in excelsis, the type of white musician who connected extravagant, imitation hot music out of a strident tone, a limited imagination and a slight technic. Essentially a magnificent showman, rather than a remarkable musician (a fact that he would be the first to concede) his vogue was extensive among those who found his gyrations as he played the clarinet even more diverting than the music he produced. Exaggeration and distortion were the ear-marks of this type of performance, rather than inventiveness and good musical taste. Nevertheless, he commanded an enormous following during the lush years of the early 20*s, and still retains a respectable measure of it. However, as a group of talented white players grew up who modeled themselves on the great Negro musicians, the popularity of the spurious hot players steadily diminished. The name of Lewis has long been synonymous with an inimitable version of "When My Baby Smiles at Me." It is

also interesting to note that Goodman's public career as a clarinetist virtually began with his impersonation of Lewis in Chicago vaudeville houses fifteen years ago.

SHINE .... **Mack-Brown-Dabney**

Greatest of all trumpet players and one of the most inventive spirits among all hot players, Louis Armstrong has a public career of nearly twenty years as a jazz player behind him. Perhaps the most remarkable fact of his history is that his hot style developed as early as 1920, years in advance of the general trend to that manner of playing, and tremendously influenced a whole generation of jazz musicians, white and Negro alike. Most of his time from 1920 to 1928 was spent in Chicago where he was heard by many young musicians; and it is no mere coincidence that a large proportion of the best jazz musicians either originated in Chicago or formulated their style while employed in that city.

Widely known today for his ability to take endless F's and G's above the staff, for his extraordinary glissandi (legitimate musicians who hear his records refuse to believe they are played on a trumpet), the best of Armstrong's talent is undoubtedly contained in his records of a decade ago. There one finds these devices rarely employed merely for the purpose of astonishing the laity, but only as the crisis of a series of remarkable variations or because no other expression will contain his marvelous fertility of thought. As the performance of a typical Armstrong chorus of "Shine" indicates, his style combines brilliance, volatility, and great variety. As a technician, Armstrong has an established place in the still unwritten history of jazz music, for he did with incredible ease and nonchalance feats that other trumpet players had previously not considered possible. It is, nevertheless, merely accurate reporting to say that his spirit, fervor and originality far outweighed his pure virtuosity.

BLUE REVERIE (Ellington) .... **Ellington**

What Armstrong was to the improvisers of jazz, Duke Ellington has been to its best written accomplishments; save that Armstrong's manner is more susceptible to imitation than Ellington's, and the latter has thus remained even more distinctly an individual. Needless to say this is not the Ellington of "Solitude", "Sophisticated Lady", "Mood Indigo" and other tunes of wide popular appeal, but the Duke of such solid jazz as "Black and Tan Fantasy", "Creole Rhapsody", "Lazy Rhapsody", "The Mooche", etc. Even in so quiet a work as this "Blue Reverie", there is the internal heat (without which jazz is pointless), expressed with great refinement and subtlety. As for swing, it may be recalled that long before the term attained its present specialized meaning, Ellington wrote a grand rhythmic tune whose first words were: "It don't mean a thing if it ain't got that swing."

It Is well known that Ellington's writing is to a considerable extent a reflection of the particular musicians with whom he has been associated for the last ten years; that is to say, the tune and its orchestral expression are not (as in the case of ninety-five per cent of jazz) separable elements, but actually part of a single idea formulated with a consciousness of the tone produced by a certain section of his orchestra or the characteristics of a particular soloist (Bigard on Clarinet, "Cootie" Williams on trumpet, Hodges on saxophone, etc.). Thus, the most characteristic parts of "Blue Reverie" (which is primarily an arranged "Blues") are plainly expressive of Williams' skill in the use of mutes, Ellington's own piano style and Hodges' saxophone. Moreover, it is always difficult to know in an Ellington piece how much has been conceived by the Duke, and how much has been contributed, in performance, by the players themselves; which is perhaps the highest praise, in jazz terms, that could be lavished on a composer.

LIFE GOES TO A PARTY (Goodman) .... Harry James-B. Goodman

The functioning of a contemporary swing orchestra is excellently exemplified by this vigorous piece written recently by Harry James, trumpet player of the orchestra, and Benny Goodman. (The title was borrowed from the series of picture stories appearing in "Life" magazine, and has no connotations other than the obvious ones). "Life Goes to a Party" is particularly interesting for its balancing of arranged and improvised passage in which the freest and most involved elaborations of the theme are maintained against the background of the accompanying instruments without harmonic distortion or conflict. Rhythm being the foundation of swing, the pulse is established by a solo cymbal from the drums followed by a brief introduction by the whole orchestra. The principal theme, sharply punched out by the brass, is then heard, answered by an accompanying figure from the reeds. Logically, this first occurrence is fairly unadorned, with the attack of the brass and an occasional off-beat from the drum providing a contrast of weak and strong accents. The same instrumentation is maintained for a repetition of the idea, with variety provided by a shift to minor, stronger rhythm from the drums, brass, guitar and piano. Also, the tenor saxophone has a four-measure solo. A new impetus is given to the piece with a feverish solo from the clarinet, prolonged through a whole chorus and backed by a solid rhythm foundation. This is succeeded by a trumpet solo (muted by a derby hat) of the same intensity, in which occurs a phrase that is picked up by the three trumpets, inverted and used as the basis of a variation that carries the piece to a climax. This five-note phrase heard from the brass is echoed by the drums, two, three, four times. The clarinet is heard in the middle section solo, then the trumpet and drums resume their duel, finally piling up eight repetitions of the idea in a powerful climax. (James Arrangement)

JAM SESSION

A jam session without stale air, tobacco fumes and drinks within easy reach is no doubt the greatest contradiction a swing program could offer, but in deference to the evening's surroundings, the players have consented to forego these indispensables. Though the phrase has recently attained an esoteric vogue suggesting proceedings of almost a ritualistic flavor, a jam session is nothing more than a meeting of hot musicians for the pleasure of mutual improvisation. Since the amount of improvisation tolerated on the usual commercial job is limited, a jam session frequently serves as a safety valve for the musical energy stored up in a player during seven or eight hours of routine playing. In the company of five or six others of equal skill and imagination, he can relax completely, let his fancy range as widely as it will, and produce the kind of music which is swing or hot jazz at its best.

When the jam session is properly intimate, the procedure is invariable. One of the players or one of the enthusiasts listening in (a small, appreciative audience is a desirable stimulus) will suggest a tune — some such perennial as "Dinah", "Lady Be Good", "Sweet Sue", "Who", a blues, or any one of a hundred others — and the piano and rhythm swing into it, with the other instruments outlining the tune lightly. As the feel of the harmonic background sketched by the piano begins to assert itself more definitely, one player or another will take a solo chorus. Without perceptible sign, the other instruments give way to him, and work out accompanying patterns, based on their feeling for the harmonic background, frequently complementing the line evolved by the solo player with a subordinate one of their own. A characteristic phrase from one solo may be picked up in the succeeding one by a different instrument, elaborated in more individual style, or simplified.

As the warmth of the playing increases, the solos may lengthen, with a player taking two or three choruses in succession, developing his ideas more fully. Invariably there is a heightening tension as solo follows solo, with the music moving more widely away from the starting tune, which has now been skeletonized completely. Finally, as if by mutual consent, there will be an ensemble chorus in which the whole sequence will be summed up, rounded off and concluded. When the players are properly sympathetic to each other, and the mood is a congenial one, with the skill of the performers approximately even, a jam session will be filled with instances of almost telepathic understanding between the players of what a soloist is going to do before he does it. Thus the progress of a solo will be anticipated, and built up by the other instruments in a manner that defies analysis or explanation.

It is understood that a hall of this size is far from the most appropriate setting for the best results in this type of playing, and that tension or excessive effort are death to the spontaneity which is the life blood of improvisation. Moreover, the length of the jam session cannot be predicted; it may cover five choruses or twenty-five, one tune or three, depending on the reactions of the players to each other and to the audience. Thus the audience is asked to accept the jam session in a spirit of experimentation, with the hope that the proper atmosphere will be established.

GOODMAN TRIO

The Goodman trio owes its existence to a chance meeting at a party given at the home of Mildred Bailey, the jazz vocalist, in June, 1935. Krupa and Goodman were then associated in the orchestra, of course, but Wilson was free-lancing, making records, etc. The results of this impromptu session was perpetuated in several records made a few days later, but it was not until the following winter that Wilson was added to the Goodman organization and the trio made a permanent feature of the band's performances. Thus the trio has a history of slightly more than two years' consecutive playing; and has already managed to amass a dozen imitators.

However, the trio is unique in the realm of jazz for several reasons, not the least of which is the fact that none of its performances have been written down, though many of them have been recorded. Thus each of its two or three performances in an evening is in effect a new jam session, though the routine and procedures of the older numbers they play have now been fairly well stabilized. Nevertheless, none of these is ever played exactly the same way twice, for there is always a considerable proportion of improvisation in every performance. It is also a most unusual association of three outstanding performers on their instruments, yielding a subtlety, variety, and polish to their interpretations which no other jazz playing has duplicated. Further, it is a rare example of a band leader participating in a small ensemble on a footing of equality with the other members of his organization.

GOODMAN QUARTET

The Goodman trio became a quartet late in the summer of 1936, during a visit by the band to the West Coast. Lionel Hampton has long been a celebrity in jazz, particularly as a drummer, playing with many prominent Negro orchestras and leading his own orchestra. However, he had also devoted himself to specialization on the vibraphone (or vibra harp), an instrument which might be described as a mechanized xylophone. In addition to having steel bars instead of the wooden one of the xylophone, each bar is tapped by a resonating metal tube in which the tone is focused and expanded. In each tube is a small disk rotated by power furnished from a small electric motor attached to the instrument It is the spinning of these disks which gives the tone of the vibraphone its characteristic vibrato and depth. A pedal arrangement (which employs the damper principal utilized in the piano) permits the performer to control the length of time a note will sound. Since the player can use two striking hammers in each hand, the vibraphone may also produce complete chords and harmonies. Moreover, the performer has the choice of using hammers with felt or glass heads, which considerably effect the kind of tone produced.

Inasmuch as its dynamic range and color possibilities are so great, the vibraphone adds a valuable resource to the piano-clarinet-drums trio, without effacing the individual qualities of any of the instruments. It is also flexible enough to be classed as either a percussion or a melodic instrument, depending on the choice of the player. The nervous energy and essentially brilliant style of Hampton's playing also have a pronounced influence on the playing of the other members of the quartet.

BLUE SKIES .... Irving Berlin

Over a period of years (dating back to the pre-war "Alexander's Rag-time Band")) few jazz composers have turned out so many and varied tunes as living Berlin. It is appropriate thus to cite his "Blue Skies" as an example of a popular ballad treated in the swing manner. The original tune flowed smoothly, with only a moderate rhythmic variety, and the arranger has thus supplied a crisp, varied pattern from the first chorus, written for ensemble, with only brief solo passages. The second chorus begins similarly, with brass and reeds exchanging places in the rhythmic scheme, and the tenor coming out for a solo in the last eight measures. In the third chorus the trumpet gets further away from the melodic line, which is brought to the front again by the ensemble in the last sixteen bars. An abrupt modulation leads directly to a clarinet solo, which is varied by replies from the brass. Saxophones and trombones follow each other in the second half of the last chorus, with the ensemble building up the last measures. The arrangement is throughout a model of what can be done with rhythmic figuration of a smooth tune, without losing the basic pattern. (Henderson Arrangement).

LOCH LOMOND .... Traditional Scotch
The vogue for singing Scotch ballads with swing feeling was initiated recently by Maxine Sullivan, Negro vocalist of the Onyx Club. Most aptly suited for this purpose is "Loch Lomond", here heard in the arrangement originally made for her by Claude Thornhill. There is a clever simulation of a Scotch bagpipe at the outset, with the tom-tom to provide the color of the large bass drum. The first vocal fragment is then heard, followed by a reasonably straight version of the folk-song, with a piano background. The trumpet then offers his treatment of the tune. Again bagpipes, and this time both the verse and chorus of the song are heard, with a few rhythmic exchanges in conclusion. (Thornhill Arrangement).

BLUE ROOM (from The Girl Friend) .... Richard Rodgers-Lorenz Hart
Prominent among the songwriters who have contributed most substantially to the gayety of the Broadway musical comedy stage during the last decade and a half is the inseparable pair of Rodgers and Hart, whose "I'd Rather Be Right" is current now. They have written an impressive number of tunes suitable for hot treatment, among them "I've Got Five Dollars", "You Took Advantage of Me", and "Thou Swell", though the early "Blue Room" need not defer to any of these. The arrangement used tonight, by Fletcher Henderson, is the most recent example of his work, and was made for this occasion.

It has some of the same traits of workmanship to be found in "Blue Skies", rather differently applied. Notable among these is the rhythmic pattern of the first chorus, which is principally for the ensemble. The clarinet leads in the second chorus against an alternating saxophone and brass background. It defers briefly to the trombone in the middle section, thereafter resuming for the last eight bars. The whole orchestra works at the intricate rhythmic figures of the last chorus, with a short interlude for the solo clarinet. (Henderson Arrangement).

SWINGTIME IN THE ROCKIES .... Mundy
Mundy is the present staff arranger for the Goodman orchestra. Previously he did similar work for the orchestra of the Negro pianist Earl Hines. So far as the title is concerned, it has no other meaning than a mild play on words, and the fact that it is distinctive. Since the library of jazz includes such sequences of words, in tides, as "Humpty Dumpty", "Skip the Gutter", "Prince of Wails", "Duck Wucky" and "Diga Diga Doo", it may be seen that "Swingtime in the Rockies" is in an estimable tradition.

The piece begins immediately with its most characteristic phrase, a rhythmic figure which comprises both the first sixteen measures of the tune and its last eight. The middle section provides a more melodic phrase and a harmonic change. Both the first and second occurrences are for the ensemble, with only brief solos. However, the trombones have the lead in the third chorus, spelled briefly by the clarinet. The latter then has a solo chorus, followed by one for the trumpet. The ending is much the same as the beginning. (Mundy Arrangement).

BEIMIR BIST DU SCHOEN .... Jacobs-Secunda-Cahn-Chaplin

As these words are written, the name of Sholom Secunda and the tune he wrote a year ago for a Yiddish musical comedy of Second Avenue are in the ears of millions of Americans. Whether they will still be a week or a month hence, is a question no man can answer, the vogue of a jazz tune being as brief as it familiarly is. However, its adaptability for swing treatment suggests that it might be added to the list of the songs to which jazz players revert over the years.

The arrangement follows a progression of: ensemble for the first chorus, a vocal refrain for the second, a clarinet solo for the third, with the piano heard in the middle section, succeeded by the ensemble for the last eight measures. What follows is Jewish dance music in its purest form (scholars of such matters refer to it as a "froelich") warmly treated by the Messrs. Elman, Krupa, and Goodman. The last sixteen measures of vocal refrain are added as conclusion. (Jim Mundy Arrangement).

SING, SING, SING .... Louis Prima

The elaboration of this tune in several ways sums up the procedures, the spirit, and the technical devices that have been incorporated into practically every one of the interpretations heard on this program. If one prefers orthodox musical terminology, it is a free fantasy, based on two themes, with an indeterminate number of solos (depending, as has been said before, on the mood of the performers). The first of these is the tune which gives the work its name; the second is Fletcher Henderson's "Christopher Columbus", utilized because its pace parallels the tempo of the name tune, and because its characteristic phrase provides an appropriate contrast. "Sing, Sing, Sing" began, so far as the Goodman interpretation is concerned, during an engagement at the Palomar Ballroom in Los Angeles, in the summer of 1936. It was taken up again and extended for a tour of movie houses initiated at the Paramount Theatre in New York last February. The original arrangement by Jim Mundy covered scarcely a third of its present length, the rest being built up by the players in innumerable performances.

Throughout the piece, the tom-tom is used instead of the more conventional snare-drum and bass, and it is this instrument which provides the initial impetus with a solo. An extensive introduction follows, appropriate to the length of the piece of a whole. "Sing, Sing, Sing" is then heard from the saxophones, virtually in its original form. A clarinet variant follows, leading to a tom-tom bridge, which arrives at "Christopher Columbus", pronounced by the brass. Another tom-tom solo prefaces a brass chorus on "Sing, Sing, Sing . The development then reverts to "Christopher Columbus", much altered. When the ensemble has finished another dissection of "Sing, Sing, Sing", the tenor has the lead in the first of a group of solos, followed by the clarinet (over a growling brass background), trumpet, and piano. By now both tunes have been reduced to their rhythmic outline, with little to indicate whether one or the other is momentarily under consideration. The drum tapers down to a faint patter. Then the ensemble bursts forth in one exuberant transformation of "Sing, Sing, Sing", bringing the piece to a close. (The order of the solos may be altered as the occasion suggests.) (Mundy Arrangement)

    These notes would not be complete without an acknowledgement to John Hammond, whose suggestions have been of substantial value; and to Hugues Panassie, whose "Hot Jazz" (M. Witmark and Sons, New York, 1936) is an invaluable guide.

CONCERT DIRECTION
(*By arrangement Music Corporation of America*)
HUROK ATTRACTIONS, INC.
30 ROCKEFELLER PLAZA, N. Y. C

– Notes on the Program –

CARNEGIE HALL 1978

APPENDIX 2

Benny Goodman's Carnegie Hall Appearances

Benny visited Carnegie Hall on many occasions, here is the complete list.

16 January 1938
Benny Goodman, *Clarinet*. Gene Krupa, *Drums*. Jess Stacy, *Piano*. Teddy Wilson, *Piano*. Lionel Hampton, *Vibraphone*. Harry James, Ziggy Elman, Gordon Griffin, *Trumpets*. 'Red' Ballard, Vernon Brown, *Trombones*. Allan Reuss, *Guitar*. Babe Russin, Hymie Schertzer, *Alto Saxophones*. George Koenig, Arthur Rollini, *Tenor Saxophones*. Harry Goodman, *Bass*. Martha Tilton, *Vocals*. Guests: Count Basie, *Piano*. Lester Young, *Tenor Saxophone*. Cootie Williams, *Trumpet*. Johnny Hodges, *Alto and Soprano Saxophones*. Bobby Hackett, *Cornet*. Freddie Green, *Guitar*. Buck Clayton, *Trumpet*. Walter Page, *Bass*. Harry Carney, *Baritone Saxophone*.

January 9 1939
First performance of the Rhapsody for Clarinet and Violin (Contrasts) by Béla Bartók. Endre Petri, *Piano*. Joseph Szigeti, *Violin*. Benny Goodman, *Clarinet*.

October 6 1939
ASCAPS's 25th Anniversary concert.
Benny Goodman, *Clarinet*. Jimmy Maxwell, Ziggy Elman, Johnny Martel, *Trumpets*. 'Red' Ballard, Vernon Brown, Ted Vesely, *Trombones*. Toots Mondello, Buff Estes, *Alto Saxophones*. Bus Bussey, Jerry Jerome, *Tenor Saxophone*. Fletcher Henderson, *Piano*, Arnold Covey, *Guitar*. Art Bernstein, *Bass*. Lionel Hampton, *Drums*. Charlie Christian, *Electric Guitar*. Nick Fatool *Drums*.
Also on the bill that day were Paul Whiteman and his orchestra, Fred Waring and his Orchestra, Glenn Miller and his orchestra

24 December 1939 Spirituals to Swing.
Benny Goodman, *Clarinet*. Charlie Christian, *Electric guitar*. Art Bernstein, *Bass*. Fletcher Henderson, *Piano*. Lionel Hampton *Vibraphone*. Nick Fatool, *Drums*

The cover of the program for the 1978 anniversary concert.

12/13 December 1940
Debussy - First Rhapsody and Mozart - Clarinet Concerto. John Barbirolli conducting the New York Philharmonic.

29 April 1941
Prokofieff's Variations on Yiddish Themes with Feri Roth, Rachmael Weinstock, Julius Shaier and Oliver Edel of the Roth quartet and Andor Foldes *Piano*.

10 May 1948 Jazz Septet
Benny Goodman, *Clarinet*. Stan Hasselgard, *Clarinet*. Teddy Wilson, *Piano*. Wardell Gray, *Tenor Saxophone*. Joe Bushkin, *Piano*. Jonah Jones, *Trumpet*. Morey Feld, *Drums*. Fred Robbins *Host*.

17 April 1953 Jazz with Louis Armstrong
Willie Smith, Clint Neagley, *Alto Saxophones*. George Auld, Sol Schlinger, *Tenor Saxophones*. Ziggy Elman, Charlie Shavers, Al Stewart, *Trumpets*. Vernon Brown, Rex Peer, *Trombones*. Teddy Wilson, *Piano*. Israel Crosby *Bass*. Steve Jorden, *Guitar*. Gene Krupa, *Drums*. Helen Ward *Vocalist*.

19 January 1955
With Leonard Bernstein. Hindemith Clarinet Concerto.

16 November 1960
Copeland Concerto for Clarinet, String Orchestra and Harp. Aaron
Richard Korn Orchestra of America. Copland, Concerto for Clarinet, Strings, Harp and Piano. Copeland's sixtieth birthday and he was in the audience.

3 April 1961 Carnegie Hall salutes Jack Benny
Benny Goodman, *Clarinet*. Red Norvo, *Vibraphone*. Jim Wyble, *Guitar*. Mickey Sheen, *Drums*. Chuck Israels, *Bass*. Tony Aless, *Guitar*.

10 April 1963
Poulenc memorial concert – Premier of the Poulenc Sonata for Clarinet and Piano. Leonard Bernstein, *Piano*. Benny Goodman, *Clarinet*.

May 6 1964 Jazz Quartet
Benefit for Wiltwyck School for Boys. Benny Goodman, *Clarinet*. Dick Shreve, *Piano*. Monty Budwig, *Bass*. Colin Bailey *Drums*.

29 June 1973 Newport Jazz Festival. Jazz Quintet
Benny Goodman, *Clarinet*. Lionel Hampton, *Vibraphone*. Slam Stewart, *Bass*. Gene Krupa, *Drums*.

27 January 1974 Monsanto special. Jazz Concert
Benny Goodman, *Clarinet*. Marvin Stam, Johnny Frosh, Chris Griffin, Bernie Privin, *Trumpets*. Buddy Morrow, Edie Bert, *Trombones*. Toots Mondello, Walt Levinsky, *Alto Saxophones*. Zoot Sims, Al Klink, *Tenor Saxophones*. Sol Schlinger, *Baritone Saxophone*. Bucky Pizzarelli, *Guitar*. Slam Stewart, *Bass*. Grady Tate, *Drums*. Guests, Cleo Laine *Vocals*, Johnny Dankworth *Alto Saxophone*.

3 April 1974
Benefit for NYU Medical Centre. Benny Goodman, *Clarinet*. Eubie Blake, *Piano*. Carmen De Lavaville, *Dancer*. Rachel Wiesman, *Piano*. Peter Appleyard, *Vibraphone*. Hank Jones *Piano*. Remo Palimeri, *Guitar*. Bucky Pizzarelli, *Guitar*. Paul Quinchette, *Tenor Saxophone*. Zoot Sims, *Tenor Saxophone*. Slam Stewart, *Bass*. Grady Tate, *Drums*. Paul Williams, *Trumpet*.

13 September 1974
Benny Goodman, *Clarinet*. Zoot Sims *Tenor Saxophone*, Bobby Hackett, *Cornet*. Urbie Green *Trombone*. Chris Griffin, Hank Jones, *Piano*. Peter Appleyard, *Vibraphone*. Bucky Pizzarelli, *Guitar*. Slam Stewart, *Bass*. Grady Tate, *Drums*.

13 February 1976 Jazz
Benny Goodman, *Clarinet*. Roy Eldridge, *Trumpet*. Bobby Hackett, *Cornet*. Hank Jones, *Piano*. Slam Stewart, *Bass*. Bucky Pizzarelli, *Guitar*. Peter Appleyard, *Vibraphone*. Urbie Green, *Trombone*. Al Klink, *Tenor Saxophone*. Grady Tate, *Drums*.

28 June 1976 Newport Jazz Festival
Tommy Fay, Teddy Wilson, *Piano*. Eddie Duran, *Guitar*. Mike Moore, *Bass*. Peter Appleyard, *Vibraphone*. Connie Kay, *Drums*.

17 January 1978 40th Anniversary
Benny Goodman, *Clarinet*. Lionel Hampton, *Vibraphone*. Jimmy Rowles, John Bunch, Mary Lou Williams, *Piano*. Martha Tilton, Debi Craig *Vocals*. Mike Moore, *Bass*. Connie Kay, *Drums*. Cal Collins, Wayne Wright, *Guitar*. George Young Mel Rodon, *Alto Saxophones*. Buddy Tate, Frank Wess Tenor *Saxophones*. Sol Schlinger *Baritone Saxophone*. Victor Paz, Jack Sheldon, Warren Vache, *Trumpet*. Wayne Andre, George Masso, John Messner, *Trombones*.

March 24 1979 Jazz with Stephan Grappelli
Staphane Grappelli, *Violin*. John Bunch, *Piano*, Major Holly, *Bass*. Cal Collins, *Guitar*. Buddy Tate, *Tenor Saxophone*. Peter Appleyard, *Vibraphone*. Connie Kay, *Drums*.

June 24 1979 Newport Jazz Festival
Benny Goodman, *Clarinet*. Buddy Tate, *Tenor Saxophone*. Wayne Andre, *Trombone*. Roland Hanna, *Piano*. Warren Vache, *Cornet*. Slam Stewart, *Bass*.

June 5 1980 Jazz

Benny Goodman, *Clarinet*. Warren Vache, *Cornet*. Bill Ramsey, *Tenor Saxophone*. Ray Tutle, *Trombone*. Don Haas, *Piano*. Eddie Duran, *Guitar*. Al Obidinsky, *Bass*. John Markham, *Drums*. Rare Silk, *Vocal Ensamble*.

June 25 1982 Kool Jazz Festival

Benny Goodman, *Clarinet*. Lionel Hampton, *Vibraphone*. Teddy Wilson. *Piano*. Panama Francis, *Drums*. Phil Flanigan, *Bass*.

– Benny Goodman's Carnegie Hall Appearances –

Benny's last performance at Carnegie Hall. Benny Goodman, Teddy Wilson, Lionel Hampton and Phil Flanigan in 1982.

SELMER
THE SOUND OF HISTORY

BENNY GOODMAN

THE TIME: JANUARY 16, 1938

THE PLACE: CARNEGIE HALL

THE EVENT: THE BENNY GOODMAN CONCERT

THE SOLOIST: BENNY GOODMAN

THE HORN: SELMER (PARIS) CLARINET

Try today's Selmer – better than ever!

The Selmer Company
Post Office Box 310 • Elkhart, Indiana 46515

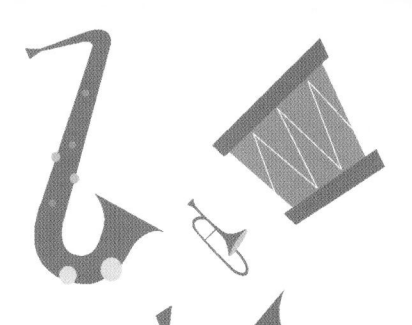

Index

Aless, Tony, 208
Alexander, Willard, 23, 27, 28, 36, 109, 201
Allen, Steve, 181
Allen, Walter, 85, 185
Amos, James, 165, 166
Amundsen, Roald, 16
Anderson, Edmund, 88, 126
Anderson, Ivie, 81
Anderson, Marion, 25
Andre, Wayne, 209
Appleyard, Peter, 209
Armstrong, Louis, 72, 93, 96, 125, 158, 165, 198, 208
Astaire, Fred, 22
Auld, George, 189, 208
Avakian, George, 145, 158, 165, 169, 173, 177, 185, 190
Bailey, Colin, 208
Bailey, Mildred, 37, 101, 200
Baldwin, Hope, 77
Ballard, Red, 48, 85, 86, 88, 93, 95, 107, 108, 110, 112, 113, 119, 121, 123, 207
Balliett, Whitney, 29, 44, 146, 185
Barbirolli, Jack, 125, 208
Barnet, Charlie, 31
Bartók, Bela, 8, 178, 207
Basie, William 'Count', 11, 29, 31, 33, 35, 38, 41, 45, 77, 88, 89, 97, 98, 99, 125, 126, 185, 186, 196, 207
Bechet, Sydney, 95
Beecham, Thomas, 15
Beiderbecke, Bix, 91, 92, 96, 197
Berigan, Bunny, 17
Berkeley, Busby, 38
Berlin, Irving, 107, 108, 185, 201
Bernstein, Leonard, 16, 207, 208
Berry, Chu, 119
Bert, Eddie, 209
Biederbecke, Bix, 19
Big John - Meetball, 123
Bigard, Barney, 199

Blake, Eubie, 209
Block, Martin, 12, 13, 36
Bowers, Ronnie (Dick Powell), 38
Brackman, Al, 90, 121
Braff, Ruby, 182
Brahms, 7, 8
Breck, Rachel, 157, 182
Brinckerhoff, 100
Brown, Vernon, 25, 31, 42, 43, 85, 86, 88, 89, 90, 91, 92, 93, 94, 95, 97, 98, 101, 107, 108, 110, 112, 113, 119, 121, 123, 145, 207, 208
Brunis, George, 44
Budwig, Monty, 208
Bunch, John, 182, 209
Bushkin, Joe, 181, 208
Bussey, Bus, 207
Cahn, Sammy, 113, 203
Calloway, Cab, 31
Cantor, Eddie, 22
Carnegie, Andrew, 15
Carney, Harry, 77, 94, 95, 96, 97, 112, 133, 138, 207
Carter, Benny, 33
Casa Loma - Orchestra, 21, 25
Chaplin, Saul, 113, 203
Cheatham, Doc, 182
Chilton, John, 85
Chopin, 67, 193, 194
Christian, Charlie, 90, 207
Churchill, Winston, 16
Clayton, Buck, 11, 97, 100, 101, 123, 138, 174, 177, 185, 207
Cobain, Kurt, 7
Collier, James Lincoln, 12, 23, 27, 28, 47, 89, 105, 178, 185, 188
Collins, Cal, 209
Conan Doyle, Arthur, 16
Condon, Eddie, 44, 185
Confrey, Zev, 16
Coniff, Frank, 157

This Advert for Selmer clarinets used the Carnegie concert as 'The Sound of History'.

Connor, Russell, 12, 36, 41, 91, 96, 120, 126, 161, 181, 185
Conover, Willis, 157
Cook, Will, 197
Coolidge String Quartet, 38, 129, 130, 177
Copland, Aaron, 208
Covey, Arnold, 207
Coward, Noel, 35
Craig, Debi, 209
Crampton, Savington, 22, 82, 100, 174
Crosby, Bob, 31, 47, 147
Crosby, Israel, 208
Damrosch, Leopold, 15
Damrosch, Walter, 15, 146
Dankworth, Johnny, 209
Davis, Rufe, 23
De Lavaville, Carmen, 209
DeAngelis, Bob, 182
Debussy, 7, 208
Dolan, Pat, 165
Dorsey, Tommy, 17, 18, 19, 22, 31, 36, 147
Downes, Olin, 81, 99
Dragoi, Sabin, 43
Driggs, Frank, 89
Duncan, Isadora, 25
Duran, Eddie, 209, 210
Dylan, Bob, 35
Edel, Oliver, 208
Edelson, Rachel, 5, 9, 142
Edwards, E, 196
Edwards, Eddie, 91
Eldridge, Roy, 18, 125, 209
Ellington, 'Duke', 11, 17, 29, 31, 33, 35, 41, 77, 81, 86, 88, 89, 94, 95, 96, 97, 126, 182, 185, 196, 198, 199
Elman, Ziggy, 12, 25, 78, 85, 86, 88, 93, 95, 107, 108, 110, 112, 113, 119, 121, 123, 138, 145, 203, 207, 208
Enesco, Georges, 42, 43, 99, 146
Estes, Buff, 207
Esty, William - Advertising Agency, 22, 28, 29, 37, 38, 51, 82, 91, 100
Europe, James Reese, 16
Ewing, Annemarie, 99, 149
Fatool, Nick, 207
Faye, Alice, 22
Feather, Leonard, 115, 116, 185
Feld, Morey, 181, 208
Ferguson, Otis, 102, 103, 121, 185
Firestone, Ross, 12, 19, 86, 150, 153, 157, 163, 185
Fitzgerald, Ella, 126
Fizdale, Tom, 27, 123

Flanigan, Phil, 210
Flora, Jim, 165, 166, 185
Foldes, Andor, 208
Francesconi, Gino, 182
Francis, Panama, 182, 210
Franklin, Aretha, 35
Frazier, 43, 91, 178, 185
Freeman, Bud, 44, 177
Frosh, Johnny, 209
Gabler, Milt, 43, 45
Gale, Moe, 125
Garland, Judy, 22
Gershwin, George, 16, 104, 112
Gilbert, Douglas, 37, 42, 110
Glantz, Harry, 87
Golden Hill Chorus, 45
Goode, Gerald, 27, 28, 82, 118, 161, 186
Goode, Morte, 123
Goodman, Charlie - Benny's brother, 93
Goodman, Harry, 48, 82, 85, 138
Goodman, Rachel, 157
Goodman, Saul - No relation to Benny, 106
Goodman-Edelson, Rachel, 157, 182
Goodwin, Bill, 23
Grant, Cary, 23
Grappelli, Stephan, 18, 209
Gray, Glen, 25, 208
Gray, Wardell, 181
Green, Freddie, 45, 97, 98, 101, 112, 123, 207, 209
Greer, Sonny, 86
Grey, Al, 182
Grieg, 119
Griffin, Chris, 18, 82, 85, 86, 87, 88, 93, 95, 107, 108, 110, 112, 113, 119, 121, 138, 186, 207, 209
Grofé, Ferde, 16
Haas, Don, 210
Hackett, Bobby, 35, 41, 44, 90, 91, 92, 93, 96, 101, 113, 178, 186, 197, 207, 209
Hammond, John, 22, 28, 33, 35, 43, 44, 45, 77, 81, 91, 95, 99, 108, 145, 155, 157, 158, 165, 177, 181, 182, 185, 186, 204
Hampton, Lionel, 19, 32, 38, 42, 81, 86, 93, 103, 104, 112, 114, 115, 116, 126, 129, 133, 142, 182, 185, 201, 207, 208, 209, 210
Handy, William Christopher, 16, 32
Hanlon, Allan, 41
Hanna, Roland, 209
Hardy, Rex, 26, 186
Hart, Lorenz, 202
Hasselgard, Stan, 181, 208

Index

Heck, Rudolph, 71
Heck, Walter, 71
Heifetz, Jascha, 82
Heller, Ben, 177
Henderson, Fletcher, 7
Henderson, Flethcer, 13, 85, 86, 87, 107, 108, 110, 111, 112, 113, 129, 185, 186, 195, 196, 202, 203, 207
Henderson, Horace, 86
Hess, Myra - Dame, 48
Heywood, Donald, 197
Hines, Earl, 113, 202
Hodges, Johnny, 11, 43, 77, 86, 94, 95, 96, 97, 99, 112, 133, 138, 199, 207
Holiday, Billie, 38, 41, 72, 86, 101, 102, 123, 126
Holly, Major, 209
Horowitz, Vladimir, 15, 71
Howard, Tom, 37
Hunt, Frances, 23
Hurok, Sol, 16, 25, 26, 27, 28, 29, 31, 33, 36, 72, 118, 181, 182, 186
Inman, Bob, 77, 119, 121, 186
Israels, Chuck, 208
Jackson, Edgar, 195
Jacobs, Jacob, 113, 203
Jacobs, Phoebe, 9
James, Harry, 12, 18, 36, 37, 41, 42, 47, 71, 82, 85, 86, 87, 88, 89, 91, 93, 94, 95, 96, 97, 101, 107, 108, 110, 112, 113, 119, 120, 121, 123, 125, 181, 186, 199, 207
James, Jesse, 94
Jerome, Jerry, 207
Jones, Hank, 209
Jones, Jo, 98, 99
Jones, Jonah, 181, 208
Kammen, J, 113
Kay, Connie, 209
Kemp, Hal, 23
Klink, Al, 209
Koenig, 85, 86, 88, 93, 95, 107, 108, 110, 112, 113, 119, 121, 177, 207
Kolodin, Irving, 12, 18, 19, 27, 28, 33, 67, 82, 90, 95, 96, 98, 99, 111, 149, 150, 185, 193
Krupa, Gene, 18, 19, 36, 37, 38, 41, 42, 47, 49, 81, 82, 85, 86, 88, 89, 90, 91, 93, 94, 95, 96, 97, 98, 99, 101, 103, 104, 106, 107, 108, 110, 112, 113, 114, 115, 118, 119, 120, 121, 137, 138, 145, 153, 161, 177, 186, 200, 203, 207, 208
LaCentra, Peg, 23

Laine, Cleo, 209
Lane, Lola, 38
Lane, Rosemary, 38
Lang, Eddie, 91
LaRocca, Nick, 91, 196
Levine, 169
Levinsky, Walt, 209
Lewis, Ted, 93, 197
Lillie, Beatrice, 35, 36
MacEachern, Murray, 25
Mahler, Gustave, 15
Markham, John, 210
Martel, Johnny, 207
Marx, Albert, 23, 81, 89, 146, 147, 149, 161, 177
Marx, Lawrence, 81, 133, 152
Masso, George, 209
Maxwell, Jimmy, 207
Mayer, Alexander Mayer Chorus, 23, 109
McCrae, Margaret, 23
McDonough, John, 13, 147, 153, 173, 181, 182, 186
McNaughty, William, 51
McNeil, Don, 21
Menhuin, Yehudi, 71
Mercer, Johnny, 147
Merman, Ethel, 78
Messner, John, 209
Miller, Glen, 13, 22, 85, 87, 147, 207
Mitcham, Robert, 121
Moldavan, Nicolas, 129
Mondello, Toots, 93, 207, 209
Monte, Pee Wee, 142
Moore, Mike, 209
Morrow, Buddy, 209
Moten, Bennie, 196
Mozart, 7, 8, 38, 43, 51, 129, 130, 177, 208
Mundy, Jimmy, 100, 109, 112, 113, 119, 126, 129, 133, 190, 202, 203, 204
Nash, WW, 86, 120
Nathanson, Wynn, 27, 28, 123
Neagley, Clint, 208
Newman, Marion, 23
Nichols, Red, 49
Nielsen, 8
Norvo, Red, 31, 41, 126, 208
Oakie, Jack, 21, 22, 23
Oakley, Helen, 18, 43, 125
Oberstein, Eli, 86
Obidinsky, Al, 210
Oistrakh, David, 86
Page, Walter, 97, 98, 99, 101, 123, 153, 165, 207

Paige, Raymond, 22
Paley, William, 165
Palimeri, Remo, 209
Panassie, Hugues, 204
Pavlova, Anna, 25
Paz, Victor, 209
Perkins, Francis, 36, 99, 103, 106
Petri, Endri, 178, 207
Piastro, Mishel, 42, 146
Pizzarelli, Bucky, 209
Poe, Jim, 77
Pollack, Ben, 19, 23, 36, 120
Poulenc, 208
Powell, Dick, 38
Prima, Louis, 23, 31, 119, 203
Privin, Bernie, 209
Quinchette, Paul, 209
Rachmaninoff, 15
Ramsey, Bill, 210
Rare Silk, 210
Reagan, Ronald, 38
Reeves, 'Buzz' Hazard, 158
Reuss, Alan, 18, 41, 85, 86, 88, 91, 93, 94, 95, 107, 108, 110, 112, 113, 119, 120, 121, 177, 207
Reuss, Allan, 75, 102
Reynolds, RJ Cigarette Company, 21, 27, 51, 130, 189
Rheinhardt, Django, 18
Riesenweber's, 196
Robbins, Fred, 181, 208
Rodgers, Richard, 202
Rodon, Mel, 209
Rollini, Arthur, 48, 82, 85, 86, 87, 88, 93, 95, 107, 108, 110, 112, 113, 119, 121, 186, 207
Roosevelt, Theodore, 16
Roth, Feri, 208
Rubinstein, Arthur, 25
Russe, Ballet, 25, 26
Russell, Pee Wee, 44
Russin, Babe, 32, 49, 85, 86, 88, 89, 91, 93, 95, 107, 108, 110, 112, 113, 119, 121, 137, 207
Saint Saens, 42
Salemme, Attillio, 169
Sampson, Edgar, 37, 82, 85, 86, 115, 123, 195
Sauter, Eddie, 90
Savory, Bill, 133, 145, 150, 157, 161, 163, 174, 186
Sbarbaro, Tony, 91
Schaap, Phil, 90, 96, 98, 100, 121, 146, 169, 173, 174
Schertzer, Hymie, 48, 82, 85, 86, 88, 93, 95, 107, 108, 110, 112, 113, 119, 121, 123, 207
Schiff, Andras, 152
Schilgan, Bobby Van, 77
Schlinger, Sol, 208, 209
Schneider, Alexander, 177
Schoenberg, Loren, 89, 104
Schoepp, Franz, 129
Scholl, Warren, 90, 105, 186
Scott, Howard, 161, 173, 174
Scott, Raymond, 153
Seconda, 113
Seymour, Dan, 38, 129
Shackleton, Ernest, 16
Shaier, Julius, 208
Shane, Ted, 47, 113
Shan-Kar, Ravi, 118
Shan-Kar, Uday, 16, 118
Shapiro, Art, 44, 186
Shavers, Charlie, 208
Shaw, Artie, 22, 119, 123, 186
Sheen, Mickey, 208
Sheldon, Jack, 209
Shelton, George, 37
Shields, Larry, 90, 91, 196
Shiraly, Vishnudas, 119
Shoepp, Hans, 7
Shreve, Dick, 208
Simon, George, 47, 85, 90, 95, 96, 99, 104, 109, 112, 125, 133, 141, 186
Sims, Zoot, 209
Smith, Harry, 81, 147, 149, 153, 174, 177
Smith, Stuff, 23, 86
Smith, Willie, 208
Speiden, Rachel - Later Rachel Breck, 157
Springstein, Bruce, 35
Stacy, Jess, 12, 39, 42, 43, 44, 48, 85, 86, 87, 88, 89, 90, 91, 93, 94, 95, 102, 107, 108, 110, 112, 113, 114, 119, 120, 121, 139, 146, 150, 185, 207
Stam, Marvin, 209
Stearns, Marshall, 43, 89, 186
Steinweiss, Alex, 165, 186
Sterling, 197
Stern, Isaac, 141, 182
Stewart, Al, 208
Stewart, Slam, 208, 209
Stokowski, Leopold, 33, 88
Stoll, George, 21
Strauss, Johann, 193, 194
Strauss, Richard, 15, 67

Index

Sudhalter, Richard, 44, 85, 93, 186
Sullivan, Maxine, 109, 110, 202
Sykes, Guy (Marshall Stearns), 43, 106, 115, 120, 121
Szigeti, Joseph, 81, 120, 129, 178, 186, 207
Tate, Buddy, 182, 209
Tate, Grady, 209
Tatum, Art, 31
Taylor, Billy, 86
Tchaikovsky, Petr Ilich, 15, 141
Templeton, Alec, 51, 146, 190
Thompson, Burnett, 182
Thompson, J. Walter, 22
Thornhill, Claude, 109, 202
Tilton, Martha, 23, 36, 108, 113, 133, 138, 146, 149, 152, 182, 207, 209
Toscanini, Arturo, 37, 75, 86, 105, 106, 110
Totten, John, 41, 142
Tough, Dave, 115, 177
Turner, Joe, 32
Tuthill, William Burnet, 17
Tutle, Ray, 210
Underhill, 71
Vache, Warren, 209, 210
Van Lake, Turk, 49, 88, 97, 98
Van, Betty, 23
Vannerson, Lenard, 142
Vesely, Ted, 207
Vleck, Nancy Van, 77
Wallenstein, Alfred, 78
Waller, Thomas 'Fats', 16, 31, 97, 98, 102, 116
Wallerstein, Ted, 158, 165
Ward, Helen, 23, 81, 119, 146, 186, 208
Waring, Fred, 207
Watkins, Frank, 9
Webb, Chick, 31, 35, 77, 115, 125, 126, 195
Weber, 7
Weinstock, Rachmael, 208
Wess, Frank, 209
West, Mae, 72
Wettling, George, 44
Whiteman, Paul, 16, 22, 92, 207
Wiesman, Rachel, 209
Wilber, Bob, 182
Williams, Cootie, 43, 77, 94, 95, 97, 112, 199
Williams, Mary Lou, 32, 209
Williams, Paul, 209
Williams, William B., 109, 181
Wilson, Teddy, 19, 36, 37, 38, 41, 42, 81, 86, 88, 94, 96, 98, 101, 102, 103, 104, 112, 113, 114, 115, 120, 121, 123, 125, 133, 139, 181, 186, 200, 207, 208, 209, 210
Wright, Wayne, 209
Wyble, Jim, 208
Young, George, 209
Young, Lester, 11, 12, 45, 97, 101, 112, 123, 207
Zuckerman, Muriel, 8, 9

Photograph Credits

Cover photo:	Columbia LP Courtesy of Sony BMG Music Entertainment.
6:	Courtesy of Rachel Edelson
14:	Courtesy of Frank Alkyer, Publisher, Down Beat Magazine.
20:	Courtesy of Dr. Richard Savington Crampton.
32:	Courtesy of the Yale Music Library MSS 53 The Benny Goodman Papers, photo 1510.2
50, 68, 192:	The concert program and Notes are from the author's collection, reproduced courtesy of The Carnegie Hall Corporation.
72:	Courtesy of the Yale Music Library MSS 53 The Benny Goodman Papers, box 44, folder 1.
79:	Frank Driggs
87:	(L): Courtesy of Frank Alkyer, Publisher, Down Beat Magazine. (R): From the author's collection.
92:	(Top): Photo montage ©2009 Jon Hancock. (Bottom): Rhythm Magazine.
101:	(L) Courtesy of Frank Alkyer, Publisher, Down Beat Magazine. (R) From the author's collection.
111:	Library of Congress, New York World-Telegram & Sun Photograph Collection.
124:	(Top): Frank Driggs (Bottom): From the author's collection, reproduced courtesy of The Carnegie Hall Corporation.
138:	(Top): From the author's collection. (Bottom) RCA Victor BX 44 manual.
147:	Metronome Magazine.
150:	Lebrecht Images.
151:	RCA Victor BX 44 manual.
153:	Courtesy of John Hornsby.
163:	Courtesy of the Audio Engineering Society — New York.
164, 168, 184:	Courtesy of Sony BMG Music Entertainment.
180:	Everett Collection — Rex Features.
206:	From the author's collection, reproduced courtesy of The Carnegie Hall Corporation.
211:	Associated Press.
212:	Courtesy of Conn-Selmer.
32, 160, 162:	Courtesy of the Estate of Benny Goodman.
95, 99:	Rhythm Magazine, from the author's collection.
24, 30, 40, 42, 44, 97, 122, 134:	Courtesy of the Carnegie Hall Corporation.
27, 43, 45, 46, 74, 102, 132, 144, 176:	Getty Images
48, 67, 76, 80, 84, 94, 98, 106, 107, 109, 116, 117, 118, 120, 128, 135:	From the author's collection, reproduced courtesy of the Lawrence Marx archive, The Carnegie Hall Corporation.
10, 26, 36, 70, 73, 97, 100, 108, 136, 140, 142, 148, 154, 156, 170, 171, 172, 177:	From the author's collection.